Y0-CFT-767

CONTENTS

WEIGHTS AND MEASURES

Weights and Measures

1 teaspoon = 1/3 tablespoon
1 tablespoon = 3 teaspoons
2 tablespoons = ⅛ cup (1 ounce)
4 tablespoons = ¼ cup
5-1/3 tablespoons = 1/3 cup
8 tablespoons = ½ cup
16 tablespoons = 1 cup
⅜ cup = 5 tablespoons
⅝ cup = 10 tablespoons
1 cup = ½ pint
2 cups = 1 pint
2 pints = 1 quart
4 quarts = 1 gallon
8 gallons = 1 peck
4 pecks = 1 bushel
1 pound = 16 ounces
1 fluid ounce = 2 tablespoons
16 fluid ounces = 1 pint
1 jigger = 1½ fluid ounces (3 tablespoons)
1 fifth = 16 jiggers
1 quart = 20 jiggers

Approximate Can Sizes

Can Size	Weight	Contents
6 ounces	6 ounces	¾ cup
8 ounces	8 ounces	1 cup
No. 1	11 ounces	1-1/3 cups
12 ounces	12 ounces	1½ cups
No. 303	16 ounces	2 cups
No. 2	20 ounces	2½ cups
No. 2½	28 ounces	3½ cups

PREFACE

Seasons in the Sun is the realization of a dream, plus two and a half years of hard work by the members of Beaux Arts. The recipes contained in *Seasons in the Sun* were gathered by Beaux Arts members from their own kitchens and from those of their friends and local restaurants. Each recipe was tested and evaluated before being accepted for inclusion in this book. Over 1200 recipes were prepared and judged. In testing, emphasis was placed on the use of fresh ingredients, especially those native to South Florida. Beaux Arts regrets that every recipe could not be used because of the lack of space or similarity.

Beaux Arts provides civic support for the Lowe Art Museum, located on the campus of the University of Miami. Beaux Arts is a group of 100 young women dedicated to promoting and creating interest in art and art appreciation throughout the Miami area. The Lowe Art Museum contains one of the eighteen regional Samuel Kress Collections on permanent exhibit and offers the community an active schedule of changing exhibitions drawn from its own collection and from galleries and museums throughout the world. The Museum is free to all.

The members of Beaux Arts invite you to use and enjoy the recipes in *Seasons in the Sun.*

Seasons in the Sun is dedicated in memory of Carla Atkins Schulte, a member of Beaux Arts who represented the high standards and best qualities that Beaux Arts strives to achieve.

Appetizers

APPETIZERS

A Southeast Asian gilded figure from the collection of the Lowe Art Museum gazes down at an assortment of appetizers. A gift to the museum from the Leon Dix Estate, the figure was photographed in Coral Gables at one of the intersections of Coral Way. Coral Way has been designated as a Historic Roadway and many of the intersections are decorated with Mediterranean gates and arches.

ANGELS ON HORSEBACK

Serves 6
12 slices bacon
1 pint oysters, well drained
Toothpicks
Salt, pepper and paprika to
taste
Parsley

Wrap bacon around oysters. Secure with toothpicks. Sprinkle each oyster with salt, pepper and paprika. Place a rack on a shallow baking pan. Brown slowly at 350° for about 15 - 20 minutes. Serve on a bed of parsley.

Mrs. John Renuart

ANNE'S ARTICHOKES

Serves 8
8 artichokes
1 clove garlic, minced
½ teaspoon salt
1 tablespoon lemon juice
SAUCE:
2½ cups mayonnaise (see Index)
½ cup fresh parsley, finely
chopped
½ cup dried chives
¼ cup capers, finely chopped
3 tablespoons dried tarragon

Rinse artichokes. Place in large pot. Add 1 ½ inches water. Add garlic, salt, and lemon juice. Cover and bring to a boil. Steam until done. Remove artichokes when cool and remove choke.

Sauce: Mix all ingredients together. Chill at least 6 hours or overnight. Serve sauce in small dish alongside the artichoke or spread artichoke open and fill middle with sauce.

Mrs. Taffy Gould Beber

ASPARAGUS ROLL-UPS

Serves 20
8 ounces cream cheese, softened
4 tablespoons sour cream
¼ teaspoon dill seed
¼ teaspoon pepper
1 loaf white bread, sliced thin
14 ounce can thin asparagus,
drained
4 tablespoons butter, melted

Mix cream cheese, sour cream, dill, and pepper. Remove bread crusts. Roll slices flat with rolling pin. Spread cheese mixture on bread. Place asparagus spear at end of bread and roll jelly-roll style. Seal with cheese. Place seam side down on cookie sheet. Brush butter over rolls. Brown in oven at 350° for 15 - 20 minutes. Turn to brown all sides. With sharp knife, cut into bite size pieces.

Mrs. Edgar Jones, Jr.

AVOCADO SHRIMP PASTE

1 ripe avocado
¼ pound shrimp, cooked and cleaned
½ cup mayonnaise (see Index)
1 teaspoon capers
1 tablespoon ketchup
¼ teaspoon seasoned salt
Pepper to taste
½ teaspoon dry mustard
1 teaspoon curry powder
Lemon juice to taste

Mash avocado with a silver fork. Mince the shrimp and add to the avocado. Add the remaining ingredients and stir thoroughly to blend. Serve with crackers or chips.

Mrs. Alan Greer

BISCUIT SAUSAGE

Makes 150
3 cups Bisquick mix
1 pound ground sausage
10 ounces Cheddar cheese, grated

Mix all of the ingredients with your hands and roll into balls about the size of large marbles. Bake at 400° for 15 minutes on ungreased cookie sheet. These may be frozen, after baking, and re-heated for 10 minutes at 375°.

Mrs. Fred E. Luhm

BOLLOS

A special delight of Key West

½ pound black-eyed peas, dried
2 cloves garlic
Tabasco to taste
Cooking oil
Salt to taste

Soak black-eyed peas in water to cover overnight. Drain peas and rub handfuls of them between layers of paper towels to remove the husks. Add garlic and chop twice with the fine blade of a food chopper. Pour the chopped beans into a sauce pan with Tabasco and cook over low heat, adding water if the beans become too dry, for about 15 - 20 minutes or until creamy. Pour the oil into a deep fat fryer to a depth of 3 inches and heat to 375°. Drop the bean mixture by teaspoons into the hot oil and fry until golden brown. Drain on paper towels and sprinkle with salt before serving. Serve hot.

Mrs. John Renuart

BROCCOLI DIP

2 onions, chopped
1 stick butter
2 cups celery, chopped
1 package frozen chopped
  broccoli
1 roll garlic cheese
1 can cream of mushroom soup
8 ounces cream cheese, softened
1 package slivered almonds

Sauté onions in butter. Add celery, simmer until tender. Add remaining ingredients and heat thoroughly. Serve hot in chafing dish with crackers or chips.

Mrs. Jane Warren

CAVIAR MOUSSE

1 cup boiling water
2 tablespoons gelatin, softened
  in 4 tablespoons cold water
2 tablespoons lemon juice
4 tablespoons mayonnaise (see
  Index)
Pinch of dry mustard
1 tablespoon Worcestershire
1 pint sour cream
8 ounce jar fresh caviar
  (Icelandic lumpfish is a
  good substitute)
4 hard cooked eggs, chopped
¼ cup onion, minced

Add boiling water to gelatin. Stir until dissolved. Add remaining ingredients and mix well. Pour into a shallow glass pan or mold. Chill several hours or overnight. Serve with squares or triangles of dry toast.

Mrs. John Klein

CLAM CANAPES

Serves 20
7½ ounce can minced clams
2 tablespoons onion, minced
1 tablespoon butter
1½ tablespoons flour
1 clove garlic, minced
¼ teaspoon Worcestershire
  sauce
12 slices bread
2-3 tablespoons butter, melted

Drain clams and reserve the liquid. Cook the onion in 1 tablespoon butter. Remove from heat and blend in flour. Gradually stir in clam juice. Add garlic and Worcestershire. Cook until thickened. Add clams. Remove the crusts from the bread slices and roll thin with a rolling pin. Brush bread with melted butter, spoon on 1 tablespoon clam mixture and roll up. Brush each roll with melted butter. Freeze. Cut into 4 pieces. Bake frozen at 425° 8 minutes or until light brown. Serve hot.

Mrs. Lawrence E. Lewis, II

CLAMS CASINO

Serves 4

8 ounce can diced or minced clams, drained

2 tablespoons olive oil

4 ounce can chopped mushrooms, drained

½ cup Progresso Italian bread crumbs

1 ½ tablespoons parsley flakes

1 heaping tablespoon pimiento, finely chopped

¼ cup grated Romano or Parmesan cheese

Salt and pepper to taste

Accent to taste

4 slices of Provolone or Mozzarella cheese

Paprika

In a large bowl mix first 9 ingredients together thoroughly. Mixture should be moist and heavy. Divide evenly and spoon into clean scallop shells. Place a slice of cheese on each portion. Sprinkle with paprika. Refrigerate until serving time. Bake at 350° for 15 minutes. Serve very hot.

Mrs. Linda Zack

HOT CLAM DIP

2 jars Old English Cheddar cheese

1 small can clams, drained

Dash of garlic powder

¼ cup mayonnaise (see Index)

Mix ingredients. Put mixture into baking dish. Bake at 350° for 25 minutes, stirring occasionally until smooth and heated through. Serve in chafing dish with melba rounds or Fritos.

Mrs. Frank C. Sargent, III

CHEESE BALL

Makes 2 balls

5 ounces Vera sharp cheese

¼ pound Blue cheese

4 small packages cream cheese

1 tablespoon Worcestershire sauce

1 teaspoon Tabasco

1 clove garlic, minced

1 cup pecans, chopped

1 cup parsley, chopped

Mix softened cheese together. Add seasoning and blend thoroughly. Shape cheeses into 2 balls and roll in nuts and then in the parsley. Refrigerate or freeze until ready to serve. Serve cold with melba toast.

Mrs. Tom Pennekamp

CHEESE BUREKS

½ pound Ricotta cheese
1 pint cottage cheese
½ pound Feta cheese
1 bunch fresh parsley, minced
4 eggs, beaten
1 tablespoon sugar
1 pound fillo dough, commercial
½ cup butter, melted

Combine the 3 different cheeses and mix thoroughly. Add parsley, eggs and sugar and beat well. Open fillo dough and cut lengthwise into 3 inch wide strips. Using 3 strips at a time, brush melted butter lightly over dough. Place ample teaspoonful of cheese mixture at one end of strip. Fold one corner of the strip over the cheese to form a small triangle. Then fold the opposite way to form another triangle and continue folding until you reach the end of the strip and the cheese is encased in a tiny triangle of dough. (Flags are folded in this manner.) Brush the top of each triangle with butter and place on greased baking sheet. Bake at 350° for 15 minutes until browned. The bureks can be made ahead and frozen. Increase the cooking time for frozen bureks to 20 - 25 minutes.

Mrs. Steve Pease

CHEESE CANAPES

1 pound sharp Cheddar cheese, grated
3 strips bacon, well cooked and broken into small pieces
1 small green pepper, chopped
1 small onion, chopped
1 dash Worcestershire sauce
2 tablespoons mayonnaise (see Index)
Party rye

Mix cheese, bacon, pepper, onion, and Worcestershire with mayonnaise. Spread on sliced party rye. Bake at 400° until cheese melts.

Mrs. Jane Warren

CHEESE CRUNCHES

Makes 6 dozen
½ pound sharp Cheddar cheese, grated
½ pound butter, softened
2 cups flour
2 cups Rice Krispies
¼ teaspoon cayenne pepper
½ teaspoon salt

Mix cheese and butter together. Add other ingredients. Form small balls. Flatten out with fork on an ungreased cookie sheet. Bake at 350° 15-20 minutes. Store in air tight container.

Mrs. Fred E. Luhm

CHEESE PATÉ

8 ounces cream cheese
4 ounces Cheddar cheese, grated
½-1 teaspoon curry powder
¼ cup sauterne, dry vermouth or dry sherry
1 bottle chutney
1 bunch scallions, minced
Wheat crackers

Cream the cheeses together. Add curry powder and wine and blend thoroughly. Mount cheese mixture on a serving platter making an oval about ½ inch thick. Cover and refrigerate until serving time. Before serving cover the cheese with the chutney, chopped fine if necessary, and sprinkle the scallions generously over the chutney. Serve with wheat crackers.

Mrs. John Renuart

ICE BOX CHEESE WAFERS

Makes 6-8 dozen
½ pound sharp Cheddar cheese, grated
¼ pound butter, creamed
½ teaspoon salt
Heavy pinch cayenne pepper (at least ½ teaspoon)
1 ½ cups sifted flour
Pecan halves (optional)

Cream cheese, butter, salt, and pepper together. Add flour. Make into logs. Wrap in waxed paper and place in refrigerator; will keep a month. Slice thinly. Bake at 350° 12-15 minutes. Press a pecan half into each wafer before baking for a decorative variation.

Mrs. Leon L. Rich

CRAB COCKTAIL

8 ounce package cream cheese, softened
1 tablespoon milk
8 ounces crabmeat, picked over and cleaned
2 tablespoons onion, finely chopped
½ teaspoon cream style horseradish
¼ teaspoon salt
Dash pepper
Sliced almonds for garnish

Mix all of the ingredients together. Put the mixture into a baking dish. Sprinkle with sliced almonds. Bake at 370° for 15 minutes. Remove from the oven. Place over a low flame in a chafing dish. Serve with Bremner Wafers.

Mrs. James A. Sawyer

CRAB-CHEESE DIP

13-15 ounces Alaskan King crab, check for shells
20 ounces sharp Cheddar cheese
16 ounces sharp processed cheese, sliced
½ cup of butter
1 cup sauterne

Shred crabmeat and put aside. Cut Cheddar into small pieces. In sauce pan combine cheeses, butter, and sauterne. Over low heat stir until cheese melts. Stir in crabmeat (saving a little for garnish.) Cook until heated. Pour into chafing dish and garnish with reserved crabmeat. Serve with shredded wheat wafers. This may also be used as a fondue.

Mrs. Joe Abrell

EMILIO'S CONCHITAS

Serves 5
1 pound crabmeat, picked over for shell
20 small green olives, finely chopped
4 ounce jar pimiento strips, finely chopped
1 teaspoon dry mustard
Juice of 1 lemon
¾ cup mayonnaise (see Index)
½ small jar capers
Salt and pepper to taste
20 clam shells, small size
Plain bread crumbs

Mix all ingredients, except bread crumbs, together, using enough mayonnaise to make mixture stick together, but not making it too soft. Fill clam shells. Smooth top with a little mayonnaise. Sprinkle with bread crumbs. Bake at 350° for 10 minutes. Then place under broiler until golden brown.

Emilio Cerrotta

GREEK CRABMEAT PASTRIES

Makes about 72
4 tablespoons butter
½ medium onion, minced
¼ pound mushrooms, minced
1 pound fresh crabmeat
8 sprigs parsley, minced
15 sprigs dill, minced
1 pimiento, chopped fine
Dash Tabasco
Salt and pepper to taste
½ pound fillo sheets
1 cup clarified butter

Melt 4 tablespoons butter in a heavy skillet. Add onion and cook over low heat until transparent. Stir in the mushrooms and cook, stirring 3-5 minutes. Combine all remaining ingredients except fillo and clarified butter. Mix well and cook 3 - 5 minutes more. Remove from the heat and set aside until dish reaches room temperature. Cut sheets of fillo pastry in half. Refrigerate ½ of pastry, covered. Cover other ½ with a damp towel. Take one sheet at a time; using a feather brush, coat sheet with clarified butter. Place 1 tablespoon of crabmeat mixture 1 inch from narrow edge of sheet. Fold the 1 inch margin over crabmeat. Then fold the opposite side over to edge of crabmeat mixture. Butter folded pastry again on exposed parts and roll up like a rug. Place in baking dish. Continue same procedure with remaining pastry sheets. At this point pastries can be frozen. Defrost before using. Bake at 425° for 20 minutes. Serve warm. Shrimp or lobster may be substituted for the crabmeat.

Mrs. Lindsey D. Pankey, Jr.

HOT CRABMEAT DIP

8 ounce can white crabmeat
8 ounce package cream cheese, softened
1 medium onion, finely chopped
1 tablespoons sherry, more if desired
Dash Worcestershire sauce

In a non-stick pan over low heat, cook all of the ingredients together slowly. Serve in a chafing dish with slices of French bread or light crackers.

Mrs. Linda Zack

COCONUT CHIPS

1 coconut
Salt

Crack coconut and remove meat from the shell. Cut the coconut meat into very thin slices. Spread coconut in a layer on a cookie sheet and sprinkle with salt. Toast in a slow 200°-250° oven until golden brown, turning often. Store in *airtight* container to keep crisp.

Mrs. Tom Pennekamp

CURRY DIP

Makes 1½ cups
1 cup mayonnaise (see Index)
½ cup sour cream
1 tablespoon lemon juice
1 teaspoon Worcestershire sauce
1 tablespoon Spice Island salad
   herbs
½ teaspoon curry
½ teaspoon paprika
1 clove garlic, crushed

Mix together well and serve with raw vegetables.

Mrs. John Fullerton

MRS. SMITH'S EGG RING

Serves 10
1 package unflavored gelatin
½ cup cold water
½ cup boiling water
6 eggs, hard cooked
1 tablespoon lemon juice
1 tablespoon ketchup
1 cup mayonnaise (see Index)
Salt and pepper to taste

Soften gelatin in cold water. Add boiling water and stir until dissolved. Chop the eggs very fine and add to the gelatin mixture. Stir in the remaining ingredients and mix thoroughly. Pour into a mold that has been lightly greased with mayonnaise. Refrigerate until serving time. Unmold, by dipping mold in hot water for a few seconds, on serving platter and serve with crackers.

Mrs. Leonidas Dowlen

EGG SALAD SPREAD

Serves 10
6 hard boiled eggs, chopped
1 cup Cheddar cheese, grated
1 tablespoon onion, minced
½ cup green pepper, chopped
½ cup black olives, chopped
4 slices crisp bacon bits
½ cup mayonnaise (see Index)

Combine the eggs with the rest of the ingredients while they are still warm. Spread on bread or crackers, or chill for use as a cocktail spread.

Mrs. Larry Stewart

EGGPLANT CAVIAR

1 large eggplant, unpeeled
1 medium onion
1 ripe tomato, peeled and seeded
1 clove garlic
1 teaspoon sugar
2 tablespoons vinegar
2 tablespoons olive oil (1 tablespoon, if mixture seems too liquid)
Salt and pepper to taste

Boil eggplant, do not overcook. Put the eggplant, onion and tomato through a meat grinder, or chop finely. Add seasonings and chill. (If too juicy, drain in a sieve until the consistency to stay on cracker.) Excellent on triangles of Pita bread.

Mrs. William Vass Shepherd

DEEP FRIED INDIAN EGGPLANT

Serves 12
1 eggplant (about 1 pound)
1 tablespoon salt
1 cup unbleached flour
¼ cup rice flour
1 teaspoon ground cumin
¼ teaspoon cayenne
1 cup cold water
1 bottle peanut oil

Wash eggplant, do not peel, halve lengthwise. Slice each half crosswise into 12 pieces, and sprinkle with salt all over evenly. Set aside at least 30 minutes. Combine flour and seasoning in a bowl. Add water and stir thoroughly. Fill deep fat fryer with oil 2 to 3 inches deep. Heat oil to 350°. Pat eggplants dry with paper towels. Dip 1 piece of eggplant at a time into batter. Fry in batches of 5 or 6 till golden, about 5 minutes. Drain on paper towels. Sprinkle with salt and serve at once.

Mrs. Robert Vale

SMOKED FISH

Do not place fish directly over fire—fish at one end, charcoal at other end.

½ gallon water
½ cup salt
3 pounds fish fillets
⅛ cup salad oil

Mix water and salt to form a brine. Pour over fish and let stand 30 minutes. Remove fish and rinse. To smoke fish use a charcoal barbecue with hood. Let fire burn down low. Cover with wet hickory chips. Place fish, skin side down, on well greased grill. Cover and smoke 1½ hours, adding more wet chips, as necessary. Increase temperature by adding charcoal and opening the draft. Brush fish with oil. Repeat oil at least twice during cooking.

Tom Pennekamp

GREEN CHILIES AND CHEESE DIP

4 ounce can green chilies
12 ounce package Cheddar cheese
12 ounce package Monterey Jack cheese
1 egg, beatened

Wash and seed green chilies. Drain and chop. Grate cheeses. In a 1½ quart baking dish alternate layers of green chilies, Monterey Jack, green chilies, Cheddar cheese. Repeat layering till dish is filled. Pour egg over top layer using a fork to penetrate all layers. Bake at 375° for 25 minutes. Serve hot with party rye bread.

Mrs. Lawrence R. Imber

LIPTAUER WITH ACCOMPANIMENTS

Serves 10-12
LIPTAUER:
16 ounces cream cheese,
  softened
¼ cup butter, softened
2 tablespoons heavy cream
Paprika
Lettuce cups
ACCOMPANIMENTS:
Scallions, sliced
Capers, drained and chopped
Radishes, minced
Cucumbers, finely chopped
Anchovies, chopped
Bacon, well fried and crumbled
Caviar
Brown or rye party bread

Combine cream cheese, butter, heavy cream and paprika thoroughly. Mound in center of chilled platter. Surround with lettuce cups. Fill cups with accompaniments of your choice.
Mrs. Harry Taylor

LIPTAUER CHEESE

1 large package cream cheese
½ cup butter, room temperature
2 teaspoons capers, minced
2 teaspoons paprika
1 teaspoon anchovy paste
1 teaspoon caraway seeds
2 tablespoons chives, chopped

Blend all the ingredients until thoroughly mixed. Shape into a ball or desired shape. Refrigerate until firm. Allow to reach room temperature before serving.
Mrs. John Brendle

MANGO DELIGHT

2 ripe mangoes, peeled and
  sliced
2 tablespoons lime juice
1 pound cream cheese, room
  temperature
1 cup coconut, shredded
1 cup pecans, chopped
Wheat crackers

Puree the mango with the lime juice in a blender. Add the cheese, cut into small pieces and blend until thoroughly mixed. Pour into a bowl and stir in the coconut. Garnish with pecans and refrigerate until serving time. Serve cold with wheat crackers.
Mrs. Frank Marston

BARBECUED MEATBALLS

Makes 40 1 inch meatballs
SAUCE:
1 cup smoked sauce
¼ cup ketchup
¼ cup molasses
4 tablespoons butter
1 tablespoon vinegar
2 tablespoons lemon juice
1 teaspoon dry mustard
2 teaspoons Worcestershire sauce
MEATBALLS:
1 pound pork sausage
¼ pound ground beef
1 egg, slightly beaten
¼ cup dry bread crumbs
5 ounce can water chestnuts

Combine all of the sauce ingredients until well blended and set aside. Mix sausage, beef, egg and bread crumbs thoroughly. Form mixture into 1 inch balls, placing a water chestnut in center of each meatball. In skillet brown on all sides. Drain. Add sauce. Serve hot in a chafing dish. May remain in sauce 3 hours before serving.
Mrs. Harold Neas

MUSHROOMS GRUYERE

Serves 4
½ cup butter
2 cloves garlic, minced
2 shallots, chopped
1½ pounds mushrooms, caps
    quartered and stems sliced
3 tablespoons fresh lemon juice
¾ cup celery, finely chopped
Salt to taste
Fresh ground pepper to taste
½ cup grated Gruyere cheese
3 tablespoons fresh parsley,
    finely chopped

Melt butter in large skillet. Sauté garlic and shallots until tender. Add mushrooms and lemon juice; cook, stirring, for 5 minutes. Add celery, salt and pepper. Cook 1 minute more. Remove from heat. Stir in the cheese and parsley and continue stirring until the cheese is just melted. Serve immediately with toast points.
Mrs. Taffy Gould Beber

MARINATED MUSHROOMS

1/3 cup wine vinegar
2/3 cup olive oil
1 tablespoon parsley, chopped
½ teaspoon salt
½ teaspoon pepper
½ teaspoon sugar
1 tablespoon lemon juice
1 clove garlic
2 pounds small fresh
  mushrooms, washed

Combine all ingredients and marinate several hours in refrigerator. Remove garlic clove, drain and serve. Leftovers can be used in a tossed salad.

Mrs. Hagood Clarke

MUSHROOM ROLL

Good hot or cold. May be prepared in advance and reheated.

Serves 6-8
Oil
1½ pounds mushrooms
6 eggs, separated
¼ pound butter
½ teaspoon salt
¼ teaspoon freshly ground
  pepper
2 tablespoons lemon juice
4-5 fluted mushrooms
Butter
Lemon juice
Parsley, chopped
Hollandaise sauce (see Index)

Oil a jelly roll pan and line with oiled waxed paper. Wipe mushrooms clean, chop finely and wring in cloth to remove excess moisture. Beat yolks until fluffy. Combine with the mushrooms, butter, salt, pepper and lemon juice. Beat whites until soft peaks form. Fold in mushroom mixture. Pour into the pan and smooth flat with rubber spatula. Bake at 350° for 15 minutes. Cool. Turn out onto a sheet of waxed paper and peel off top paper. Roll up by holding remaining waxed paper as a guide. Sauté fluted mushrooms in butter. Add lemon juice. Arrange on top of roll. Sprinkle with parsley. Serve with Hollandaise sauce.

Mrs. John C. Sullivan, Jr.

CHICKEN LIVER PATÉ

10 tablespoons butter
½ cup onion, minced
2 small apples, peeled, cored & diced
1 pound chicken livers
3 tablespoons brandy
1½ teaspoons lemon juice
2 tablespoons heavy cream
½ teaspoon curry powder
Salt and pepper to taste

Melt 6 tablespoons butter in a heavy skillet over high heat. When foam subsides, add onion and apple. Sauté until apple is soft enough to be mashed with a spoon. Pour contents of skillet into a blender. In skillet melt the remaining butter and add livers. Cook over high heat until the livers are browned, about 5 minutes. Add brandy and flame. When the flame subsides pour the contents into the blender with the apples and onion. Add cream and blend until smooth. Add seasonings and blend about 30 seconds more. Pour the mixture out and shape into a mound. Surround with parsley and serve with Melba toast.

Mrs. Hillard Willis

COUNTRY PATÉ

Serves 24
2 slices bacon, ground fine
1 pound pork, fat removed, ground 2 times
1 pound sausage, ground 2 times
½ pound chicken liver, ground 2 times
½ pound veal, ground 2 times
2 tablespoons brandy
2 cloves garlic, minced
1 small onion, minced
Salt, pepper and ginger to taste
1 pound bacon, minus 2 slices

All meats should be ground uniformly. Mix all ingredients except pound of bacon, thoroughly. Line a loaf pan with strips of bacon. Fill with the paté mixture and bake at 350° for 1½ hours. Remove from oven and pour off fat; cover with foil and refrigerate. Unmold onto a serving platter and garnish with watercress and curls of bacon. Serve with French bread and whipped butter.

Mrs. John Renuart

PATÉ ESSO

Serves 8
PATÉ:
1 recipe pastry dough (see Index)
½ pound bacon, sliced
1½ pounds veal, ground 2 times
1 cup water packed tuna, drained
¼ cup capers
½ cup dry white wine
1 onion, minced
1 can anchovie fillets, minced
3 tablespoons pimiento, chopped
¼ cup green olives, chopped
½ cup flour
¼ cup whipping cream
6 tablespoons butter
Juice of 1 lemon
Salt and pepper to taste
2 eggs
½ pound veal loin, cut into 2 inch square strips to equal 6 strips of meat
ASPIC FILLING:
2 tablespoons clear gelatin
2 cups clear chicken broth
3 tablespoons parsley, chopped

Line paté mold with dough which has been rolled thin. Let it hang over the sides. Layer inside of dough with over-lapping strips of bacon. Mix all of the other ingredients, except veal loin, together thoroughly. Fill the mold with 1/3 of paté mixture, spreading evenly. Lay 3 strips of veal loin lengthwise on paté mixture. Make another layer of paté, using ½ of remaining paté mixture and then add 3 more strips of veal loin. Cover the veal with remaining paté mixture and wrap bacon over the top. Fold the remaining dough over the paté and crimp the edges together to seal. Cut the scraps of left-over dough into flower and leaf shapes for decoration. Adhere the dough decorations to the top of the pate with a mixture of 1 egg beaten with 1 tablespoon water. When decorated, coat the entire paté with the egg water mixture. Insert 2 pastry cones into the top of the paté (through the center of a flower decoration). Place paté in hot 400° oven. Immediately lower oven heat to 325° and cook ½ hour or until done. Test as you would a cake. Allow paté to cool in its pan on a rack. When cool remove pastry cones and pour, through a funnel, the aspic filling. Place paté in refrigerator and chill at least 48 hours. Unmold and serve cold, sliced.

John Baratte

PATÉ IN JELLY

Serves 50
2 pounds smoked goose liver
½ pound cream cheese, softened
1 tablespoon brandy
¼ cup Madeira
1 envelope gelatin, unflavored
2 tablespoons cold water
2 cans consommé

Grease paté mold lightly with butter. Mix liver and cream cheese together until smooth. Add brandy and half of the Madeira and mix thoroughly. Soften the gelatin in the water. Heat the consommé, then add remaining Madeira and gelatin, stirring until the gelatin is dissolved. Pour ¾ inch of consommé into the mold and chill until set. Spread paté in the middle of the mold on the consommé layer. Be careful to allow space around the sides of the paté for the consommé. Pour remaining consommé over paté and refrigerate until firm. To unmold, dip mold in hot water for a few seconds and invert on serving tray. Garnish with watercress and serve cold with French bread or Melba toast.

Mrs. Conway Hamilton

FRIED PLANTAIN CHIPS

Serves 6-8
Vegetable oil
3 or more green plantains
Salt to taste

Fill deep fat fryer or heavy sauce pan with oil to depth of 2 or 3 inches. Using a deep frying thermometer, heat to 375°. Peel plantains and cut in crosswise sections, as thin as possible. Deep fry 3-4 minutes until golden brown on both sides. Drain on paper towels. Flatten cooked plantains between layers of waxed paper and fry again until crisp. Sprinkle with salt. Serve hot.

Mrs. Lindsey D. Pankey, Jr.

SALMON MOUSSE

1 envelope unflavored gelatin
½ cup cold water
1 pound can red salmon
½ cup mayonnaise (see Index)
¾ cup sour cream
½ teaspoon salt
1 tablespoon lemon juice
1¼ cups celery, finely chopped
1 tablespoon capers

Sprinkle gelatin over ¼ cup cold water to soften. Dissolve in ¼ cup boiling water. Let cool. Put all ingredients except capers and celery in blender; whip until smooth. Add capers and celery. Pour into a buttered mold or individual molds. Chill. Serve with plain Bremner wafers.

Mrs. William Vass Shepherd

SMOKED SALMON

1 pound Nova smoked salmon
1 medium onion, thinly sliced
1 tablespoon capers, chopped
2 teaspoons chopped fresh dill
1 cup sour cream or ½ cup sour
    cream and ½ cup mayonnaise
Black pepper, freshly ground
Chopped parsley

Cut salmon in thin strips and mix with onion, capers, dill and sour cream and if you wish with mayonnaise. Blend well and spoon into 8 ounce crocks and top with pepper and chopped parsley. Cover and chill. Serve with saltines or crackers of your choice.

Mrs. John C. Sullivan, Jr.

SALSA FRIA AND GUACAMOLE

SALSA FRIA:
1 large sweet onion, finely
    chopped
2 green bell peppers, finely
    chopped
3 jalapeño peppers, finely
    chopped
Pinch of coriander
2 tablespoons wine vinegar
4 tablespoons minced parsley
1 clove garlic, crushed
3 tomatoes, squeezed and seeds
    removed
GUACAMOLE:
2 ripe avocados
4 tablespoons Salsa Fria
Lime juice
Salt and pepper to taste

Salsa Fria: Combine onion, green peppers and jalapenos. Add coriander, vinegar, parsley, garlic and tomatoes. Salsa Fria may be made several days in advance and stored in a jar in the refrigerator.

Guacamole: With a silver fork mash the avocados together with the Salsa Fria. Add the lime juice, salt and pepper to taste. Avocados may be frozen mashed with lime juice for later use.

Mrs. Hillard Willis

APRICOT SAUSAGE BALLS
May be made ahead and frozen.

Makes 200 balls
5 pounds hot sausage, ground
3 eggs, beaten
1 large onion, minced
1½ cloves garlic, minced
2 or 3 cans apricot nectar

Combine sausage, eggs, onion, and garlic. Shape into 1 inch balls. Broil or pan fry until brown. Drain on paper towels. Put the balls into a large sauce pan and add the apricot nectar. Simmer for 2 hours. Reheat at serving time.

Mrs. Fred E. Luhm

SCALLOPS AND MUSHROOMS

Serves 6
1 pound scallops
2 tablespoons onion, minced
1 bay leaf
½ teaspoon salt
¼ teaspoon pepper
1 pound mushrooms, sliced
6 tablespoons lemon juice
½ cup olive oil
Tabasco, to taste
½ cup parsley, chopped

Cover the scallops, onion, bay leaf, salt and pepper with water in a medium sized pot. Bring the mixture to a boil over moderate to low heat. Turn off the stove and let the scallops stand for 5 minutes. Transfer the scallops and onion to a serving bowl with a slotted spoon. Place the thinly sliced mushrooms in another bowl. In a large measuring cup, put 3 tablespoons of the lemon juice and add the oil in a steady stream while beating constantly. Toss the scallops with 1/3 of the dressing. Add the remaining 2/3 of the dressing to the mushrooms and toss to mix. Combine the mushrooms with the scallops and add the other 3 tablespoons of lemon juice and Tabasco. Taste for correct seasonings, adding more lemon juice, Tabasco or salt if necessary. The dressing should be spicy. Sprinkle the chopped parsley over the scallops and chill several hours before serving.

Mrs. G. William McMillian

SOUTH FLORIDA SCALLOPS

Serves 6
½ pound scallops
1/3 cup key lime juice
2 teaspoons Tabasco
Salt and pepper to taste
4 tablespoons scallions, chopped
½ cup sour cream
¾ cup coconut milk*
¼ cup parsley, chopped

Combine the key lime juice, Tabasco, salt and pepper in a glass bowl. Taste to make sure the liquid is spicy. Add the scallops and toss well to coat. Cover the bowl and refrigerate for 2-3 hours to "cook" the scallops. Meanwhile, combine the scallions, sour cream, and coconut milk. Mix well and refrigerate 2-3 hours. At serving time, drain the scallops, reserving the liquid. Add the scallops to the coconut milk mixture, tossing to mix. Add the marinade from the scallops, 1 tablespoon at a time. Do not use more than 4 tablespoons, the exact number depends on personal tastes. Spoon the mixture into scallop shells and garnish with the chopped parsley.
***Coconut milk:** Combine equal parts of fresh coconut and milk and blend very well. Strain through 2 layers of cheese cloth and refrigerate. This will keep up to 5 days.
Mrs. J.W. Lotspeich

SEVICHE DOMNING

2 pounds firm fleshed white fish (such as grouper fillets)
Lime juice to cover fish
Bitter orange (optional)
2 cups onion, thinly sliced
8 cloves garlic, crushed
2 Aji, jalapeños or hot cherry peppers, finely chopped
Pinch of coriander
3 tablespoons parsley, minced
1 teaspoon salt or more, to taste

Cut the fillets into uniform bite sized pieces. Place in a bowl. Cover the fish with lime juice or a mixture of lime and bitter orange. Add the onion, garlic, peppers, coriander, parsley and salt. (No black pepper should be used so if not hot enough add more hot pepper or Tabasco sauce.) Marinate overnight. Serve very cold, arranged on a lettuce lined platter. Have toothpicks available.
Mrs. John Renuart

SEAFOOD IN DILL PESTO

Serves 6
¼ cup white wine
¼ cup water
¼ teaspoon MSG
3 peppercorns
1 small bay leaf
½ onion, sliced
½ teaspoon salt
½ pound shrimp, shelled and cleaned
½ pound scallops
¼ cup olive oil
2 cloves garlic
¾ cup fresh dill or 1¼ tablespoon dill weed
½ cup fresh parsley (optional)

In saucepan combine first 7 ingredients. Bring to a boil and simmer for 5 minutes. Add shrimp and scallops. Simmer till shrimp turn pink and scallops lose translucency, about 4-5 minutes. Remove seafood and set aside. Turn heat up high and reduce liquid to 3-4 tablespoons. While liquid is reducing, pour olive oil into blender. Add garlic and dill. Whirl in blender, adding as much dill or parsley as oil will absorb. When it will not absorb any more, add reduced liquid. Blend. Pour over warm seafood and mix. Chill before serving with crackers.

Mrs. William Taylor

SHRIMP DIP

16 ounces cream cheese
½ cup mayonnaise (see Index)
2 cloves garlic, crushed
2 teaspoons prepared mustard
1-2 teaspoons onion, grated finely
2 teaspoons sugar
¼ teaspoon seasoned salt
¼ cup plus 2 tablespoons sauterne or cooking sherry
12 ounces small shrimp

Melt the cheese over low heat. Add the mayonnaise, garlic, mustard, onion, sugar and salt. Blend well. Stir in the sauterne and shrimp. Heat. Serve in chafing dish with sesame seed crackers.

Mrs. Andrea Ferguson
Mrs. Boyce Ezell, III

MARINATED SHRIMP

Serves 40
5 pounds shrimp, cooked and cleaned
15-20 tiny white onions, thinly sliced
1 dozen lemons, thinly sliced
2 pints olive oil
1½ pints tarragon vinegar
2 large bottles capers
Salt, sugar, Tabasco and Worcestershire sauce to taste

Layer the shrimp, onions and lemons in single layers until all are used up. Mix the marinade ingredients together until blended and pour over the shrimp, onions and lemon. Refrigerate at least 12 hours, stirring occasionally.
Mrs. John Renuart

PICKLED SHRIMP

Serves 6
1½ cups salad oil
1½ teaspoons dry mustard
2 tablespoons sugar
Little over 1/3 cup white vinegar
Little over 1/3 cup ketchup
Freshly ground pepper to taste
2-3 cloves garlic
2 teaspoons Worcestershire sauce
Tabasco to taste
2-3 pounds shrimp, cooked and cleaned
1½ medium sweet onions, thinly sliced
3 bay leaves

Prepare 2 days in advance of serving. Combine first nine ingredients in blender. Arrange in deep serving dish; half of shrimp, half of onion, half of bay leaves, and half of oil mixture. Repeat layering. Cover and refrigerate until serving time.
Mrs. James Hauf

SPICEY SHRIMP COCKTAIL

Serves 6
1 pound fresh shrimp, medium size
2 tomatoes, peeled and finely chopped
1 large Spanish onion, minced
½ cup bottled French dressing
1½ teaspoons lemon juice
½ teaspoon salt
Dash cayenne

Boil shrimp in salted water 8 minutes or until pink. Shell and devein; cut in half if large. Combine shrimp with other ingredients. Cover and chill overnight.
To Serve: drain off liquid and serve over toasted bread squares or retain liquid and serve in large scallop shells with crackers.
Mrs. Lindsey D. Pankey, Jr.

DELICIOUS SPINACH
May be served as a salad.

Makes 8 cups
5 packages frozen chopped
   spinach, cooked and drained
1 stalk celery, finely chopped
1 cup onion, finely chopped
2 cups Cheddar cheese, cut into
   small pieces
8 hard cooked eggs, chopped
1 cup mayonnaise (see Index)
1 tablespoon white vinegar
Tabasco to taste
Salt and pepper to taste
Watercress

Remove as much liquid from
spinach as possible; may take
several hours to squeeze and
drain thoroughly. Mix all
ingredients together. Mound on
a platter and chill. Serve with
crackers or toasted rounds.
Garnish with watercress.

Mrs. Ed Goldstein

ORIGINAL SPINACH

1 cup uncooked spinach,
   chopped and drained
1 cup fresh parsley, minced
2 scallions, tops and bottoms
   chopped
Salt and pepper to taste
¼ cup mayonnaise (see Index)
3 eggs, hard cooked
Cherry tomatoes
Cucumbers, sliced thin

The day before, dry the spinach
as much as possible. Combine
the spinach, parsley, scallions,
salt and pepper and add enough
mayonnaise to bind the mixture.
Cover and refrigerate over night.
Before serving, mound the
spinach on a tray. Finely grate
the hard cooked eggs and
sprinkle over the spinach to
cover. Make a ring around the
mound with the tomatoes and
cucumber slices and serve cold
with crackers.

Mrs. Edwin C. Lunsford, Jr.

SPANOKOPITA

Serves 16

¼ cup olive oil

½ cup onions, chopped

¼ cup chopped scallions, including 2 inches of tops

2 pounds fresh spinach, washed thoroughly, drained and finely chopped

¼ cup finely cut fresh dill leaves, or 2 tablespoons dried dill weed

¼ cup parsley, minced

½ teaspoon salt

¼ teaspoon pepper

1/3 cup milk

½ pound Feta cheese, finely crumbled

4 eggs, lightly beatened

½ pound butter, melted

16 sheets (½ pound) fillo pastry, each about 16 inches long and 12 inches wide

In a 10 or 12 inch skillet, heat olive oil over moderate heat until a light haze forms above skillet. Add onions and scallions, stirring frequently. Cook for 5 minutes. Stir in spinach, cover tightly and cook for 5 minutes. Add dill, parsley, salt and pepper; stirring and shaking almost constantly. Cook uncovered 10 minutes or until most of the liquid in pan has evaporated and spinach sticks lightly to pan. Transfer spinach mixture to deep bowl. Stir in milk. Cool to room temperature. Add cheese and slowly beat in eggs. Preheat oven to 300°. With a pastry brush coat bottom and sides of a 12x7x2 inch baking dish with melted butter. Line dish with a sheet of fillo, pressing edges of pastry firmly into corners and against sides. Brush entire surface of pastry with 2 or 3 teaspoons butter, spreading to outside edges. Place another sheet of fillo on top. Continue layering butter and fillo until there are 8 layers of fillo in all. Spread spinach mixture evenly over last row of fillo. Smooth into corners. Place a layer of fillo on top. Spread with buter and continue until 8 more layers are completed. Trim excess pastry from rim of dish with scissors. Bake at 300° for 1 hour or until pastry is crisp and browned. Cut into squares. Serve hot or at room temperature.

Mrs. Kenneth Claussen

STEAK TARTARE BARATTE

Serves 24

5 pounds sirloin, all fat
  removed, ground 3 times
5 tablespoons Worcestershire
  sauce
½ teaspoon sea salt
¾ tablespoon freshly ground
  pepper
1 tablespoon mustard
½ tablespoon ground nutmeg
¼ teaspoon anise
¼ teaspoon cloves
3 garlic cloves, pressed
½ cup onion, minced fine
2 tablespoons capers
4 drops Tabasco
Juice of 1 lemon
4 tablespoons cognac
2 eggs, slightly beaten

A few hours before serving mix
all the ingredients thoroughly.
Press into a deep pottery bowl.
Cover and refrigerate until ready
to use. Unmold on platter and
garnish with parsley. Serve with
toast points or Melba toast.
John Baratte

STEAK TARTARE SHEPHERD

Serves 10

2 pounds sirloin, fat removed,
  ground 3 times
2 egg yolks, slightly beaten
Juice of 2 lemons
1 small tin anchovies, mashed
1 teaspoon Tabasco
1 teaspoon Worcestershire sauce
1 large onion, minced
1 small bottle capers
Salt and pepper to taste
Parsley
Watercress

A few hours before serving mix
all ingredients together
thoroughly. Shape into a mound
on a serving platter, cover and
refrigerate until serving time.
Serve very cold. Garnish with
parsley and/or watercress and
serve with Melba toast.
Mrs. William Vass Shepherd

PARTY TOMATOES

Serves 8
30 cherry tomatoes
Salt to taste
½ cup mayonnaise (see Index)
⅛ cup shallots or scallions,
** finely chopped**
1 tablespoon fresh chives,
** chopped**
1 teaspoon tarragon
½ tablespoon basil
½ tablespoon garlic, finely
** minced**
1 hard boiled egg, finely sieved
½ pound lump crabmeat
Freshly ground pepper to taste
Parsley sprigs

Core tomatoes and scoop out pulp. Salt the inside of the tomatoes, and place cut side down to drain on a rack on paper towels. Combine the remaining ingredients except parsley. Fill the tomatoes and refrigerate. Serve chilled on a platter garnished with parsley sprigs.

Mrs. Orin Ford Pearson

ANN'S RAW VEGETABLE DIP

2 cups mayonnaise (see Index)
2 garlic cloves, chopped
2 teaspoons curry powder
1 teaspoon Tabasco or to taste
1 tablespoon mustard
½ cup ketchup
1 teaspoon Worcestershire sauce
2 tablespoons horseradish
1 small onion, finely chopped

Mix all of the ingredients together and refrigerate. This dip is better if it is made a day before serving. Use as a dip for cauliflower, celery, carrots, cherry tomatoes and bell peppers.

Mrs. Kenneth Ryskamp

COFFEE PUNCH

Serves 48
6 ounce jar instant coffee
1½ cups sugar
1 quart boiling water
1 gallon vanilla ice cream
2 cups light rum
2 quarts milk
2 quarts cold water

Dissolve coffee and sugar in 1 quart boiling water and stir well and refrigerate. When ready to serve combine the cold coffee-sugar syrup with the remaining ingredients and pour into a punch bowl. (Leave the ice cream in a large piece.) Serve in punch cups.

Mrs. Robert M. McKey, Jr.

BLOODY BULLS — Palace Hotel — St. Moritz

Makes 2 quarts
18 ounce can Sacramento tomato juice
18 ounces beef bouillon
½ teaspoon salt
2 teaspoons Tabasco
2 tablespoons Worcestershire sauce
1 scant teaspoon Spice Islands black pepper, medium grind
6 ounces lemon juice
18 ounces vodka
Aromat or Spice Islands seasoning salt for garnish

Mix all of the ingredients well and chill. Serve over a generous amount of ice in over sized wine glasses. Sprinkle with Aromat.
John R. Renuart

CHRISTMAS WASSAIL

Makes 9 cups
6 sticks cinnamon
18 whole cloves
1 teaspoon whole allspice
3 medium oranges
6 cups apple juice
1 pint cranberry juice
¼ cup sugar
1 teaspoon bitters
1 cup rum

Divide cloves and stick equal amounts in three oranges. Add all ingredients, except rum, to a large saucepan and simmer for 10-15 minutes. Remove the loose spices, add the rum and serve hot.
Mrs. Boyce Ezell, III

FORD MILK PUNCH

Serves 24
1½ gallons ice milk
1 gallon milk
2 fifths bourbon
1 fifth rum
1 cup white Creme de Cacao

Let one gallon of ice-milk get mushy. Add milk and liquors and mix thoroughly. Place in freezer and freeze. Two hours before serving remove from freezer and place in punch bowl. Add ½ gallon ice milk just before serving as "ice" for punch. Serve in cups.
Mrs. Fred E. Luhm

FROZEN DAIQUIRI PUNCH

3 medium cans pink lemonade
36 ounces 7-Up
Fifth light rum

Mix all ingredients and freeze until slushy.

Mrs. Frederick A. Alders

HOT BUTTERED RUM

1 pound butter
2 pounds light brown sugar
1 teaspoon cinnamon
1 teaspoon ground cloves
1 teaspoon allspice
1 teaspoon nutmeg
3 eggs, beaten
Rum
Cinnamon sticks

Melt butter, add spices and pour over brown sugar stirring well. Set aside to cool. Add eggs and beat thoroughly. To serve pour 1½ ounces rum into mug. Add a generous tablespoon of the brown sugar syrup and enough boiling water to fill the mug. Stir well with a cinnamon stick and serve immediately.

Mrs. Fred E. Luhm

REMOS FIZZ

Makes 4 large or 8 small drinks
1 small can frozen lemonade
1 lemonade can of gin
½ lemonade can of heavy cream
Whites of 2 eggs
2-3 drops vanilla
Dash orange flower water
   (optional)

Combine ingredients in blender. Fill blender with ice and blend until the ice is completely combined with the ingredients. Serve immediately in chilled stemmed glasses or julep cups.

John R. Renuart

SANGRIA

1 large bottle red wine
1 jigger cognac
1 jigger Kirschwasser
2 shakes cinnamon
16 ounces seltzer
1 jigger Cointreau
1 jigger whiskey
8 ounces fresh orange juice
Sugar to taste
Lots of fresh fruit, cut up
   (peaches, oranges, bananas,
   etc.)

Mix all of the ingredients and chill for several hours. Serve over ice in tall glasses.

Mrs. Orin Ford Pearson

Chowders & Soups

CHOWDERS AND SOUPS

Each May and June, Miami is ablaze with the flowers of the Royal Poinciana tree. These beautiful flowers supply the background for a nineteenth century Navajo blanket, part of a very large collection of American Indian blankets in the collection of the Lowe Art Museum.

NEW ENGLAND CLAM CHOWDER

Serves 10-12 or makes 3 quarts
½ pound lean pork, diced
1 cup onions, chopped
3 cups raw potatoes, diced
1 teaspoon salt
⅛ teaspoon white pepper
4 cups clam liquid
3 cans minced clams (10½ ounces each)
2 cups half and half cream
2 cups milk
2 tablespoons butter
Dash of Tabasco or to taste

Fry the pork in a large kettle until golden. Remove the pork and reserve. Drain off all but ¼ cup of fat. Add the onion and cook for 5 minutes. Add the potatoes, 4 cups of clam liquid, and salt and pepper. (Reserve the liquid from the clams and add clam broth or water.) Simmer until the potatoes are tender. Then add the clams and all of the remaining ingredients. Heat thoroughly and serve.

Mrs. Jack Courtright

FLORIDA STYLE FISH CHOWDER

Serves 8
4 tablespoons butter or salt pork drippings
1 cup onions, sliced
1 teaspoon dried thyme
3 cups potatoes, diced
1 cup celery, sliced
8 cups hot water
2 teaspoons salt
⅛ teaspoon pepper
2 pounds tomatoes, canned or fresh
1½ cups carrots, diced
2 pounds fish, scallops or crawfish, or a combination

Melt the butter or fat in a deep kettle and add the onions and thyme. Cook until tender but not brown. Add the potatoes, celery, water, salt and pepper. Cover and simmer for five minutes. Add the tomatoes and carrots and simmer, uncovered, for one hour or so. Cut the fish into chunks or halve the scallops. Add the seafood to the kettle. Cook for 30 minutes longer or until done. Correct the seasonings and serve.

John Pennekamp

BEACHCOMBER FISH CHOWDER

Serves 8
½ stick of butter
2 Spanish onions, chopped
3-4 garlic cloves, minced
**1 green pepper, seeded and
    chopped**
½ cup celery, chopped
Olive oil (optional)
**2 pounds ripe tomatoes, peeled,
    seeded and chopped**
2 cups tomato sauce
2 quarts clear fish stock
10 bay leaves
1 tablespoon oregano
1 teaspoon basil
Salt and pepper, to taste
Tabasco sauce, to taste
**4 ears fresh corn, kernels
    removed**
4 medium potatoes, diced
**4 pounds fresh fish — grouper or
    any combination of fish**

Cook the first five ingredients in butter until the onion is tender (transparent). If more oil is needed, add olive oil, instead of butter, 1 tablespoon at a time. Combine the rest of the ingredients except the corn, potatoes, and fish. Simmer for about one hour. Add the fish, corn and potatoes and simmer for ½ hour or until the potatoes are done. Correct the seasonings and serve.

Mrs. Lindsey D. Pankey, Jr.

SHRIMP AND CLAM CHOWDER

Serves 6
**¼ pound salt pork, cut into ⅛
    inch pieces, or bacon**
1 cup onions, chopped
4 cups potatoes, diced
3 cups cold water
3 cans clams and juice
2 cups light cream
⅛ teaspoon thyme
**1-1½ pounds shrimp, cooked
    and clean**
Salt and pepper to taste
2 tablespoons butter
Paprika to taste

Fry the salt pork or bacon for 3 minutes, reduce the heat, and stir in the onions. Cook for 5 minutes longer. Add the potatoes and the water. Bring to a boil; reduce the heat and simmer with the pan half covered for 15 minutes. Add the clams, cream, thyme, shrimp and salt and pepper. Keep warm until ready to serve. At the last minute, add the butter and the paprika.

Mrs. James Hauf

AVOCADO SOUP

Serves 4
1 recipe cream of chicken soup
(see Index)
1 cup avocado, mashed
1 pinch of ground ginger
1 orange rind, grated
1 lime, thinly sliced

Stir or blend the mashed avocado into the cream of chicken soup until the mixture is smooth. If a thinner soup is desired, thin with chilled cream. Add the ginger and orange rind and season to taste. Serve cold in chilled cups garnished with diced avocado and slices of lime.

Mrs. Murray McClain

NAVY BEAN SOUP (U.S. Senate Restaurant)

Serves 6
1 pound dry navy beans
1 ham hock, with some meat
2 cups onions, chopped
1 cup celery, chopped with
leaves
2 cloves garlic, pressed
¼ cup parsley, chopped
1 cup potatoes, mashed
Dash of Tabasco
1 teaspoon salt
⅛ teaspoon white pepper

Cover the beans in water and soak over night. Place the ham hock and the drained beans in 3 quarts of water in a Dutch oven. Bring to a boil. Reduce the heat and simmer, covered, for 2 hours. Add the remainder of the ingredients and simmer covered, for another hour. Remove the ham hock, dice the meat, and return the meat to the pot. Adjust the seasonings and serve.

Mrs. Jack Courtright

SPANISH BEAN SOUP

Serves 6-8
1 pound Italian sweet sausage
1 large onion, chopped
1 clove garlic, minced
1 tablespoon Bija-Bekal
(Spanish seasoning)
¼ teaspoon turmeric
¼ teaspoon sweet basil
1 teaspoon salt
2-3 potatoes, peeled and cubed
2 cans garbanzo beans
(chick peas)
1 can chorizas, sliced (optional)
1 pinch saffron
3 cups water or chicken broth
½ cup white wine

Brown the sausage in a large Dutch oven, remove and slice. Drain all but 2 tablespoons of the fat and sauté the onions and garlic. Add the remaining ingredients and simmer slowly for at least 1 hour.

Mrs. Larry Stewart

PUREÉ OF CARROT SOUP

Serves 6
4 carrots
¼ pound of butter
2 tablespoons onions, chopped
Pinch of salt
Pinch of sugar
1 quart consommé
1/3 cup rice, uncooked
Croutons

Cut 4 carrots into thin slices and cook until tender in 3 tablespoons of butter, using a heavy covered pan. Add the chopped onion, the salt, and the sugar. Add one quart of consommé and 1/3 cup of rice. Simmer gently with the lid on. Shortly before serving, pureé the mixture in the blender. Reheat and add the remaining butter. Serve in cups garnished with croutons, sauteed in 1 tablespoon of butter.

Mrs. George Hero

CREAM OF CHICKEN SOUP

Serves 4
4 tablespoons butter
½ cup flour
4 cups chicken stock
Salt and pepper to taste
1 egg yolk
½ cup cream

Melt the butter over low heat. Stir in the flour until the mixture is smooth, but not brown. Add the chicken stock gradually, stirring constantly until the soup begins to thicken. Reduce the heat and cook from 15 to 30 minutes, stirring occasionally. Cool the soup slightly, then correct the seasonings and chill. After the soup is cooled, stir in the egg yolk beaten with the cream.

Mrs. Murray McClain

CURRIED CHICKEN SOUP

Serves 2-3
2 tablespoons onion, chopped
1 tablespoon celery, diced
1-2 teaspoons curry powder
1 tablespoon butter
1 recipe cream of chicken soup
    (see Index)
Toasted almonds, crushed

In a saucepan, cook the onion and celery with the curry powder in butter until tender. Blend into the soup and heat, stirring occasionally. Garnish with crushed almonds.

Mrs. William Atwill

CARD SOUND CRAB SOUP

Serves 8
1 pound fresh blue crab
  crabmeat
¼ cup key lime juice
2 tablespoons butter
2 tablespoons flour
3 cups clear fish stock
1½ cups light cream or half and
  half
1½ cups whole milk
Salt and white pepper to taste
¼ cup pale dry sherry

Pour the key lime juice over the fresh crabmeat. In a heavy soup pot melt the butter over moderate heat. Stir in the flour, mix thoroughly and let it bubble for a minute. Pour in ½ cup of fish stock and stir constantly with a wire whisk until the mixture is thick and bubbly. Add the remaining stock, cream, milk, salt and pepper. Bring almost to a boil; then simmer. Add the crab meat and the sherry. Simmer for 2-3 minutes to blend the flavors and serve. Extra sherry added at the table is often preferred.

Mrs. Lindsey D. Pankey, Jr.

COLD CUCUMBER-YOGURT SOUP

Serves 4 (small)
1½ cups cucumbers, peeled and
  diced
2 teaspoons fresh dill, chopped
2 tablespoons onion, minced
1 clove garlic, minced
2 tablespoons olive oil
1 teaspoon salt
¼ teaspoon black pepper,
  medium grind
⅛ cup fresh parsley, chopped
1 cup plain yogurt

Combine all of the ingredients, except the yogurt, in a non-metallic bowl at least 3 hours before serving. Stir to blend and allow the mixture to marinate in the refrigerator. Just before serving, add the yogurt and put the entire mixture in the blender for a few seconds on low speed. Blend just long enough to mix the ingredients and chop the cucumber chunks. The soup is a thick pureé. Serve in chilled cups garnished with fresh parsley.

Mrs. Robert Hartnett

COURT BOUILLON

Serves 10
2 carrots, sliced
2 celery stems
2 small onions, sliced
10 coriander seeds
½ teaspoon thyme
8 whole peppercorns
1 clove garlic
½ teaspoon fresh lemon juice
½ cup olive oil
2 quarts cold water

Combine all of the ingredients in a large pot. Simmer for 10 minutes before adding chicken or vegetables.

John Baratte

CUCUMBER AND SPINACH SOUP

Serves 8
7 small or medium whole
  scallions, sliced
¼ cup butter
4 cups cucumbers, peeled and
  diced
3 cups chicken broth
1 cup fresh spinach, chopped
½ cup potatoes, peeled and
  sliced
½ teaspoon salt
Pepper to taste
lemon juice, to taste
1 cup light cream

Sauté the scallions in buter until soft. Add the cucumbers, chicken broth, spinach, potatoes, lemon juice and salt and pepper. Simmer until the potatoes are tender. Transfer, in thirds, to a blender and pureé. Place the pureé in a bowl and stir in the light cream. Chill for several hours or overnight. Garnish with slices of cucumber, radishes, scallions or a drop of sour cream.

Mrs. Stanley Wasman

BUTTERMILK SURPRISE

Serves 2-3
½ pound shrimp, cooked,
  cleaned, and finely chopped
¼ medium cucumber, peeled
  and finely diced
1 teaspoon fresh dill, minced
1 teaspoon prepared mustard
½ teaspoon salt
½ teaspoon sugar
2 cups buttermilk

Mix the shrimp, the cucumber, and the seasonings. Stir in the buttermilk thoroughly. Chill and serve.

Mrs. Orin Ford Pearson

COLD FRESH FRUIT SOUP

Serves 12
1 medium cantalope
1 quart strawberries
½ pound green grapes
4 cooking apples, quartered, cored, peeled and coarsely chopped
¾ cup fresh lemon juice
½ cup sugar
6 cups water
1½ cups fresh orange juice
Sour cream as soup topping (optional)

Cut the cantalope in half and remove the seeds. Scoop out the pulp with a large spoon and chop coarsely. Wash the strawberries, remove and discard the stems. Combine all of the fresh fruit with ½ cup lemon juice, sugar and water in a 4 to 6 quart saucepan. Boil over high heat. Reduce the heat to low and simmer uncovered for 15 minutes. Pureé the soup through a food mill, or pour the contents of the pan into a large fine sieve over a bowl and force the ingredients through with the back of a spoon. Press down hard on the fruits before discarding any remaining pulp. Stir the remaining ¼ cup of lemon juice and the orange juice into the soup and chill for at least 2 hours. Serve in soup plates, garnished with sour cream. This recipe can also be used as a punch or tropical drink with vodka or rum.

Mrs. Kenneth Claussen

GARBANZO SOUP

Serves 4
Stock from ham bone
3 medium potatoes, diced
2 medium onions, diced
2 cans garbanzo beans (chick peas)
1 teaspoon turmeric or pinch of saffron
Salt and pepper
Hard salami, diced

Cook the potatoes and onions in the ham stock until tender. Add the garbanzo beans and spices. Add the diced salami just before serving.

Mrs. William Harward

GAZPACHO I

Serves 10
½ cup olive or Wesson oil
½ cup lime juice
6 cups V8 juice
2 cups beef broth
½ cup onion, finely minced
2 cups celery, finely minced
1½ cucumbers, finely diced
¼ teaspoon Tabasco, or to taste
2 teaspoons salt
½ teaspoon pepper, freshly
  ground

Beat the oil and lime juice together. Stir in the V8 juice, beef broth, and vegetables. Adjust the seasonings and chill for at least three hours. Serve with gazpacho garnishes, listed after Gazpacho II.

Mrs. Murray McClain

GAZPACHO II

Serves 8
1½ cups white bread, cubed and
  toasted
1 teaspoon salt
1½ teaspoons cumin, powdered
  or ground
3 tablespoons olive oil
2 large garlic cloves, peeled and
  pressed
1½ cups ripe tomatoes, peeled,
  cored, and roughly chopped
1½ cups canned tomatoes,
  drained
½ cup beef bouillon, undiluted
½ teaspoon Tabasco sauce
3 tablespoons wine vinegar
Black pepper to taste
GAZPACHO GARNISHES:
Croutons
2 cups green pepper, diced
2 cups scallions, chopped
2 cups cucumbers, diced

In the electric blender, pureé the bread with the salt, cumin, olive oil, and garlic. Add the tomatoes, bouillon, Tabasco sauce, vinegar, and black pepper. Blend at high speed. Taste the mixture and correct the seasonings. This gazpacho is rather thick and has a strong bite or peppery taste. Chill thoroughly. Serve the garnishes in separate bowls, so that each guest may stir what he likes into his soup.

Note: If serving from a tureen or punch bowl, freeze one or two ice trays full of Clamato juice. The frozen juice will keep the gazpacho cold, without diluting the flavor.

Mrs. Robert M. McKey, Jr.

MARY FRANCES WHITESIDE'S GUMBO

Serves 8-10 (makes 2 quarts)
1 pound fresh okra or 2 packages
  frozen okra, thawed
1 pound claw crabmeat
1 pint oysters
2 pounds medium shrimp
1 large green pepper, chopped
½ cup celery, chopped
1 large onion, chopped
6 cloves garlic, minced
Parsley, finely chopped
  (optional)
20 ounces whole tomatoes
3-4 bay leaves
2½ tablespoons salt
1 tablespoon white pepper
1 teaspoon ginger
1 cup butter
½ cup flour
Gumbo Filé to taste,
  approximately 1-2 teaspoons

Wash the okra. Clean and shell the seafood. Chop the celery, onion, green pepper, and parsley. Mince the garlic and set all aside. In a shrimp boiler, add tomatoes and water (use oyster water if available) and heat to boiling. Add the bay leaves, salt, pepper, parsley and ginger. Blend well and reduce the temperature to simmer. Melt the butter in a frying pan, and add the vegetables and garlic; sauté until transparent. Add the flour and blend well. Raise the heat and cook until golden brown, 5-8 minutes. When the roux is cooked, add it to the tomatoes and water mixture and blend all together. Bring to a boil in a covered boiler, skimming off the foam. Add the shrimp and crab and simmer for one hour. Stir occasionally. Add the okra and continue to cook for 30 minutes. If oysters are to be used, add them during the last 20 minutes. Reduce the heat to just below boiling and add Filé powder to taste. *Do not boil* after Filé has been added. Serve over hot rice.

This recipe may be frozen in individual portions and reheated. However, be careful *not* to boil.

Mrs. Douglas Oppenheimer

COLD LEMON SOUP

Serves 6
2 quarts chicken consommé
1 cup raw rice
4 egg yolks
½ pound butter
Juice of 2 lemons
Salt to taste
Dash of cayenne pepper
Grated rind of 2 lemons
2 tablespoons parsley, minced

Simmer the consommé and rice until the rice is very soft. Chill. Whisk small pieces of the butter into the egg yolks in the top of a double boiler until the mixture begins to thicken. Add 1 teaspoon of lemon juice to the yolks and continue to whisk until the rest of the butter is absorbed. Add more lemon juice to taste and season. Strain the consommé and discard the rice. Add the remainder of the lemon juice and the rind to the soup. Spoon a large dollop of the lemon-egg mixture into the soup and sprinkle with parsley.

Mrs. Murray McClain

LENTIL SOUP WITH MUSHROOMS

Serves 8-10
4 tablespoons butter
1 cup celery, minced with leaves
2 cups onion, minced
5 garlic cloves, crushed
½ pound boiled ham, cut into thin strips
5 cups tomatoes, seeded and chopped
1½ teaspoons oregano
Salt and pepper to taste
2½ cups dried lentils, washed
6 cups chicken stock
4 cups water
1 pound mushrooms, sliced
Tabasco to taste
2-3 tablespoons butter
Parmesan cheese, freshly grated
Croutons

Sauté the celery and onion in butter until soft. Add the crushed garlic. Add the ham and sauté for a few minutes. Add the tomatoes, oregano, salt and pepper and simmer 6 minutes. Transfer all to a soup kettle and add the lentils, the chicken stock and the water. Add the sliced mushrooms and the chopped stems. Simmer the soup 2 hours or more. Add Tabasco, additional butter and correct seasonings. Serve with freshly grated Parmesan cheese and sautéed croutons. Excellent as a first course with lamb or as a main course with a salad and French bread.

Mrs. John Renuart

CREAM OF LETTUCE SOUP

Serves 8
8 scallions, chopped
6 tablespoons sweet butter
1 clove garlic, crushed
2 tablespoons parsley, chopped
1¼ teaspoons salt
¼ teaspoon Tabasco
3 heads of Boston lettuce,
   washed and cleaned
2 cups water
5 cups chicken stock
1 cup heavy cream, heated
3 egg yolks

Sauté the scallions in butter until clear. Add the garlic, parsley, salt, Tabasco, lettuce leaves, and water. Cover the pan and simmer for 15 minutes. Pour the mixture into a blender and puree. Add the 5 cups of chicken stock to the lettuce puree. Bring this mixture to a boil. Beat the egg yolks with the hot cream and add to the soup gradually. *Do not boil.* Serve at once.

Mrs. John Renuart

MUSHROOM SOUP

Serves 6-8
1 tablespoon butter
1 tablespoon olive oil
1 medium onion, grated
1 garlic clove
1 pound of mushroom caps,
   thinly sliced
2½ tablespoons tomato paste
3 cups chicken broth
4 tablespoons sweet Marsala
Salt and pepper to taste
4 egg yolks
3 tablespoons Parmesan cheese,
   grated
2 tablespoons parsley, finely
   chopped

Sauté the onion and garlic in the butter and olive oil until lightly brown. Remove the garlic. Add the mushrooms and sauté for 4 to 5 minutes. Stir in the tomato paste. Add the 3 cups of chicken broth with the sweet Marsala. Season with salt and pepper and simmer for 10 minutes. Beat the egg yolks and mix with the parsley and grated cheese. Blend this mixture quickly into the boiling soup. Serve immediately with toasted French bread spread with Parmesan butter.

Mrs. Murray McClain

CREAM OF MUSHROOM SOUP

Serves 8
1 pound mushrooms, thin sliced
1 quart chicken broth
2 tablespoons butter
2 tablespoons flour
6 tablespoons cognac
2 cups coffee cream, heated
Salt to taste

Simmer the mushroom stems with the chicken broth for 30 minutes. Strain the broth and add one cup of the broth to the paste made by mixing the butter and flour and blend. Add this mixture to the rest of the broth and stir until slightly thickened. Slice the mushroom caps thinly, add to the broth, and simmer for 8-10 minutes. Add the cognac and then the heated cream. Use salt if needed.

Mrs. Murray McClain

ONION SOUP

Serves 6
¼ cup butter
4 cups onion, thinly sliced
5 cups beef bouillon
3-4 tablespoons cognac
4-6 slices French bread,
  one inch thick
¼ cup Gruyere cheese, freshly
  grated
2 tablespoons Parmesan cheese,
  freshly grated

In a large skillet, sauté the onion in the butter over medium heat until golden — about 8 minutes. In a medium saucepan, combine the bouillon, the cognac and onions. Bring to a boil. Reduce the heat and simmer, covered for 30 minutes. Toast the French bread on both sides. Sprinkle each slice with grated cheese and broil until the cheese is just bubbly. Pour the soup in a tureen or soup bowls and float the toast, cheese side up. This soup is very good refrigerated and reheated.

Mrs. Orin Ford Pearson

MONGOLE GLACÉ GEORGE DICKERSON

Serves 2
1 can pea soup
1¼ cup light cream
1 teaspoon curry powder
¼ teaspoon salt
Chives or scallions, minced

Blend all of the ingredients except chives or scallions and chill thoroughly. Serve in chilled cups, garnished with fresh chives or minced scallions.

Mrs. John Renuart

POCAHONTAS SOUP

Serves 8
3 tablespoons butter
1 cup onions, minced
¼ cup carrots, grated
Salt, white pepper to taste
2 medium white potatoes, peeled and cubed
2 acorn squash, peeled and cubed
4 cups chicken broth
½ cup heavy cream
½ cup milk
1 teaspoon salt
¼ teaspoon white pepper
Cayenne pepper

In a saucepan, melt the butter. Add the minced onions and grated carrots. Sprinkle the vegetables lightly with salt and white pepper. Cover the pan with a sheet of buttered waxpaper and the lid, and cook the vegetables for 10 minutes until tender. (Do not allow to brown.) Add the potatoes and acorn squash, and the chicken broth. Discard the waxpaper. Simmer covered over low heat about 25 minutes or until the potatoes and the squash are very tender. Place the mixture in a blender and pureé a few seconds until smooth. Return it to the pan and add heavy cream and milk. Cook the soup until it is heated through and add salt and white pepper. Pour the soup into a tureen and serve it in heated cups. Sprinkle with cayenne pepper. This soup is excellent with Thanksgiving dinner. It can be prepared ahead and reheated before serving.

Mrs. Robert M. McKey, Jr.

PUMPKIN SOUP

Serves 12
6 tablespoons butter
8 scallions, chopped
1 large sweet onion, sliced
4 tablespoons flour
3 pounds of pumpkin puree, fresh or canned
8 cups chicken stock
Pinch of coriander, ginger, nutmeg and cinnamon
1 pint half and half
½ pint heavy cream
GARNISH: lightly salted whipped cream

Melt the butter and cook the onion and scallions until soft, not brown. Add the flour and cook a few minutes more. Then add the pumpkin pureé and as soon as it is mixed well, add the chicken stock. Bring the soup to a boil. Cook and blend in the blender. Add the spices and the half and half, return to the pan, and cook for five more minutes. Add the salt and pepper to taste. Before heating to serve, add the heavy cream. Do not boil. Top each serving with a dollop of lightly salted whipped cream.

Mrs. John Renuart

CLEAR FISH STOCK

Serves 12
5 pounds fish heads, bones,
    tails, and fins
2 pounds white fish
2½ quarts water
2 carrots, sliced
1 cup mushrooms, sliced
1 large onion, chopped
2 leeks, sliced
1 bay leaf
1½ tablespoons thyme
2 teaspoons salt
¾ teaspoon lemon juice
2½ cups dry white wine

Wash the fish and place with all of the above ingredients in a large saucepan. Cover and bring to the boiling point. Reduce the heat and simmer for 1 hour. Periodically skim off the grey residue. Strain through a fine sieve or double cheese cloth, wrung out in cold water. Refrigerate and use as needed. This recipe can be served as a soup or used as a sauce base. However, it is a strong stock, so use small amounts.

John Baratte

AGNES NEWTON'S CREAM OF TOMATO SOUP

Serves 12
6 cups medium white sauce (see
    Index)
6 cups tomato purée, hot
3 tablespoons onion juice
3 tablespoons celery juice
1/3 cup butter, melted
Croutons

Make the white sauce just before serving and add the tomato puree to the hot white sauce. The tomato pureé should be hot too, as the soup will curdle if both liquids are reheated. Pour the soup into a tureen and add the juices and butter and stir gently to mix. Serve with the croutons.

Mrs. George W. Cornell

TOMATO AND ORANGE BROTH

Serves 4
2 cups tomato juice
2 cups orange juice, freshly
    squeezed
¼ cup lemon juice
Pinch of coriander
Tabasco to taste
Salt to taste

Blend together all of the above ingredients and serve, ice cold, in chilled cups.

Mrs. John Renuart

GREEN TURTLE SOUP

Serves 10-12
1 pound turtle meat, minced
1½ pounds veal stew meat,
    approximately, minced
1 large Spanish onion, minced
1 large clove garlic, minced
1 cup celery tops, chopped
1 bay leaf
2 cloves, whole
2 allspice, pounded
Salt and black pepper, to taste
Dash of cayenne
Sprig of thyme or 1 teaspoon
2 eggs, hard boiled
1 cup sherry
1 lemon, sliced thin
¼ cup parsley, chopped fine

Put all but the last 5 ingredients in 3 quarts of cold water. Season with the salt, black pepper and a dash of cayenne; simmer for 6 hours. Half an hour before serving, add the thyme. Slice hard boiled eggs and add them to the soup. When the soup is removed from the heat, add the sherry. Float a slice of lemon and chopped parsley on top of each serving.

Mrs. Lindsey D. Pankey, Jr.

ITALIAN SPRING VEGETABLE SOUP

Serves 6
2 tablespoons butter
1 medium onion, chopped
2 small stalks of celery with
    leaves, chopped
6 cups chicken broth
1 large unpeeled zucchini, thinly
    sliced
½ cup green peas
½ cup broccoli flowerets
½ cup cut green beans
½ cup chopped spinach
½ cup soup pasta
Salt and pepper to taste
½ cup Parmesan cheese, grated

Heat the butter and sauté the onion and celery until soft. Add the onions and celery to the broth and bring to a boil. Add the vegetables and the pasta. Cook for 10 minutes. Do not overcook. Add salt and pepper to taste. Serve topped with grated Parmesan cheese.

Mrs. Charles Miller

VICHYSSOISE

Serves 8
2 pounds of potatoes, diced
½ pound leeks, chopped fine
2 bay leaves
½ cup chicken stock
1 teaspoon sugar
2 teaspoons salt
2 quarts water
Corn starch as needed
Heavy cream
Chives, freshly chopped

Combine all of the first 7 ingredients and simmer, covered, for 1½ hours. Thicken the mixture with the corn starch, 1 tablespoon at a time until the desired consistency. Force the mixture through a strainer and measure the amount of liquid. Add an equal amount of cream stirring well. Refrigerate until serving time. Serve the soup cold sprinkled generously with the chopped chives.

Mrs. Orin Ford Pearson

COLD YOGURT SOUP

Serves 8
3 cups yogurt
1½ cups cold chicken broth
2½ cucumbers, peeled, seeded and coarsely grated
½ cup red radishes, minced
3 tablespoons white wine vinegar
3 tablespoons olive oil
Salt and a little red pepper, to taste
GARNISH: minced radishes and scallions

Combine all of the ingredients and chill thoroughly. Serve in chilled tea cups or in mugs and pass before dinner.

Mrs. John Renuart

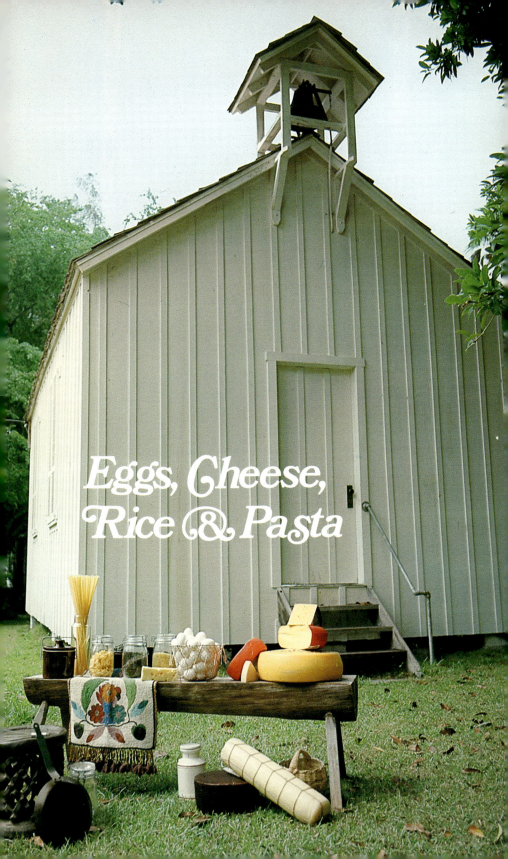

Eggs, Cheese, Rice & Pasta

EGGS, CHEESE, RICE AND PASTA

Coconut Grove's Old School House, built in 1887 and listed on the National Register of Historic Places, adds local history to an African Bamoum man's stool. The stool, carved from a solid log, was donated to the Lowe Art Museum by Raymond Ball. On the log bench is a North American Indian beaded pouch that was made in the nineteenth century. The pouch was a gift to the Museum from Mr. Alfred I. Barton.

EGGS EUROPEAN

Serves 6
1 package frozen chopped
  spinach
2 tablespoons butter
2 teaspoons lemon juice
1/4 teaspoon celery salt
Salt and pepper to taste
1 cup medium cream sauce (see
  Index)
1 1/2 teaspoons onion, grated
Pinch nutmeg
6 eggs
1 cup Swiss cheese, grated

Cook spinach according to package directions and drain well. Season with butter, lemon juice, celery salt, salt and pepper. Add cream sauce, grated onion and nutmeg to spinach and mix thoroughly. Place in shallow 1 1/2 quart baking dish. Break eggs over spinach mixture. Sprinkle cheese over eggs. Bake at 350° for 25-30 minutes or until eggs are set.

Mrs. John Slaton

FAVORITE EGGS

Serves 4
2 tablespoons (or more) butter
1 small package cream cheese,
  diced
8-10 eggs, beaten with whisk
2 tablespoons chives, minced
Salt and pepper to taste

Melt butter in skillet. Add diced cream cheese. When cheese softens, add eggs and chives. Scramble until done.

Mrs. Fred E. Luhm

EGGS HUSSARDE

Serves 2
4 large thin slices of grilled ham
4 Holland rusks or 2 English
  muffins, split and toasted
1 cup Marchand de Vin sauce
  (see Index)
4 slices grilled tomatoes, salted
4 soft poached eggs
1 cup Hollandaise sauce (see
  Index)
Paprika
Parsley, chopped

For each serving, place slice of ham on rusk or muffin. Cover with Marchand de Vin sauce. Add grilled tomato slice; then poached egg, Hollandaise sauce, dust with paprika and garnish with parsley.

Mrs. George W. Cornell

MORNING GLORY EGGS

Serves 4
4 hard cooked eggs
1 recipe medium white sauce (see Index)
4 slices Canadian bacon, lightly broiled
4 slices toast

Crumble egg yolks and set aside. Chop whites and set aside. Add chopped egg whites to hot white sauce. Place a piece of Canadian bacon on each slice of toast. Top with ¼ cup creamed mixture. Sprinkle crumbled egg yolks over top.

Mrs. Maurine T. Pagan

EARLY BIRD OMELET

Serves 4
1 small onion, sliced
½ red pepper, sliced
½ green pepper, sliced
4 tablespoons butter
8 eggs, separated
1/3 cup milk
¼ teaspoon salt
Dash pepper
½ cup Cheddar cheese, grated

Preheat oven to 350°. Sauté onion and peppers in 2 tablespoons butter until tender. Keep warm. Beat egg whites until they form soft peaks. Beat yolks until creamy and thick. Stir in milk, salt, and pepper. Fold into beaten egg whites. Melt 2 tablespoons butter in 12 inch frying pan with an oven-proof handle. Pour in egg mixture. Cook over medium heat for 5 minutes or until underside is golden. Then bake at 350° for 10 minutes or until puffed and golden. Remove from oven. Make a cut through center of omelet not quite to bottom with a sharp knife. Spoon pepper mixture and Cheddar cheese over half of omelet. Fold other half over filling. Lift onto a heated serving platter. Slice crosswise into quarters.

Mrs. John Patterson

EGGS RIO GRANDE

Serves 6
2 tablespoons olive oil
½ cup tomato, diced
½ cup pepper, diced
½ cup onion, minced
6 eggs
Jalapeño or Tabasco, to taste
Salt and pepper to taste

Sauté vegetables in oil until tender. Add eggs, letting them simmer on top until they turn white. Stir continuously until eggs are done. Season with Jalapño, salt and pepper.

Mrs. Orin Ford Pearson

TEXAS EGGS

Serves 6
6 large hard cooked eggs
1 recipe medium white sauce
   (see Index)
Buttered bread crumbs

Grate white and yolks of eggs separately. Mix grated whites with cream sauce and pour into buttered 1½ quart round casserole. Cover with layer of buttered bread crumbs. Add grated yolks and top with another layer of bread crumbs. Bake at 350° for 30 to 45 minutes.

Mrs. John Slaton

SCRAMBLED EGGS WITH CRABMEAT

Serves 6
1 pound white crabmeat
¼ cup bacon, chopped
¼ cup onion, chopped
4 eggs, beaten
¼ cup cream
¾ teaspoon salt
Cayenne to taste

Pick over crab for shell pieces. Fry bacon until light brown. Add onions and sauté until tender. Combine rest of ingredients and cook until eggs are firm, stirring occasionally.

Mrs. John Renuart

SCRAMBLED FRENCH TOAST

Serves 4
4 eggs beaten
½ cup milk
Dash salt
8 slices white bread, cubed
5 tablespoons butter

Add milk and salt to beaten eggs, then stir in bread cubes. Melt butter in large frying pan over medium heat. When butter foams, add egg mixture and cook until done, stirring constantly. Serve with syrup.

Mrs. Larry Stewart

EGGS VELOUTE SHIRLEY

Serves 6
6 slices Canadian bacon, ¼ inch
    thick
6 slices French bread, 1 inch
    thick
½ pound chicken livers
2 tablespoons butter
2 tablespoons white wine
1 teaspoon scallions or shallots,
    minced
1 pound fresh mushrooms,
    sliced thin
Veloute sauce (see Index)
6 fresh extra large eggs

Saute Canadian bacon until well done. Remove bacon from pan and place on paper towel. Brown slices of bread in bacon fat left in pan and set bread aside. Rinse chicken livers well, dry off, and saute in left over bacon fat (adding butter if needed) until well done. Slice livers and place on paper towel. In clean pan melt butter. Add wine and scallions or shallots. Saute mushrooms in this mixture until done. Drain mushrooms. Place bread in a single layer in a 2 inch deep baking dish. Put a piece of bacon on each slice. Spoon on chicken livers and mushrooms. Cover with Veloute sauce. Bake at 350° for 10-15 minues or until warmed through. Meanwhile, poach 6 eggs and place poached eggs on top of warmed through casserole. Serve immediately.
Mrs. Frank Marston

EGGS WILLIAM

3 dozen pullet or small eggs,
    hard boiled
4 large cucumbers, peeled,
    seeded, and grated
3 tablespoons anchovy paste
1 cup celery, minced
2 tablespoons onion, grated
2 tablespoons or more dill,
    minced
½ cup or more mayonnaise (see
    Index)
Salt to taste
Cayenne to taste
18 capers
18 sprigs of fresh dill

Cut eggs in half. Remove yolks. To yolks add cucumbers, anchovy paste, celery, onion, minced dill and enough mayonnaise to make desired consistency. Mound into egg whites. Place a caper on the middle of half of the eggs and a sprig of dill on the other half.
Mrs. John Renuart

QUICHE LORRAINE I

Excellent luncheon dish.

Serves 5
9 inch pie crust (see Index)
½ pound bacon, fried crisp
½ cup onions, chopped and
   browned in bacon fat
1 cup Swiss cheese, diced
6 Vienna sausage links, diced
6 eggs
1 cup coffee cream
½ teaspoon salt

Line pie plate with pastry. Fill half full with bacon, onion, Swiss cheese, Vienna sausage. Beat together eggs and coffee cream. Pour in mixture. Bake at 350° for 45 minutes or until knife comes out clean.

Mrs. Joe Abrell

QUICHE LORRAINE II

Serves 6
1-1/3 cups plus 1 tablespoon
   flour
Pinch of salt
¼ pound butter
3 ounces cream cheese
8 thin slices cooked ham or fried
   smoked bacon
8 ounces Swiss cheese, thinly
   sliced
2 cups sour cream
3 eggs and 1 yolk
½ teaspoon salt
1 tablespoon butter
Nutmeg (optional)

Sift 1-1/3 cups flour with salt. Add butter and cream cheese. Mixture is crumbly, but eventually forms a single large ball. Set aside for 30 to 60 minutes. Roll out and line a deep pie pan. Cut ham or bacon and cheese into 1 inch x 1½ inch pieces. Cover pastry, alternating the ham and cheese. Combine remaining ingredients. Pour over ham and cheese. Sprinkle with nutmeg, if desired. Bake at 375° 35 to 40 minutes until set.

Mrs. Dwight Plyler, Jr.

QUICHE LORRAINE III

Serves 10 — 2 pies
2 pie crusts, baked (see Index)
10 cooked and crumbled slices of bacon
3 whole eggs
3 egg yolks
1¼ cups heavy cream
1¼ cup Swiss or Gruyere cheese, grated
¼ cup Parmesan cheese, grated
½ teaspoon salt
1 tablespoon onion, minced
White pepper to taste
Nutmeg, pinch
4 tablespoons butter, cut into tiny pieces

Place crumbled bacon on bottom of baked pie shell. Combine all other ingredients except butter. (This may be prepared in advance). About 30 minutes before serving, pour ingredients into pie shell over bacon and dot with butter. Bake at 375° for 25 minutes, test with a knife. Can be served up to 10 minutes after removal from oven.

Mrs. Vincent Damian
Mrs. Art Roberts
Mrs. Arthur Weller

ONION QUICHE

Serves 6
1 teaspoon butter
1 cup ham or Canadian bacon, diced
1 medium onion, grated
1 unbaked pie crust (see Index)
½ cup Swiss cheese, grated
2 large eggs
1 cup heavy cream
½ teaspoon salt
¼ teaspoon pepper
Pinch of nutmeg

Melt butter in skillet. Add meat and cook until golden brown. Remove meat. Add onions and cook about 5 minutes. Cover bottom of crust with meat, onion and cheese. Combine remaining ingredients and pour into shell. Bake at 350° for 25-30 minutes.

Mrs. Charles Killingsworth

CRAB QUICHE

Serves 6
CRUST:
1 recipe for pie crust (see Index)
1/4 teaspoon dill
1/8 teaspoon cayenne
2 tablespoons dry white wine
1 tablespoon softened butter
FILLING:
2 cups Swiss cheese, grated
1 1/2 cups crab meat
1 1/2 cups light cream
4 eggs, beaten
1 tablespoon flour
1/2 teaspoon salt
2 tablespoons sherry
Pinch cayenne
Pinch nutmeg

Preheat oven to 375°. Stir together pie crust, dill and cayenne. Combine with wine. Roll out on a lightly floured board and place in a 9 inch pie pan. Spread with soft butter. Cover crust with cheese and crabmeat. Mix cream and eggs. Combine flour, salt, and sherry; add remaining ingredients to egg mixture. Pour into pie shell. Bake 40 minutes at 375°. Let stand 20 minutes before serving.

Mrs. Kenneth Claussen

CRAB AND OLIVE QUICHE

Serves 6
9 inch pie crust, baked (see Index)
4 eggs
1-1/3 cups half and half
2 tablespoons Madeira
1/8 teaspoon nutmeg
1/8 teaspoon salt
1 pound crabmeat
1-1/3 cup Swiss cheese, grated
1/4 cup pimiento-stuffed green olives, sliced
1 tablespoon butter, melted

Beat eggs until blended and mix in half and half. Add Madeira, nutmeg and salt. Distribute crabmeat (pick out any shells or cartilage) over partially baked shell. Sprinkle shredded Swiss cheese and sliced olives over crab. Pour in custard mixture. Sprinkle surface with 1 tablespoon melted butter. Bake at 350° for 30 minutes or until custard is set and slightly puffed. Cut into wedges and garnish with parsley.

Mrs. Robert M. McKey, Jr.

MUSHROOM QUICHE

Serves 6
9 inch pie crust (see Index)
1 cup fresh mushrooms, sliced
2 tablespoons butter
2 cups natural Swiss cheese,
   grated
4 eggs
1½ cups half and half
½ teaspoon salt
¼ teaspoon white pepper
Dash nutmeg

Sauté mushrooms in butter until golden brown. Sprinkle cheese evenly over bottom of prepared pie shell. Arrange sautéed mushrooms over cheese. In medium bowl, with rotary beater, beat eggs with half and half, salt, pepper, and nutmeg, until frothy, but not bubbly. Pour into pie shell. Bake at 375° for 40 to 45 minutes or until top is golden and center seems firm when gently shaken. Remove to wire rack to cool 10 minutes before serving.

Mrs. Barbara Bachmann

BLUE CHEESE QUICHE

Serves 6
6 ounces cream cheese, softened
3 ounces blue cheese
2 tablespoons butter, softened
3 tablespoons heavy cream
2 eggs, slightly beaten
½ teaspoon onion or chives,
   minced
Salt and pepper to taste
9 inch pastry shell, partially
   baked (see Index)

Mash and blend cheeses. Add butter, cream, eggs, onions or chives, salt and pepper and mix well. Pour into pastry shell. Bake at 375° for 30 minutes or until quiche is puffed up and golden brown on top.

Mrs. James Sheley

VICKI'S QUICK CHEESE SOUFFLÉ

Serves 4
4 eggs yolks
4 slices white bread, remove
   crusts and crumble
1-1/3 cups milk
1½ cups Cheddar cheese, grated
½ cup butter
1 teaspoon Worcestershire sauce
Dash paprika
1 teaspoon baking powder
Salt and pepper to taste
4 egg whites

Beat egg yolks and mix everything except egg whites in double boiler until it thickens. Beat egg whites until very stiff. Fold together gently. Place in buttered soufflé dish (about 6½ inches x 7 inches in diameter.) Place soufflé dish in pan of boiling water. Bake at 350° until brown 45-50 minutes.

Mrs. Robert Harnett

CHAMPAGNE CHEESE FONDUE

24 ounces Gruyere cheese
½ to 1 cup champagne
1 loaf French or Italian bread

Cut Gruyere into small pieces and place in fondue pot with enough champagne to moisten cheese. Heat on top of stove at medium-high, adding champagne as needed. Stir until smooth, adding enough champagne for desired consistency. Cut bread into ½ inch chunks, each piece having some crust (so fondue fork can spear and hold it easily.) Put pot over flame. Serve with bread chunks.

Mrs. Blackwell Stieglitz

BASIC CHEESE STRATA

This dish tastes best prepared at least 6 hours in advance and baked just before serving.

Serves 8
10 slices day old white bread
2½ cups Cheddar cheese, grated
4 eggs, slightly beaten
2½ cups milk
1 teaspoon salt
¼ teaspoon white pepper
4 tablespoons butter

Trim crusts and quarter each slice. Alternate layers of bread and cheese in a well greased 11 x 17 x 1 inch baking dish, ending with cheese. Combine eggs, milk, and salt and pepper. Pour over cheese and bread layers. Dot with butter. Bake at 325° until firm 45-60 minutes. Let set 5 minutes before cutting.

Variations:
1. Add ¼ teaspoon dry mustard to liquid for tangy taste.
2. Add 1 cup chopped ham
   ¼ cup stuffed green olives, sliced
   ½ cup onion, chopped
   Combine above and spread over cheese layer.
3. Add 2 tomatoes, sliced on top

— 5 minutes before strata is done. Return to oven and finish cooking.
4. Sprinkle 1½ cups sliced mushrooms over cheese layer.
5. Sprinkle 1½ cups crabmeat or shrimp over cheese layer.

Mrs. Don Leitner
Mrs. R. Layton Mank
Mrs. Frank C. Sargent, III

BREAKFAST STRATA

Serves 12-14
1 pound hot spicy sausage (bulk or 1½ pounds link sausage, cut in 1 inch pieces)
1 pound bacon
12 slices bread, cubed
2½-3 cups sharp cheese, grated
8 eggs
Worcestershire sauce to taste
1 teaspoon salt
1 teaspoon dry mustard
1 quart milk

Fry sausage and bacon. Drain, dry, and crumble and mix together. Butter a lasagna casserole dish. Place ½ bread cubes, ½ cheese and all sausage mixture in casserole. Cover with remaining bread cubes and cheese. Beat eggs and add a little Worcestershire sauce, salt, dry mustard and milk. Pour over casserole and refrigerate overnight. Bake 1 hour at 325°.

Optional Topping:
1 can mushroom soup diluted with ½ cup milk spread on casserole. Bake 1½ hours at 300°.

Mrs. Carole Boulter
Mrs. Steve Pease
Mrs. William H. Walker

GREEN CHILI STRATA

Serves 6
6 thick bread slices, crusts removed and buttered
2 cups Cheddar cheese, shredded
2 cups California green chilies, chopped
2 cups Monterey jack or brick cheese, shredded
6 eggs
2 cups milk
2 teaspoons salt
2 teaspoons paprika
½ teaspoon oregano
½ teaspoon pepper
¼ teaspoon garlic salt
¼ teaspoon dry mustard

Place buttered bread downside in large casserole dish. Layer Cheddar cheese and 1 cup chilies on top. Add layer of Monterey jack or brick cheese, 1 cup chilies. Beat eggs. Add milk and seasonings. Pour over. Cover with plastic wrap and refrigerate overnight. Bake uncovered at 325° for 50 minutes until brown. Let set for 10 minutes. Cut and serve.

Mrs. Emery Johnson

BAKED CHEESE GRITS

Serves 8
1 cup grits
4 cups water
1 teaspoon salt
3-4 egg, beaten
1 cup sharp cheese, grated
1 cup milk
2 tablespoons Worcestershire
   sauce (optional)
½ cup butter
Black pepper to taste
1 teaspoon garlic salt, optional

Cook grits in salt and water until thick. Cool and add the beaten eggs, ¾ cup cheese, milk, Worcestershire sauce, butter, pepper, and garlic salt. Pour into a buttered baking dish and sprinkle the remaining cheese on top. Bake at 350° for 1 hour.
Variation:
Sprinkle the top with Parmesan cheese and paprika for color.
Mrs. Robert Gillander
Mrs. Dwight Plyler, Jr.

CANNELLONI

Serves 8 (3 crepes per person)
1 recipe basic crepes (see Index)
1 recipe tomato sauce (see Index)
3 cups thick white sauce (see
   Index)
4 tablespoons Parmesan cheese,
   grated
3 tablespoons butter
FILLING:
1 pound ground beef
1 tablespoon butter
¼ cup thick white sauce
CHEESE:
1 pound Ricotta cheese
4 ounces Mozzarella cheese,
   grated
¼ cup Parmesan cheese, grated
1 egg, beaten
SPINACH:
1 teaspoon garlic, crushed
¼ cup onion, diced
2 tablespoons olive oil
1 package chopped spinach,
   drained

Assembly: Prepare the crepes, tomato sauce and white sauce and set aside. Sauté beef in the butter and combine with ¼ cup white sauce. Combine the cheese, egg and salt and pepper in a large bowl with the beef mixture and set aside. Saute garlic and onion in oil. Add spinach and combine with the meat filling. Preheat the oven to 375°. Pour a thin film of tomato sauce on the bottom of a large baking dish. Place 1 tablespoon of the filling on the bottom third of each crepe and roll the crepe up like a rug. Place the cannelloni crepes in the baking dish. Pour the white sauce over the crepes. Spoon the tomato sauce over the white sauce leaving some of the white sauce showing. Cover the tomato sauce with the Parmesan cheese and dot with 3 tablespoons of butter. Bake at 375° for 20 minutes. Serve immediately.
Mrs. Jack Courtright

FETTUCINE WITH MUSHROOMS

Serves 6
1 pound noodles, cooked and
 drained
8 tablespoons butter
1¼ cups heavy cream
1 cup grated Parmesan cheese
Salt and pepper, to taste
Ground nutmeg
½ pound fresh mushrooms,
 sliced and sautéed

Cook noodles according to package directions. Keep warm. In a large frying pan over high heat, melt butter, add ½ cup cream, and boil rapidly, stirring. Reduce heat to medium. Add noodles. Toss with 2 forks and gradually pour in the cheese and remaining cream. Season with salt, pepper, and a little nutmeg. Add sautéed mushrooms and serve immediately.

Mrs. Charles Miller

PARTY MACARONI AND CHEESE

Serves 4
5 tablespoons butter
5 tablespoons flour
2 cups milk
½ cup heavy cream
Ground nutmeg, pinch
1 teaspoon salt
Pepper, to taste
¾ cup Parmesan cheese, freshly
 grated
¾ pound fresh mushrooms,
 thinly sliced
Fancy macaroni (twirls, shells,
 etc.)

In saucepan melt 3 tablespoons butter. Stir in flour and remove from heat. Beat in milk and cream. Return to heat and cook for 2 minutes. Remove from heat and add nutmeg, salt, and pepper. Add ½ cup grated cheese to hot mixture. Set aside. Saute mushrooms in 2 tablespoons butter for 3 to 4 minutes until light brown. Cook macaroni al dente. In a baking dish make layers of macaroni, mushrooms, and lastly, sauce. Sprinkle remaining cheese on top. Bake at 375° for 30 minutes. Serve at once.

Mrs. Hugh T.Whitehead

NOODLES WITH CUMIN

Serves 6
1 small package egg noodles
2 to 3 tablespoons butter
¼ to ½ cup heavy cream
Cumin, to taste (two teaspoons,
 or more)

Cook noodles according to package directions and drain. Do not wash. Add butter, cream, and cumin. (Serve hot with entree.)

Mrs. Sandy D'Alemberte

MACARONI AND CHEESE CASSEROLE

Serves 8
1½ cups milk
2 eggs, slightly beaten
1 cup cottage cheese
2 tablespoons Parmesan cheese, grated
1 teaspoon salt
Pepper, to taste
1 package Creamettes, cooked and drained
Cheddar cheese, grated
Bread crumbs

With a fork blend milk and eggs in a 2 quart baking dish. Add all remaining ingredients, except Cheddar cheese and bread crumbs. Stir to distribute evenly. Sprinkle Cheddar and bread crumbs on top. Bake at 350° for 1 hour.

Mrs. Richard O. Dowling

SPAGHETTI CARBONARA

Serves 6
1 pound linguine spaghetti
½ pound bacon, thick cut
1/3 cup dry vermouth
2 eggs, well beaten
½ cup Parmesan or Romano cheese, freshly grated
Pepper, freshly ground

Dice bacon in ½ inch squares. Sauté until cooked but not crisp. Remove bacon from pan. Add vermouth to drippings. Cook down and keep hot. Cook spaghetti for 8 minutes, drain, and return to kettle. Immediately add the bacon and wine. Mix well. Add eggs and cheese. Toss as you would a salad. Add pepper. Serve hot.

Mrs. Jack Courtright

BAKED RICE

Serves 6
½ cup butter
1½ cup rice, uncooked
1 medium onion, chopped, or bunch of chopped scallions
½ cup mushrooms
1 package slivered almonds
¼ cup chopped celery or ¼ cup fresh parsley
1 teaspoon parsley flakes
2 cans beef bouillon

Sauté rice, onion, mushrooms, almonds, and celery in butter until rice begins to brown. Add parsley and 2 cans of broth. Bake in covered baking dish at 350° for 1 hour and 15 minutes. (Prepare this in Corning ware or some other dish that can go from range top to oven.)

Mrs. Jane Warren

FRIED RICE

Serves 6
6 slices bacon
½ cup green onion, chopped
2 cups cooked rice
4 tablespoons soy sauce
¼ cup water
4 eggs, slightly beaten

Fry bacon until crisp. Drain, crumble, and reserve. Brown onion for 2 minutes. Add rice and stir fry for about 5 minutes. Add soy sauce, water, and bacon. Reduce heat before pouring in eggs. Stir fry 3 to 4 minutes until egg is cooked. (This recipe can be doubled. Any left-over meat may be used in place of the bacon.)

Mrs. Tom Pennekamp

KEY WEST FRIED RICE

Serves 6 for main course
1 medium onion, minced
4 tablespoons butter
2 cups cooked brown rice, cold
½ teaspoon paprika
1 teaspoon celery seed
¼ teaspoon ginger
1 tablespoon brown sugar
½ teaspoon Accent
½ teaspoon allspice
2 tablespoons soy sauce
¾ pound ham, cubed
1 pound shrimp, cooked and deveined
½ cup nuts (peanuts or almonds)
1 egg, well beaten
Parsley
Pineapple (optional)

Sauté onion in 2 tablespoons butter until limp. Add cold rice and 2 tablespoons more butter. Fry gently over low heat. Add the seasonings and the soy sauce. Add the ham, shrimp, nuts and the beaten egg. Stir until warm. Garnish with parsley and pineapple.

Mrs. Frank de Robertis

SAUSAGE AND RICE

Serves 6
1 pound bulk sausage
1 cup celery, chopped
1 onion, chopped
1 package chicken noodle soup
2 cups water
¾ cup rice, uncooked (not instant)
¼ cup almonds, slivered

Brown sausage well and drain. Remove from skillet and sauté onions and celery. Add soup mix, water and stir. Combine everything, garnish with almonds and bake at 350° for 1 hour in a covered dish.

Mrs. Larry Stewart

PEAS AND RICE, BAHAMA STYLE

Serves 10
Small hunk of salt pork
2 onions, chopped
2 bell peppers, chopped
4 cloves garlic, chopped
1½ cups rice, uncooked
3 cups water
1 can tomato paste
2 cans pigeon peas
Salt, pepper, and cayenne to
taste

Sauté salt pork and remove. Add onion, pepper, and garlic to fat and cook until tender. Add rice and mix together for a few minutes. Add remaining ingredients. Season to taste. Cook in Dutch oven or large covered skillet until water has evaporated and rice is done.
Mrs. George W. Cornell

SPANISH RICE

Serves 6
Cooking oil, to cover pan
1 onion, thinly sliced
½ green pepper, chopped
1 pound ground beef
1 cup uncooked rice, not instant
16 ounces tomato sauce
1¾ cups hot water
1 teaspoon prepared mustard
1 teaspoon salt
Pepper to taste

Heat oil. Add onion, green pepper, beef, and rice. Stir over high heat until browned. Add remaining ingredients and mix well. Bring quickly to a boil. Cover and simmer for 25 minutes.
Mrs. Ray Fisher

RICE VALENCIA

Serves 10
3 onions, chopped
4 garlic cloves, minced
4 tablespoons olive oil
2 cups rice, not instant
6 tomatoes, peeled and chopped
4½ cups chicken stock
½ teaspoon saffron, powdered
Tabasco
Salt and pepper to taste

Sauté onion and garlic in oil until golden. Add raw rice and stir well. Add tomatoes, chicken stock, saffron and Tabasco. Salt and pepper to taste. Cook uncovered over high heat for 10 minutes. Cover pan. Reduce the heat and cook rice for 10 minutes until rice is tender and the liquid is gone.
Mrs. John Renuart

WILD RICE WITH ARTICHOKE HEARTS

Serves 4-6
2/3 cup wild rice, uncooked
2 cups water
½ teaspoon salt
1 package artichoke hearts,
    frozen
3 tablespoons water
1 tablespoon lemon juice
½ teaspoon salt
1 tablespoon parsley, snipped
¼ teaspoon dried oregano leaves
Dash garlic powder
3 tablespoons butter, melted

Wash, drain and cook rice in water with salt about 45 minutes. Drain. Cook artichoke hearts in 3 tablespoons water, the lemon juice and salt. Combine the rice with artichoke hearts, parsley, oregano, garlic and butter. Heat, covered at 300° before serving.

Mrs. George Crawford, Jr.

WILD RICE CASSEROLE

Serves 6
¼ pound butter
1 cup wild rice, uncooked
½ cup slivered almonds
2 tablespoons green onions,
    chopped
2 tablespoons green pepper,
    chopped
½ pound mushrooms, sliced
3 cups chicken broth

Put first 5 ingredients in skillet and saute until rice browns and onions turn yellow. Place in covered casserole with chicken broth which has been heated. Bake at 325° for 1 hour or until all the moisture is absorbed. Add more stock if too dry. If recipe is increased it must be cooked longer. This dish can be made ahead and re-heated.

Mrs. James A. Wright, III

Fish & Shellfish

FISH AND SHELLFISH

Sailboats moored in Biscayne Bay await the arrival of the weekend sailors. Surrounded by the catch of the day, a French gilded silver tray shines in the sunlight. The tray and its elaborate cover date from the early nineteenth century and were given to the Lowe Art Museum by Mrs. C. Ruxton Love.

BAHAMIAN CONCH SALAD

Serves 12

2 pounds fresh conch; skinned, cleaned and finely chopped

2 sweet onions, large size and freshly chopped

2-3 green peppers, minced

8 ripe tomatoes, seeded and minced

2 cups lime juice

Salt and pepper to taste

Dash of Tabasco

Saltine crackers

Combine the first four ingredients and chill for at least 3 hours. At serving time, cover conch mixture with the lime juice, salt, pepper and Tabasco. Serve in chilled bowls with saltine crackers. Good idea to have additional Tabasco, salt and a pepper mill at the table for those who desire it.

Mrs. Virginia Saunders Brinson

KEYS CONCH SALAD

Serves 4

1¼ cup raw conch meat, chopped

¼ cup celery, chopped

¼ cup onion, chopped

¼ cup green pepper, chopped

½ cucumber, seeded and chopped

2/3 cup ripe tomato, seeded and chopped

1/3 cup lime juice

Dash of Tabasco

Salt to taste

Combine all the chopped ingredients in a bowl. Add the lime juice, Tabasco and salt and mix well. Cover the bowl and allow to sit for at least 30 minutes before serving. Serve cold.

Mrs. Richard Crawford

MARINATED CONCH

Serves 10

1 pound raw conch meat, chopped fine
1 medium onion, minced
3 limes, squeezed
4 or 5 ripe tomatoes, seeded and chopped fine
1 green pepper, minced
1 clove garlic, minced
2 teaspoons chopped parsley
½ teaspoon oregano
1 teaspoon salt or to taste
½ cup olive oil
1 tablespoon vinegar
⅛ teaspoon curry powder
3 drops Tabasco

Combine the conch, onion and lime juice and let the mixture rest while chopping the other ingredients. Add all the rest of the ingredients and refrigerate at least 8 hours before serving. Serve cold. This is good served in the hollow of an avocado as a luncheon dish or in a small clam shell as an appetizer with crackers.

Mrs. Lyle Roberts

CRABMEAT CREPES

Serves 12

FILLING:

24 crepes (see Index)
4 tablespoons green onions, chopped
6 tablespoons butter
1½ pounds crabmeat, cooked and picked over for shell
2 tablespoons white wine
Salt and pepper to taste

SAUCE:

6 tablespoons butter
8 tablespoons flour
Salt and pepper
4 cups chicken stock
3 egg yolks
¾ cup whipping cream
¾ cup Swiss cheese, grated

Sauté green onions in butter. Add crabmeat and wine. Season with salt and pepper. Simmer for a few minutes and turn off.
In double boiler melt butter. Add flour, salt and pepper. Slowly add boiling chicken stock, stirring sauce constantly. Cook until thick. Remove from heat. Beat yolks and cream until well mixed. Slowly add egg mixture to sauce. Correct seasonings to taste.

To assemble crepe: Add a little sauce to crabmeat mixture to hold it together. Put a small amount of this mixture on each crepe and roll. Place in a shallow buttered pan. Cover with remaining sauce. Sprinkle with cheese. Bake at 350° for 20 minutes. Brown under broiler and serve.

Mrs. Robert Ferrel

COLD CURRIED CRAB

Serves 12

2 apples, peeled, cored and
   sliced
8 shallots, chopped
½ cup butter
2 tablespoons curry powder
2 teaspoons crushed coriander
   seed
2 teaspoons flour
½ cup coconut milk*
4 cups mayonnaise (see Index)
Lemon, squeezed
Salt to taste
Cayenne, dash
Watercress
6 cups crab, cooked and picked
   over
2 cups cooked rice

Sauté apple and shallots in butter until soft. Add curry powder, coriander and flour and mix well. Slowly add coconut milk until mixture makes a thick paste. Remove from the heat and cool. Then add mayonnaise, lemon juice, salt and cayenne. Cover a bed of cooked rice with the crabmeat. Pour the curry sauce over the crabmeat and garnish with watercress. Serve cold. *To make coconut milk, combine 1 cup milk with 1 cup shredded coconut and let sit several hours in refrigerator. Strain before using.

Mrs. John Renuart

DEVILED BLUE CRAB

Serves 6

2 tablespoons onion, chopped
2 tablespoons butter, melted
2 tablespoons flour
¾ cup light cream
1½ tablespoons lemon juice
1½ teaspoons powdered
   mustard
1 teaspoon Worcestershire sauce
½ teaspoon salt
4-5 drops Tabasco sauce
Dash cayenne
1 egg, beaten
2 tablespoons parsley, chopped
1 pound crabmeat, cooked and
   picked over
1 tablespoon butter, melted
¼ cup dry bread crumbs
Dash pepper

Sauté onion in butter over medium heat until soft, then blend in flour. Add cream gradually and cook until thickened, stirring constantly. Add lemon juice and other seasonings. Stir a small amount of the sauce into the egg separately, then add the egg mixture to the sauce, stirring constantly. Add the parsley and picked over crabmeat and blend well. Spoon the mixture into well buttered crab shells (or scallop shells). Combine the melted butter with the bread crumbs and sprinkle over the crabmeat. Bake at 350° for 20-25 minutes.

Mrs. Richard Dennis

CRABMEAT MOUSSE

Serves 8

2 tablespoons gelatin, unflavored
3 tablespoons cold water
¼ cup mayonnaise (see Index)
4 tablespoons lemon juice
1 tablespoon parsley, chopped
1 tablespoon scallions, chopped, white bottom only
1 tablespoon Dijon mustard
Salt to taste
Dash of cayenne
2 cups crabmeat, cooked and picked over
¾ cup heavy cream, whipped

Soften gelatin in water, then place in top of double boiler and stir to dissolve. When dissolved, remove from heat and add mayonnaise, lemon juice, parsley, scallions, mustard, salt and cayenne and mix well. Fold in crabmeat, then fold in the whipped cream. Pour into a mold, greased with mayonnaise and chill at least half a day. Serve cold, unmolded. Garnish with thin slices of lime, avocado or minced scallion tops.

Mrs. Kermyt W. Callahan, Jr.

CRAB SUPPER PIE

Serves 6

1 pie crust, unbaked (see Index)
1 cup Swiss cheese, shredded
½ pound crabmeat, picked over
2 scallions, chopped with tops
3 eggs
1 cup light cream
½ teaspoon salt
½ teaspoon lemon peel, grated
¼ teaspoon dry mustard
Dash of mace
¼ cup almonds, sliced

Sprinkle cheese over bottom of pie shell. Top with picked over crabmeat; sprinkle with chopped scallions. Combine eggs, cream, salt, lemon peel, mustard and mace. Pour over crabmeat. Top with sliced almonds. Bake in slow oven, 325° for 45 minutes or until silver knife inserted near the center comes out clean. Remove from oven and let stand 10 minutes before serving.

Mrs. Jay Van Vechten

CRABS ROYAL

Serves 4

3 tablespoons butter
½ cup mushrooms, sliced
3 tablespoons butter
2 tablespoons flour
½ teaspoon salt
¼ teaspoon paprika
¼ teaspoon dry mustard
1 egg, slightly beaten
2/3 cup light cream
2/3 cup chicken stock
1 cup crabmeat, cooked and
  picked over

Sauté mushrooms in butter until just cooked. Drain and set aside. Melt butter over medium heat, add the flour and seasonings, stir, making a roux. As the flour mixture bubbles, add the cream, egg and stock. Cook over medium heat, stirring constantly until the mixture thickens. Remove from the heat, add the crabmeat and mushrooms and mix well. Serve immediately in scallop shells.

Mrs. R. Eugene Caldwell

SANIBEL ISLAND CRAB AND RICE

Serves 8

2 tablespoons oil
2 tablespoons butter
2-4 garlic cloves, peeled and
  crushed
½ cup chopped scallions
2 cups rice, not instant
3 cups water
1 cup white wine
2 tablespoons chives
1 bay leaf
¼ teaspoon thyme
Salt and pepper to taste
2 pounds crabmeat, picked over
2 tablespoons key lime juice
2 tablespoons parsley, chopped

In a heavy pot (4-5 quart) heat oil and butter over moderate heat. Sauté garlic until browned, then discard. Add the scallions and sauté until transparent. Add the rice and cook until milky, but not browned. Add the water, wine, chives, bay leaf, thyme, salt and pepper, stir well and reduce the heat to low. Cover and cook undisturbed for 20 minutes. Add the crabmeat, key lime juice and parsley and cook for 10 more minutes. Fluff rice and crabmeat with a fork and serve immediately with additional slices of lime and drawn butter.

Mrs. Lindsey D. Pankey, Jr.

HOT CRAB SANDWICH

This filling tastes best if made several hours in advance.

Serves 3-6
1½ cup Cheddar cheese, shredded
½ cup butter, softened
1¼ cup crabmeat, picked over
1/3 cup onion, finely chopped
¼ cup green pepper, finely chopped
1 teaspoon Worcestershire sauce
¼ cup key lime juice
3 English muffins, halved
½ cup Cheddar cheese, shredded
Paprika

Mix all of the ingredients together, except the muffins, ½ cup cheese and paprika. Spread the muffin halves with the crabmeat mixture and sprinkle shredded cheese and paprika on top. Place under the broiler for 5-7 minutes or until heated through. Serve immediately as 3 double servings or 6 single servings with a salad.

Mrs. Lyle Roberts

CRAWFISH NEWBERG

Serves 6
¾ pound Florida lobster meat, cooked
¼ cup butter
2 tablespoons flour
1 pint light cream
¼ teaspoon paprika
Dash cayenne
2 egg yolks, beaten
2 tablespoons sherry
1 teaspoon salt

Cut the lobster meat into ½ inch pieces and set aside. Melt butter over medium heat and add flour. Reduce heat to low and cook until the mixture is bubbly. Gradually add cream, stirring constantly. Add the seasonings. Stir a small portion of the sauce into the egg yolks and then pour the egg yolk mixture into the rest of the sauce. Add the lobster and sherry and heat slowly, stirring well. Serve hot on toast points.

Mrs. Peter Ray

CRAB SOUFFLÉ

This dish tastes best assembled the day before serving.

Serves 8

10 slices white bread, crusts removed and cubed

3 cups crabmeat or mixture of lobster, crab and shrimp

1 cup mayonnaise (see Index)

1 onion, minced

1 green pepper, minced

1 cup celery, minced

Salt and pepper to taste

4 eggs

3 cups milk

1 can cream of mushroom soup

1 cup Cheddar cheese, grated

Paprika

Spread bread cubes evenly on the bottom of a deep baking dish. Mix the crabmeat, mayonnaise, vegetables, salt and pepper and spoon over bread cubes. Arrange another layer of bread cubes over the crabmeat mixture. Beat the eggs and milk together and pour over the bread cubes and crabmeat. Cover and place in the refrigerator for 12 hours. Pre-heat oven to 325°, remove the cover and bake for 15 minutes. Remove from oven and spread mushroom soup over hot mixture. Sprinkle the top with the grated cheese and paprika and return to the oven. Bake 1 hour longer or until golden brown. Garnish with green pepper rings.

Mrs. William E. Greene, Jr.
Mrs. William Taylor

CRABMEAT TROPICAL

Serves 8

3 cups rice, cooked

½ pound fresh mushrooms, sliced

1 cup green pepper, minced

1 cup water chestnuts, sliced thin

3 pimientos, chopped

2 cups crabmeat

¼ cup parsley, chopped

¼ cup chives, chopped

1 cup olive oil

3 tablespoons soy sauce

3 tablespoons vinegar

½ teaspoon Tabasco sauce

2 teaspoons Dijon mustard

Lettuce

In a large bowl combine the rice, mushrooms, green pepper, water chestnuts, pimientos, crabmeat, parsley and chives. In another bowl combine the olive oil, soy sauce, vinegar, Tabasco and mustard and beat to blend. Pour the dressing over the other ingredients and toss until thoroughly mixed. Refrigerate for several hours and serve cold on lettuce.

Mrs. Karl Noonan

CRABMEAT AND WILD RICE

Serves 6
½ cup butter
2 cups mushrooms, sliced
2 cups wild rice, cooked
2 cups crabmeat, flaked
1 large can mushrooms, sliced
   and liquid
1 cup cream of mushroom soup
1 can cream of celery soup
1 cup Cheddar cheese, grated
Paprika

Sauté mushrooms in butter until soft and set aside. Arrange wild rice in a buttered casserole and make a layer of sautéed mushrooms and a layer of crabmeat. Combine the cream of mushroom soup and the cream of celery soup with the canned mushrooms. Pour over the crabmeat layer to cover. Sprinkle on the grated cheese and paprika. This constitutes one layer of the casserole. Continue layering the ingredients until they are all used up, ending with cheese and paprika. Bake in a slow oven, 325° until bubbling and slightly brown on top. Serve immediately.

Mrs. Oden Scheaffer

BISCAYNE MOUSSE

Serves 8
3 cups court bouillon (see
   Index)
2 pounds white meat fish
2 packages unflavored gelatin
1 cup mayonnaise (see Index)
1 teaspoon lemon juice
Dash Tabasco
Salt and pepper to taste
1 pint whipping cream, whipped
   to soft peaks

Simmer court bouillon 10 minutes, then add fish and cook over low heat until fish flakes when pricked with a fork. Remove fish to a platter. Strain liquid through two layers of rinsed cheesecloth. Discard vegetables and reserve 2½ cups of liquid. Soften gelatin in 1 cup of fish liquid. Add remaining liquid and over low heat stir until all of the gelatin is dissolved. Set gelatin mixture aside until it becomes the consistency of thick egg whites. Add mayonnaise and beat until fluffy. Flake the fish with a fork and add to the mayonnaise mixture, along with the lemon juice, Tabasco, salt and pepper; stirring to combine the mixture. Fold in the whipped cream. Pour into a mold greased with mayonnaise. Refrigerate until firm. Unmold and serve with cucumber sauce (see Index).

Mrs. Lindsey D. Pankey, Jr.

BARBECUED FISH

This recipe came from an old fish camp on the Florida Keys.

Serves 10
½ pound butter
1½ cups brown sugar
¾ cup fresh lemon juice
1/3 cup soy sauce
3-5 pounds white meat fish
(dolphin, snapper, grouper)

Melt butter and add sugar, lemon juice and soy sauce. Bring to a boil, stirring constantly. Then remove from the heat, set aside to cool. Skin and bone fish. Marinate fish in sauce one hour before grilling. Cook fish on a grill over low fire basting often with remaining marinade. For additional flavor, add wet hickory chips to the fire.

Mrs. Hagood Clarke

GEORGE'S FISH DISH

Serves 2
1 lemon
1 medium flounder quartered (or other white fish)
¼ cup butter
1 clove garlic, pressed
½ cup Parmesan cheese, grated
White wine
Dash Tabasco
Dash of Worcestershire sauce
½ cup Parmesean cheese, grated

Squeeze juice of one lemon over flounder quarters. Place fish in a broiler pan and dot with pats of butter. Sprinkle pressed garlic over the fish and then cover with grated Parmesan cheese. Pour white wine into the pan until it almost covers the top of the fish. Add a dash of Tabasco and Worcestershire sauce to taste. Place pan under pre-heated broiler for 8 minutes. Remove from the heat and arrange the tomato slices and more Parmesan cheese over fish and in the sauce to thicken it. Put it back under the broiler for 5 minutes more or until tomatoes are cooked. This is an excellent "hurry up" dinner.

George Whiteside

SMOKED FISH SCANDINAVIA

A good Swedish dish for a cool winter evening.

Serves 4
¾ pound smoked fish
4-5 potatoes, peeled and cubed
½ cup butter
2 leeks, sliced
1 large sour pickle, minced
3 tablespoons parsley, minced
3 tablespoons dill, minced
Salt and pepper to taste
4 egg yolks at room temperature;
reserve the shell

Cut fish into ½ inch pieces. Melt butter over medium heat in a large skillet and add the cubed potatoes. Cook the potatoes until nearly done. Add leeks and cook with the potatoes. (This part can be prepared up to 4 hours earlier.) Fold fish into the hot potatoes along with the pickle, parsley, dill, salt and pepper and mix well. Remove to a serving platter and make four indentations in the fish and potatoes. Into each indentation place ½ of the egg shell filled with the egg yolk. Each serving should have an egg yolk which is to be poured over the hot fish and stirred into the dish by the individual.

Mrs. William Taylor

FISH HATER'S FISH

Serves 4
2 pounds fish fillets
½ cup key lime juice
2 cups cold water
1 bottle Green Goddess dressing
Paprika
Salt and pepper to taste
¼ cup butter
1 can cream of mushroom soup
¼ cup dry sherry
1 cup green grapes

Place fillets of fish in bowl and add lime juice and water to cover. Let fish marinate 1 hour. Drain liquid. Place fish in a buttered baking dish. Pour Green Goddess dressing over the fish, sprinkle with paprika, salt, pepper and butter, cut into tiny pieces. Mix the mushroom soup and sherry together and pour over the fish. Garnish with the green grapes and broil until the fish flakes, about 12 to 15 minutes. Do not over cook! Serve immediately.

Mrs. Emil Gould

FISH MOUSSE

Serves 8
2 cups fish, cooked
1 cup clam chowder or lobster
   bisque
1 package unflavored gelatin
½ cup white wine
Salt and pepper to taste
2 tablespoons dill, mincd
Tabasco, dash
1 cup mayonnaise (see Index)

In a Cuisinart or blender, add the fish, chowder or bisque, gelatin dissolved in wine, salt and pepper, dill and Tabasco and mix well. Stir in mayonnaise and pour into a decorative mold and chill at least 4 hours. Unmold and decorate with remaining dill before serving.

Mrs. Edward F. Swenson, Jr.

VINEYARD BLUEFISH OR GROUPER

Serves 6
2 pounds bluefish or grouper —
   fillet and remove skin
½ teaspoon salt
¼ teaspoon pepper
3 tablespoons lemon juice
3 tablespoons chopped chives or
   scallion tops
Dash of Tabasco
2 cups sour cream
(½ cup mayonnaise may be
   substituted for part of sour
   cream)
Paprika

Wash fillets and pat dry. Rub salt and pepper on fish and arrange in buttered baking dish in a single layer. Mix remaining ingredients together. Spread over the fillets. Sprinkle with paprika and bake at 375° for 15 minutes. Place under broiler to brown and serve immediately.

Variation:
¼ cup grated Parmesan cheese may be sprinkled over fish before the paprika for extra richness.

Mrs. James W. McLamore
Mrs. Edward F. Swenson, Jr.

ORIENTAL GROUPER STEAKS

Serves 6
2 pounds grouper, fillet
¼ cup orange juice
¼ cup soy sauce
2 tablespoons ketchup
2 tablespoons butter, melted
2 tablespoons parsley, chopped
1 tablespoon lemon juice
1 clove garlic, minced
½ teaspoon oregano
½ teaspoon pepper

Cut fish into serving size portions and place in a single layer in the bottom of a shallow baking dish. Combine all the remaining ingredients and pour the sauce over the fish. Let it stand for 30 minutes. Remove the fish and either broil or bake at 350° for 12-15 minutes. Baste fish with remaining sauce.

Mrs. Charles D. Hall

CHARCOALED KINGFISH

Serves 6

3 pounds kingfish, filleted and skinned

½ cup butter, melted

2 tablespoons Worcestershire sauce

1 teaspoon pepper

½ teaspoon garlic powder

Juice of 1 large lemon

2 teaspoons soy sauce

Cut fillets into 6 individual servings. Combine the remaining ingredients for the sauce. Grill over a low charcoal fire, brushing with the sauce.

Mrs. Kenneth Claussen

LOBSTER MARCO POLO

Serves 6

2 packages frozen broccoli spears

2 leeks, sliced

3 tablespoons butter

3 whole lobster tails, uncooked

2 lemons, squeezed

1 tablespoon Worcestershire sauce

2 cups flour

1 teaspoon salt

Cayenne, dash

2 eggs, beaten

½ cup butter

2 cups Cheddar cheese sauce, (see Index)

Cook broccoli, following package instructions, with the leeks, until just fork tender. Remove from heat, drain and toss with butter. Set aside. Split the shells and remove the lobster meat, being careful to keep the meat in one piece. Cut the meat from each half tail into 6 pieces. Combine the lemon juice and the Worcestershire sauce and add to the lobster meat, tossing to mix. Mix the flour, salt and cayenne together on a piece of waxed paper. Place the lobster in flour and roll to cover. Then dip in beaten eggs and roll once more in the flour. Sauté the floured lobster meat in the butter over medium high heat. When the lobster is brown on one side, turn meat and turn heat to low, cover and cook 3-5 minutes. Meanwhile, arrange broccoli in oven-proof serving dish. Arrange cooked lobster medallions in a decorative pattern on top of the broccoli and pour the cheese sauce over the dish. Place under the broiler until browned and bubbly. Serve immediately.

Andreas Mueller

ISLAMORADA LOBSTER

Serves 4
1½ cup Florida lobster, cooked
¼ teaspoon sea salt
3 oranges, peeled and sectioned
¼ teaspoon white pepper
Tabasco sauce to taste
¼ cup orange juice
1½ tablespoons mayonnaise
  (see Index)
½ teaspoon dry mustard
½ teaspoon orange peel
½ cup whipped cream
½ teaspoon horseradish
1 key lime, squeezed
2 eggs, hard cooked
Tomatoes
Lettuce

Cut lobster meat into bite-sized pieces. Combine the lobster meat, salt, orange sections, pepper and Tabasco sauce in a bowl; cover and refrigerate several hours. Meanwhile, mix the orange juice, mayonnaise, mustard and orange peel together. Fold in the whipped cream. Add the horseradish and lime juice and refrigerate the dressing until serving time. Before serving, toss the lobster with the dressing and serve on lettuce with quartered egg and tomato slices as garnish.

Mrs. Lyle Roberts

LOBSTER THERMIDOR

Serves 8
4-6 ounces fresh mushrooms
6 tablespoons flour, heaping
1 pint heavy cream
1 pint milk
½ teaspoon Mr. Mustard
¼ pound sharp cheese, grated
1 lemon, squeezed
2 tablespoons dry sherry
Salt to taste
Dash of Tabasco sauce
4 pounds lobster meat, cooked
3 tablespoons butter
½ cup bread crumbs

Sauté mushrooms in butter, stir in flour, then add cream, milk, mustard, cheese, lemon juice, sherry, salt and Tabasco sauce and mix until combined. Remove cooked lobster from the shell and cut into bite sized pieces. Add the lobster meat to the sauce and pour into a buttered casserole dish. Melt 3 tablespoons of butter and mix with the bread crumbs to form a crumbly mixture. Add more bread crumbs if necessary. Sprinkle the bread crumb mixture over the thermidor and bake at 325° until bubbly and browned, about 30-45 minutes. Serve at once.
Note:
To serve 24, increase to:
10 pounds lobster meat
1¼ pounds sharp cheese
1¼ pounds fresh mushrooms
Triple all other ingredients

Mrs. Oden Schaeffer

LOBSTER AND FISH THERMIDOR

Serves 12
8 medium lobster tails, cooked
1 large fish fillet, steamed
1 lemon, squeezed
Salt to taste
½ cup butter
4 tablespoons flour
1 cup evaporated milk
1 tablespoon Dijon mustard
6 tablespoons dry sherry
2 teaspoons salt
Paprika, dash
Nutmeg, dash
Pepper, dash
3 egg yolks, slightly beaten
2 cups evaporated milk
1 cup water
3 tablespoons butter
½ cup bread crumbs

Remove cooked lobster meat from shells and cut into bite sized pieces. Break steamed fish into bite-sized pieces with a fork. Mix the lobster and fish together and arrange in the bottom of a buttered casserole dish. Squeeze lemon over fish and add salt to taste. In the top of a double boiler, melt the butter. Add the flour, milk, mustard, sherry and salt and combine well, but do not let the mixture boil. Add a dash of paprika, nutmeg and pepper. Combine the egg yolks, milk and water and slowly add to the sauce. Cook and stir until thickened. Pour the sauce over the fish and lobster. Melt the butter and combine with the bread crumbs, add more bread crumbs if necessary, to form a crumbly mixture. Sprinkle over the thermidor and place under a broiler until browned. Serve immediately.

Mrs. W. A. Snare

OYSTERS FLORENTINE

Serves 4
1 package frozen spinach, chopped
½ cup parsley, chopped
½ cup chives, chopped, or scallion tops
¼ teaspoon Tabasco sauce
1 teaspoon Worcestershire sauce
½ clove garlic, crushed
⅛ teaspoon nutmeg
6 tablespoons butter, melted
1 pint oysters
¼ cup bread crumbs
¼ cup Parmesan cheese

Cook spinach, following package directions, and drain carefully. When cool enough to handle, squeeze all of the additional water out of the spinach. Combine the parsley, chives, Tabasco sauce, Worcestershire sauce, garlic, nutmeg and butter and stir well. Mix the sauce with the spinach and then fold in the oysters. Pour into a buttered baking dish, top with bread crumbs and Parmesan cheese and bake at 350° for 30 minutes. Serve immediately. For a delicious addition serve the oysters with a Hollandaise or mousseline sauce.

Mrs. Hillard Willis

FLORIDA LOBSTER THERMIDOR

Serves 6
**6 Florida lobster tails,
  cooked**
6 onions, chopped
4 tablespoons butter
1½ cups white wine
12 tablespoons butter
12 tablespoons flour
1 quart milk
12 tablespoons heavy cream
**9 tablespoons Parmesan
  cheese, grated**
3 teaspoons paprika
1½ teaspoons prepared mustard
½ teaspoon salt
Dash Tabasco sauce
½ cup bread crumbs

Split lobsters carefully and reserve shells. Cut lobster meat into 1 inch cubes. Slowly cook chopped onions in butter until soft. Add the wine and quickly bring onions and wine to a boil and reduce the heat. In the top of a double boiler, prepare the cream sauce by melting the butter and adding the flour, mixing well. Add milk, cream, cheese, paprika, salt, Tabasco and mustard, stirring constantly. Add onion mixture and blend well; cook, stirring constantly until thickened. Remove from the heat and add the lobster meat. Carefully fill the reserved lobster shells with the mixture and sprinkle with the bread crumbs. Dot with butter and bake at 325° for 10 minutes or until bubbly. Serve immediately.
Mrs. George W. Cornell

SCALLOPED OYSTERS

Serves 4
½ cup butter, melted
½ cup stale bread crumbs
1 cup cracker crumbs
1 pint oysters, reserve liquid
Salt and pepper to taste
4 tablespoons heavy cream

Melt butter and add bread and cracker crumbs and mix well to form a crumbly mixture. Sprinkle 1/3 of the crumb mixture into the bottom of a buttered baking dish. Arrange ½ of the oysters in one layer over the crumbs. Sprinkle with salt and pepper. Mix the cream with the reserved oyster liquid and pour half of this liquid over the oysters. Make another layer of the crumbs and oysters and liquid just like the first. Never make more than 2 layers. Sprinkle the last 1/3 of crumbs over the top of the oysters. Bake at 450° for 30 minutes, until bubbly and browned on top. Serve immediately. More cream may be added during baking if too dry.
Mrs. Thomas P. Wenzel, Jr.

POMPANO PAPILLOTE

Serves 6
White parchment paper for
cooking
2 whole pompano filleted with
skin, head and bones removed
½ cup vermouth
3 tablespoons butter
3 teaspoons shallots
½ cup shrimp, uncooked,
chopped
3 tablespoons flour
1½ cups fumet (See next recipe)
2 tablespoons heavy cream
½ teaspoon lemon juice
Salt and pepper to taste
Dash cayenne pepper
½ cup crabmeat, optional

Pour the vermouth into a poaching pan and add water or fumet to cover the fish, about 1½ to 2 inches deep. Bring to a boil over high heat, then turn to a simmer and carefully add the fillets, wrapped in cheesecloth. Simmer for 3 minutes. Remove the fish from the liquid and set aside. Sauté the shallots and shrimp in the butter until tender, then remove the shrimp, leaving as many shallots as possible. Add flour and cook, stirring one minute. Add warm fumet and cook, stirring until sauce thickens. Add cream, lemon juice, salt and pepper and cayenne pepper. Taste for seasonings.

Cut parchment paper into 6 large hearts, about 13 or 14 inches across. Fold in half and oil the outside of the paper, then lay the oiled side flat of the table. Remove the fish from the cheesecloth and cut into 6 equal servings and place fillet along the fold, lengthwise, of the heart. Put a tablespoon of the shrimp (and crabmeat) on top of the fish. Spoon about 3 tablespoons of the sauce over the fish. To close, fold the heart over and line up the outside curve. Roll the edges of the paper with small even turns to crimp. Make sure that all the edges are firmly closed. Repeat this process for each serving. Place on oiled cookie sheet and bake at 450° for 8 minutes or until the "bags" are puffed and brown. Slide from the pan onto hot serving plates. Serve in bag, providing each guest with a very sharp pointed knife to cut the paper open.

Mrs. Jack Courtright
Mrs. Richard Dennis

FISH FUMET (Poaching Liquid)

1 pound lean fish bones and
trimmings
1 medium carrot, sliced
1 medium onion, sliced
2 tablespoons flour
Bouquet Garni (thyme, ½ bay
leaf, parsley, 1 celery stalk
with leaf)
2 cups vermouth
½ can chicken stock
Salt and pepper to taste

Wash the bones and trimmings. In a heavy pot sauté the sliced carrot and onion in butter for 5 minutes, stir in flour, cook one minute. Add the trimmings, Bouquet Garni, wine, 3½ cups water, ½ can chicken stock. Boil for 25 minutes. Strain, return to the sauce pan and reduce to 2½ cups or less if you want a stronger flavor. Taste and season. Can be kept in the refrigerator for 2 days or frozen.

Mrs. Jack Courtright

COULIBIAC

Serves 12
1 recipe brioche dough (see
Index)
12 ounces salmon
1 cup fresh mushrooms
6 tablespoons onions, minced
3 eggs, hard boiled and chopped
1½ cups rice, cooked
¼ cup butter, melted
¼ cup bread crumbs
2 cups Hollandaise sauce (see
Index)

All of the ingredients should be cold. Make brioche dough as directed, omitting the sugar. Divide the dough into two equal parts and roll each into a rectangle. Arrange in layers, in the middle of each rectangle, half of the mushrooms, onions, salmon, egg and rice, ending with the rice layer. Fold the dough over the filling, the narrow sides first and then the long sides. Moisten the dough with a little milk and pinch the edges together to seal the dough. The finished Coulibiac should resemble 2 tiny pillows. Place the Coulibiac on lightly greased baking sheets, sealed side on the bottom, in a warm place to rise for 30 minutes. Cut a tiny hole in the top of each pillow to allow the steam to escape. Brush the surface with melted butter and sprinkle with bread crumbs. Bake at 375° for 45-60 minutes. Remove from the oven and pour 2 tablespoons melted butter into each steam hole. Cut the Coulibiac into slices and serve with Hollandaise sauce.

Mrs. Paul Gimbel

SALMON LOAF

Serves 6
3 eggs, separated
6 ounces salmon, well mashed
1 cup celery, minced
2 tablespoons parsley, chopped
1 cup corn flakes, crushed
5 tablespoons butter, melted
Salt and pepper to taste

Separate the egg yolks from the egg whites and add to the egg yolks the salmon, celery, parsley, corn flakes, butter, salt and pepper, mixing well. Beat the egg whites until stiff. Fold the salmon mixture into the egg whites gently. Pour into a greased loaf pan and bake at 350° for 1 hour. Hollandaise sauce makes a delicious accompaniment (see Index).

Mrs. Barbara Bachmann

SALMON MOUSSE

Serves 6
1 cup cold water
2 packages unflavored gelatin
12 ounces salmon
3 tablespoons mayonnaise (see Index)
3 tablespoons whipping cream
Salt and white pepper, to taste
Tabasco sauce, dash
3 tablespoons lemon juice

Dissolve gelatin in cold water in a small sauce pan. Heat to a slow boil, stirring constantly until the liquid is clear. Strain off the juice of the salmon and retain for later use. Remove any bones and skin and flake the meat with a fork. Place 1/3 of all the ingredients in a blender or Cuisinart and blend for several seconds. Pour blended mixture into a fish mold greased with mayonnaise. Repeat the above procedure with the remaining ingredients 1/3 at a time. Cover and chill until firm. Remove from the refrigerator about one half hour before serving. Run a sharp knife around the edge of the mold to loosen. Unmold on a bed of lettuce. Serve cold.

Mrs. Alan Radcliff

HOW TO DECORATE A SALMON MOUSSE

1 recipe of preceding salmon
    mousse
Juice reserved from salmon, if
    canned
1 package unflavored gelatin
Salt and white pepper to taste
1 lemon, squeezed
1 stuffed green olive
1 cucumber, sliced thin

Combine the juice from salmon with water to equal 1 cup. Use 1 cup of water if using fresh salmon. Dissolve the gelatin in the liquid and bring to a slow boil in a small sauce pan. Add the salt and pepper and lemon juice and stir until the liquid is clear. Using a chilled ungreased fish mold, add enough of the gelatin to make a thin layer over the bottom of the mold. Chill until the gelatin is the consistency of thick egg whites. Arrange ½ of the green olive to form the eye. Cut the cucumber slices in half and arrange them down the body to simulate scales. Cover the olive and cucumber with another thin layer of gelatin and chill until set. Check to make sure the decorations stay in place. When the gelatin is firm, add the remaining liquid and chill until firm. Pour the salmon mixture over the gelatin layer and refrigerate until serving time. To unmold, dip the mold into very hot water for just a few seconds, then invert on a bed of lettuce.

Mrs. Alan Radcliff

BAKED SALMON STEAKS

Serves 6
6 salmon steaks
1 teaspoon salt
Pepper to taste
6 tablespoons lemon juice
6 tablespoons butter, melted
12 sprigs dill
Anchovy or cucumber sauce (see
    Index)

Place each salmon steak on the center of a piece of heavy duty aluminium foil. Sprinkle with the salt, pepper, lemon juice, butter and dill. Fold the foil loosely around each steak and seal. Bake at 400° about 30 minutes. Fish is done when it flakes easily with a fork. Reclose packet and chill several hours. Serve cold, in the foil. Accompany with a choice of anchovy sauce or cucumber sauce.

Mrs. Hillard Willis

POACHED SALMON STEAK

Serves 4

1 lemon

2 tablespoons tarragon vinegar

2 onions, sliced

2 stalks celery, chopped

1 teaspoon salt

1 teaspoon peppercorns

½ bay leaf

¾ cup carrot, sliced

6 sprigs parsley

4 salmon steaks, ¼ to ½ pound each

Cut lemon into 4 large slices. Place all of the ingredients, except the salmon, in the bottom of a poaching pan. Arrange the salmon on top of the vegetables and add enough water to barely cover the fish. Slowly bring to a gentle boil, then reduce the heat and simmer until the fish flakes easily. Be careful not to overcook. Carefully remove the fish with a perforated spatula to a heated platter. Serve immediately, accompanied by cucumber sauce, Hollandaise sauce, mousseline sauce, or egg sauce (see Index).

Francien Ruwitch

SCALLOPS IN MUSTARD SAUCE

Serves 6

4 tablespoons oil

3 pounds scallops, cut into pieces

2 teaspoons sugar

2 tablespoons Dijon mustard with seed

3 tablespoons wine vinegar

6 tablespoons sour cream

2 tablespoons parsley, minced

3 heads endive

Heat oil over moderate heat. Add the scallops and cook, stirring until the scallops become less transparent. Remove from the heat and chill. Combine the sugar, mustard, vinegar, sour cream and parsley to make a dressing. Drain any cooking liquid from the scallops and toss the scallops in the dressing. Serve cold on the endive.

Mrs. Hillard Willis

SEAFOOD CASSEROLE

Serves 12
½ pound crabmeat, picked over
½ pound lobster meat
1 pound shrimp, cleaned
1 cup mayonnaise (see Index)
½ cup green pepper, chopped
½ teaspoon salt
¼ cup onion, minced
1½ cups celery, chopped
2 teaspoons Worcestershire
   sauce
2 cups cracker crumbs
¼ cup butter, melted
Paprika

Pick over the crabmeat for shell. Cut lobster and shrimp into bite-sized pieces. Place all of the seafood into a glass bowl and toss to mix. Add the mayonnaise, green pepper, onion, celery, and Worcestershire sauce to the seafood and mix all of the ingredients together. Spoon seafood into a casserole dish. Combine the cracker crumbs with the melted butter and mix until crumbly. Spread the crumbs over the seafood and sprinkle with the paprika. Bake at 400° for 20-25 minutes. Serve hot

Mrs. D. Robert Graham

SEAFOOD CURRY

Serves 4
1 tablespoon butter
1 teaspoon curry powder
¼ cup onion, chopped
1 can cream of celery soup
1/3 cup milk
Salt and pepper to taste
1 cup shrimp, cleaned, cooked
   and chopped
½ cup crabmeat, picked over
2 cups rice, cooked or 4 patty
   shells, cooked

Melt butter over medium heat in heavy saucepan. Add the curry powder and onion. Cook until the onion is transparent. Combine the soup, milk, salt and pepper and add to the curried onions. Stir to mix together. Add the cleaned, cooked and chopped shrimp and the picked over crabmeat. Continue cooking over medium-low heat until seafood is hot. Serve over cooked rice or patty shells.

Mrs. William Atwill

ARTICHOKES STUFFED WITH SHRIMP

A delightful luncheon dish to be prepared ahead.

Serves 8

2 pounds small shrimp, cooked and cleaned

8 artichokes, trimmed

1 recipe Remoulade sauce (see Index)

1 package cornbread stuffing

10 tablespoons sweet butter

4 lemons, halved

Salt and pepper to taste

Cut half the cooked shrimp in small pieces. Cut the other half into halves by slicing them lengthwise. Refrigerate until serving time. Cook the artichokes in boiling water until tender, about 45-50 minutes. Drain them, cool them and dechoke them. It is easier to dechoke the artichokes after cooking them. Makes one recipe of Remoulade Sauce and refrigerate it. Melt the butter. Add the stuffing and toss to coat. Saute until lightly browned with salt and pepper to taste. Drain the croutons and put them in a tightly closed jar after they have cooled. The shrimp, artichokes and sauce should all be well chilled. To assemble, open the artichoke leaves a little, place the chopped shrimp in the leaves of the artichokes. Put a tablespoon of sauce in the center of each artichoke. Place 8 to 10 halved shrimp in the center of each artichoke on top of the sauce. Spoon the Remoulade sauce into the leaves and add more to the shrimp in the heart. Make sure that there is sauce in all the places where shrimp have been stuffed. Cover and refrigerate until serving time. Sprinkle croutons over the artichokes at serving time. Garnish with halved lemons which may be cut decoratively. Pass remaining croutons and sauce.

Mrs. John Renuart

ASPARAGUS AND SHRIMP AU GRATIN

Serves 6

2 pounds asparagus
½ cup scallions, minced
4 tablespoons butter, melted
4 tablespoons flour
½ teaspoon salt
Dash of pepper
2 cups light cream
¼ cup Swiss cheese, grated
2/3 cup Parmesan cheese, grated
1 tablespoon lemon juice
1½ pounds shrimp, cooked and cleaned
2 tablespoons Parmesan cheese, grated

Cut asparagus into 2 inch pieces and cook in salted water 8-10 minutes or until tender-crisp. Drain asparagus and set aside. Saute the scallions in melted butter 2 minutes; add flour, salt and pepper and mix well. Stir in the cream slowly. Cook until the sauce thickens, then simmer 1 minute. Add Swiss cheese and Parmesan cheese and stir until the cheese melts. Add lemon juice and shrimp to the sauce. Line the bottom of a baking dish with the asparagus. Pour the shrimp sauce over the vegetables. Sprinkle 2 tablespoons of Parmesan cheese over the sauce and cook at 400° for 15-20 minutes until bubbly and browned. Serve immediately.

Mrs. William E. Greene, Jr.

SHRIMP BAKED IN COCONUT

Serves 4

1½ pounds shrimp, uncooked
2 teaspoons salt
¾ cup light cream
3½ ounces flaked coconut

The day before serving, remove the shells from the shrimp but leave the tails intact. Clean the shrimp and sprinkle them with the salt. Cover and refrigerate until serving time. Place flaked coconut in a bowl and add the cream. Cover and refrigerate until serving time. About one hour before serving, remove the shrimp from the refrigerator and arrange in a baking dish. Remove the coconut from cream with a fork and sprinkle it over the shrimp. Use all of the coconut. Pour coconut cream around the shrimp. Bake at 350° for 40 minutes. Serve immediately.

Mrs. William Taylor

SHRIMP AND CRABMEAT AU GRATIN

Serves 6
1 pound shrimp
1 package artichoke hearts
¼ cup butter
½ pound mushrooms, sliced
1 clove garlic, crushed
2 tablespoons shallots, minced
½ cup flour
½ teaspoon pepper
1 tablespoon dill, chopped
¾ cup milk
8 ounces sharp Cheddar cheese, grated
2/3 cup dry white wine
2 cups crabmeat, cooked and picked over
2 tablespoons bread crumbs
½ tablespoon butter

Add shrimp to boiling water and cook until just pink, about 3-5 minutes. Drain the shrimp and place under cold water until cool enough to handle. Shell and clean the shrimp and set aside. Cook artichokes and set aside. Sauté mushrooms in 2 tablespoons butter over medium heat. Remove the mushrooms and add remaining butter and saute garlic and shallots until transparent. Remove from the heat and gradually stir in the flour, salt and pepper and dill. When mixed, add the milk and stir until blended. Add the cooked mushrooms, return to medium heat and bring to a boil, stirring constantly. When sauce becomes thickened, remove from heat and add ½ the grated cheese, gradually, stirring until melted. Stir in the wine, then the shrimp, artichokes and crabmeat and toss to mix. Pour into a casserole and sprinkle the top with bread crumbs and rest of grated cheese. Dot with butter. Bake at 375° for 30 minutes or until mixture is bubbly and browned.

Mrs. Hagood Clarke

FRIED SHRIMP

Serves 4
1½ pounds shrimp
1 cup flour
½ cup cornstarch
1 teaspoon baking soda
1 egg
Cooking oil

Remove shells from shrimp, leaving the tails in place. Clean shrimp and butterfly. Combine all dry ingredients and thin with water until batter is the consistency of pancake batter. Beat egg into batter. Holding shrimp by the tail, dip into batter and drop into hot oil. Fry until golden brown. This is a tempura-like batter.

Mrs. Lester R. Johnson, Jr.

SHRIMP CURRY

Serves 10
3 tablespoons butter
1½ cups onion, minced
3 teaspoons curry powder
3 cans frozen shrimp soup or shrimp bisque
60 jumbo shrimp or 100 small shrimp, cooked and cleaned
3 cups sour cream
9 cups rice, cooked
Salt and pepper to taste

Defrost soup. Sauté onions in butter until transparent. Add the curry powder and stir, making a paste. Pour soup into the curry, stirring to make a smooth sauce over low heat. Add shrimp, and simmer without boiling. Just before serving, add sour cream, heat through, but do not boil. Serve over cooked rice, accompanied by almonds, chutney, coconut flakes and apple slices.

Mrs. Adams Reese
Mrs. Oden Schaeffer

ICED SHRIMP CURRY

Serves 10
4 tablespoons butter
1 clove garlic, crushed
¼ cup apple, minced
¼ cup onion, minced
2 tablespoons flour
1 cup tomatoes, canned
Salt and pepper to taste
1½ teaspoon curry powder or to taste
1 tablespoon mayonnaise (see Index)
1 tablespoon lemon juice
2 pounds shrimp, cooked and cleaned
½ cup almonds, sliced and toasted

Sauté garlic, onion and apple in butter in heavy skillet. Discard the garlic. Add flour, stirring to combine, then add tomatoes, salt, pepper and curry powder. Remove from the heat and cool. Combine equal parts of mayonnaise and lemon juice and add to the curry mixture. Fold in cooked and cleaned shrimp and pour into a serving bowl. Chill at least 4 hours before serving. Just before serving, sprinkle sliced almonds over the shrimp.

Mrs. John C. Sullivan, Jr.

ISLAND SHRIMP

Serves 6

SAUCE:
4 tablespoons butter
1 onion, chopped
1 stalk celery, chopped
1 clove garlic, minced
3 tablespoons flour
1½ teaspoons curry powder
4 cups beef bouillon
1 tomato, peeled, seeded and chopped
1 apple, peeled, cored and chopped
1 banana, peeled and sliced
1 bay leaf
Pinch of thyme
½ cup chutney
Salt to taste

RICE:
1 cup rice, uncooked
¼ cup butter
¼ cup onion, chopped
8 ounces consomme
½ cup raisins
½ cup almonds, toasted

SHRIMP:
2 dozen jumbo shrimp, uncooked
Salt and pepper to taste
3 lemons
1½ cups flour
3 eggs, beaten
1 cup coconut, grated
1 cup butter

Sauce:
Sauté onion, celery and garlic in butter until transparent. Stir the flour into the butter. Add the curry powder and bouillon, stirring until smooth. Pour chopped tomato, apple and banana into sauce. Add bay leaf and thyme and simmer over low heat 20-30 minutes. Pour sauce into a blender and puree all the ingredients. Strain the sauce, add the chutney and salt to taste. Set aside, over hot water.

Rice:
Brown rice in the butter in a heavy skillet. Add the onion and cook until onion is soft. Combine the consommé with enough water to equal 2¼ cups. Pour into the rice and onion and cook, covered, 20-25 minutes or until the rice is dry. Meanwhile, plump the raisins in boiling water and drain. Just before serving, add the raisins and almonds to the rice.

Shrimp:
Remove the shell from the shrimp, leaving the tails on. Clean and butterfly shrimp. Sprinkle the shrimp with salt, pepper and lemon juice. Dip the shrimp into the flour, then beaten eggs, then into the grated coconut. Fry in the hot butter about 8 minutes or until golden brown. To serve, mound the rice in the center of a large serving platter. Surround the rice with the shrimp. Garnish with the leftover coconut, apple or parsley. Serve the sauce separately.

Mrs. George W. Cornell

JAMBALAYA

Extra seafood never hurts. Even better the next day.

Serves 10-12

4 tablespoons ham fat or butter

2 large onions, minced

2 green peppers, chopped

1 bunch celery, chopped

2 cloves garlic, crushed

2 cups okra, sliced

½ pound boiled ham, thin sliced

1 bunch parsley, snipped

4 cups tomatoes, peeled and cooked

2 tablespoons tomato paste

1 cup chicken broth

1½ pounds shrimp, shelled and cleaned

1 pint oysters

2½ cups chicken, minced

1½ cups rice, cooked

6 dashes Tabasco sauce

½ teaspoon ground mace

Salt to taste

½ cup bread crumbs

¼ cup butter, melted

Sauté onion, peppers, celery, garlic and okra in ham fat or butter until onion turns yellow. Cut the boiled ham into slivers or bite sized pieces. Add ham, tomatoes and parsley and stir thoroughly. Combine the tomato paste and the chicken broth and pour into ham mixture. Simmer 1½ hours over low heat. Add shrimp and oysters and cook for 10 minutes, then add the chicken. Boil the rice for 5 minutes, drain and rinse under cold water. Add the rice to the jambalaya and cook for 10 minutes or until the sauce becomes very thick. Add Tabasco sauce, mace and salt to taste. Pour jambalaya into a buttered casserole dish and top with the bread crumbs that have been tossed in the butter and bake at 350° for 30 minutes, until piping hot.

Mrs. James Duncan
Mrs. Charles Baker

SHRIMP ORLEANS

Serves 4

1 tablespoon butter

1 medium onion, minced

1 clove garlic, crushed

1 can cream of mushroom soup

1 cup sour cream

¼ cup tomato purée

½ pound mushrooms, sliced and sautéed

1 pound shrimp, cooked, shelled and cleaned

Salt and pepper to taste

Melt butter in skillet over low heat and sauté onion and garlic until transparent. Combine the soup, sour cream and tomato purée, then add to the onions. Add mushrooms and shrimp, salt and pepper and cook over low heat until mixture is hot. Serve over rice and garnish with chopped parsley.

Mrs. J. Michael Garner

SHRIMP DE JONGHE

Serves 6
1 cup milk
2/3 cup bread crumbs, toasted
½ cup parsley, minced
1 clove garlic, minced
1 teaspoon salt
⅛ teaspoon pepper
½ cup butter, soft
2½ pounds shrimp, shelled and cleaned
3 tablespoons Parmesan cheese
¼ cup butter

Heat milk, but do not boil. Pour hot milk over bread crumbs and let stand until all the milk is absorbed. Add more milk if needed to make bread crumbs soft. Stir in the parsley, garlic, salt, pepper, and soft butter and mix thoroughly. Spread ½ of the bread mixture on the bottom of a greased casserole dish. Arrange the shelled and cleaned raw shrimp over the crumbs. Cover with the remaining crumb mixture. Sprinkle the cheese over the top and drizzle the melted butter over all. Bake at 350° for 30 minutes then place under the broiler to brown the topping.
Variation:
Substitute ½ cup dry sherry for ½ cup milk and add 1/3 teaspoon tarragon and 1/3 teaspoon onion powder.
Mrs. Stephen A. Lynch, III

KEY WEST SHRIMP

Serves 6
2 tablespoons butter
¼ cup olive oil
2 medium onions, minced
2 green peppers, minced
2 cloves garlic, minced
2 pounds shrimp, shelled and cleaned
2 cups tomato sauce
Juice of 1 key lime
1½ cup red wine
Generous pinch bay leaf
Generous pinch oregano
Generous pinch cumin
Generous pinch chili powder
Salt and pepper to taste
Parsley

Sauté onion, green pepper and garlic in butter and oil until transparent. Add shrimp and quickly toss to coat with oil and partially cook. Remove the shrimp with a slotted spoon and keep in the refrigerator until serving time. Stir the tomato sauce, key lime and wine into the onions and green peppers. Add spices and simmer over low heat 1 hour. Sauce may be made in advance. Before serving, simmer sauce 20 minutes, adding shrimp, and cook for 10 minutes more. Serve over hot rice sprinkled with parsley
Mrs. Robert Kirkland

SHRIMP AND MUSHROOMS

Serves 8
7½ tablespoons butter
4½ tablespoons flour
½ cup milk
1 cup heavy cream
Salt and pepper to taste
Dash of cayenne pepper
Dash of nutmeg (optional)
¼ cup dry sherry
1 tablespoon Worcestershire
sauce
1 package artichoke hearts
(optional)
2 pounds shrimp, cooked,
shelled and cleaned
1 pound mushrooms, sliced
½ cup Parmesan cheese
Paprika

Melt 4½ tablespoons of the butter over low heat and stir in flour. When blended, gradually add milk and cream and stir constantly until the sauce is thick and smooth. Add salt, pepper, cayenne pepper, nutmeg, sherry and Worcestershire sauce. Remove from heat. Cook artichokes, following package instructions. Arrange a layer of artichokes in the bottom of a shallow baking dish that has been buttered. Make a layer of shrimp over the artichokes. Sauté mushrooms in the remaining 3 tablespoons of butter for 6 minutes. Make a layer of mushrooms over the shrimp. Pour cream sauce over the artichokes, shrimp and mushrooms. Sprinkle the top with the cheese and paprika and bake at 325° for 20-30 minutes.

Mrs. Reynolds Allen
Mrs. William Atwill

KEY WEST STEAMED SHRIMP

Serves 6
4-6 lemons, thin sliced
3 bay leaves
4 sprigs fresh dill
4 sprigs fresh parsley
½ teaspoon thyme
Handful of peppercorns
½ bunch celery
2 carrots, sliced
2 spanish onions, sliced
3 cans beer or 2 cups dry
vermouth or white wine
3 pounds fresh shrimp

Arrange all of the vegetables and spices in the bottom of a fish poacher or large pot. Add the beer or wine and 3 cups of water. Simmer court bouillon for 20 minutes. Add the shrimp in the shell and steam until pink. Do not overcook as shrimp will become tough. Drain shrimp and serve immediately in the shell, piping hot, with drawn butter.

Mrs. John Renuart

"SEAWEED" SHRIMP SALAD

Serves 8
DRESSING:
1 cup mayonnaise (see Index)
2 teaspoons lemon juice
1 teaspoon celery salt
1 teaspoon Beau Monde
　seasoning
Dash salt
Dash pepper
SALAD:
60 shrimp, peeled, deveined,
　cooked
32 black olives, pitted and sliced
8 celery sticks, chopped
16 baby tomatoes, sliced

Combine ingredients for dressing. Combine all salad ingredients and arrange on a leaf of Bibb lettuce. Serve cold with the chilled dressing.

Mrs. Edward Weed

SCAMPI I

Serves 4
1½ pound shrimp
1 cup flour
Dash salt
½ cup butter
2 tablespoons parsley, chopped
2 cloves garlic, crushed
1 teaspoon prepared mustard
　(Dijon)

Shell and devein fresh shrimp. Mix the flour and salt together and dust shrimp with flour mixture. Arrange a single, non-overlapping layer of shrimp in a shallow baking pan. Melt butter over low heat and add the lemon juice, parsley, garlic and mustard. When the sauce is hot, pour half of it over the shrimp. Broil the shrimp for 5 minutes and remove from the oven. Turn the shrimp and add the remaining sauce and broil 5 minutes. Remove from oven and serve immediately.

Mrs. Henry H. Bryant, III

SCAMPI II

Serves 6
2 pounds large shrimp
8 tablespoons butter
½ cup olive oil
1 tablespoon lemon juice
¼ cup shallots, minced
1 tablespoon garlic,
finely chopped
1 teaspoon salt
Fresh ground pepper, to taste
4 tablespoons parsley, chopped
3 lemons, quartered

Carefully shell and devein the shrimp, leaving tails intact. Butterfly the shrimp. Melt the butter in a sauce pan over low heat. Add the oil, lemon juice, shallots, garlic, salt and pepper. Cook, stirring for 5 minutes to allow flavors to blend. Dip the shrimp in the hot butter sauce and turn to coat. Arrange the shrimp in rows in a shallow baking dish with the tails pointing up. Broil 3"-4" from heat for 5 minutes. Turn and broil 5-10 minutes. Pour remaining sauce over the shrimp. Bake at 450° for 10 to 12 minutes. Do not overcook. Serve immediately garnished with parsley and lemon.

Mrs. Kenneth Claussen

SHRIMP AND CHICKEN SUPREME

Serves 8
¼ cup butter
½ pound mushrooms, sliced
2 tablespoons scallions,
chopped
2 cans cream of chicken soup
½ cup sherry
½ cup light cream
1 cup Cheddar cheese, grated
2 cups chicken, cooked
2 cups shrimp, cooked and
cleaned
2 tablespoons parsley, chopped

Sauté the mushrooms and scallions in butter for 5 minutes over medium heat. Stir in the soup and gradually add the sherry and cream. Do not boil. Add the grated cheese and stir until thoroughly mixed. Cut cooked chicken into bite-sized pieces. Add chicken and shrimp to sauce and simmer 10-15 minutes. Before serving, add parsley. This dish can be prepared earlier in the day and re-heated at serving time.

Variation:
Substitute crabmeat for the chicken for an all seafood dish.

Mrs. Richard R. Paige

WILD RICE SALAD WITH SHRIMP

Serves 6
2 pounds shrimp, cooked and
   cleaned
2 cups wild rice, cooked
½ cup celery, chopped
1 small can water chestnuts,
   chopped
1 large handful white
   mushrooms, sliced (squeeze
   lemon juice over mushrooms)
1 can hearts of palm, chopped
6 sprigs parsley, chopped
Mayonnaise or Italian dressing
¼ teaspoon curry powder
Salt and pepper to taste

Mix ingredients together with
mayonnaise or dressing until
moist. Chill at least 3 hours or
overnight. Add a bit more
dressing at serving time, if
desired. Serve with spiced
peaches or hot curried fruit.
Diced turkey or chicken may be
substituted for the shrimp. Add 1
cup of white grapes.
Mrs. Bill Vessels

RED SNAPPER WITH AVOCADO SAUCE

Serves 6
6 red snapper fillets
Salt and pepper to taste
1 cup flour
¼ cup olive oil
3 shallots, minced
3 cloves garlic, minced
6-8 ripe tomatoes, peeled,
   seeded and chopped
1 ripe avocado
2 tablespoons lime juice
Dash Tabasco sauce
Salt and pepper to taste

Season fish fillets with salt and
pepper and dredge in flour to
coat. Pour enough olive oil into a
heavy skillet to cover the bottom.
Sauté the fillets in the oil 2
minutes on each side. Remove
fillets to a baking dish which will
hold them in 1 layer. Saute the
shallots and garlic, adding more
oil if necessary. When lightly
browned, add the tomatoes and
cook 2 minutes, mixing
thoroughly. Pour sauce over the
fish and cover the dish with
buttered waxed paper. Bake at
325° for 15-20 minutes or until the
fish flakes. While the fish bakes,
mash the avocado with lime
juice, Tabasco sauce, salt and
pepper. Remove fish from the
oven and onto a serving platter.
Keep warm. Quickly place the
baking pan with the remaining
sauce over direct heat and boil to
reduce the liquid by 1/3. Remove
from the heat and beat in the
avocado mixture. Pour over the
warm fish and serve
immediately.
Mrs. Jerry Marcus

BAKED RED SNAPPER

Serves 8
5-7 pound red snapper
1 green pepper, minced
1 onion, minced
1 clove garlic, minced
3 tablespoons bacon fat
2 cups bread crumbs
3 eggs, beaten
$\frac{1}{2}$ cup cooked ham, chopped
6 slices bacon
$1\frac{1}{2}$ cup red wine
3 tablespoons flour (all-purpose)
$\frac{1}{2}$ cup tomato paste
Salt and pepper to taste
3 tablespoons parsley, chopped

Clean snapper, leaving head and tail. Sauté the green pepper, onion and garlic in bacon fat over medium heat until soft. Add the crumbs and remove from the heat. Stir in eggs and chopped ham. Fill the fish cavity with the crumb, egg, ham, onion mixture. Place fish in a greased shallow baking dish. Lay the bacon slices over the fish. Add 1 cup of red wine and bake at 400° for 35 minutes or until the fish flakes. Remove the fish from oven and place on a hot serving platter. Sprinkle the flour over the pan juices and stir to blend. Add remaining wine and tomato paste. Cook, stirring until sauce is smooth and thick. Season with salt and pepper to taste and pour over fish and garnish with parsley. If sauce is too thick, add a little water.

Mrs. Malcolm Weldon

KEY LIME POACHED SNAPPER

Serves 4
$3\frac{1}{2}$ cups water
1 cup key lime juice
2 tablespoons salt
2 pounds red snapper, filleted
   and skin removed
$\frac{1}{2}$ cup onions, chopped
1 clove garlic, chopped
2 bay leaves
$\frac{1}{2}$ teaspoon thyme
2 tablespoons parsley, chopped
2 tablespoons key lime juice

In a glass dish combine $1\frac{1}{2}$ cups water, lime juice and salt and stir until dissolved. Add the fish to liquid and allow to marinate 1 hour. Drain the fish. In a poaching pan combine remaining 2 cups water, onion, garlic, bay leaves, thyme and parsley and bring to a boil. Reduce heat and simmer for 5 minutes. Add the fish and simmer 10-12 minutes or until the fish flakes easily. Remove the fish from the pan. Bring the liquid to a boil over high heat and reduce the liquid to $\frac{1}{2}$ cup. Add 2 tablespoons lime juice and pour sauce over warm fish.

Mrs. W. B. Stevens

CUBAN BAKED RED SNAPPER

Serves 4

3 to 3½ pounds red snapper

1/3 cup almonds, blanched and toasted

6 tablespoons olive oil

1 cup Spanish onions, chopped

1 clove garlic, chopped

1 tablespoon parsley, chopped

1½ cup clear fish stock*

¼ cup key lime juice

Salt and pepper to taste

1 Spanish onion, sliced into rings

1 bay leaf, crumbled

½ teaspoon thyme

Clean the fish and remove the head. Set aside while making the stuffing. Put almonds in the blender and pulverize. Heat 2 tablespoons oil in a heavy skillet over moderate heat. When hot, add the almonds, onions, garlic and parsley and cook until the onions are transparent. Add ½ cup fish stock; stir thoroughly and remove from the heat. When cool, stuff the fish. Use 4 tablespoons of oil to cover the bottom of a shallow baking dish. Make a layer of onion rings, then sprinkle with the bay leaf and thyme. Place fish on the onion layer and pour key lime juice over fish. Cover the top of the fish with the remaining onion rings, salt and pepper to taste. Add remaining 1 cup of stock and bake at 400° for 40 minutes or until fish flakes.

*In an emergency, bottled clam juice may be substituted.

Mrs. R. Lowell Goldman

PENSACOLA RED SNAPPER

Serves 4

4 red snapper fillets, with skin

1 teaspoon salt

Fresh ground pepper to taste

¼ cup lemon juice

2 tablespoons olive oil

3 cloves garlic, chopped

1 teaspoon oregano

1 ripe tomato, ¼ inch slices

4 artichoke hearts, brushed with butter

1 tablespoon parsley, chopped

Pat fillets dry with paper towels and season on both sides with salt and pepper. Combine the lemon juice, olive oil, garlic, and ½ teaspoon oregano in a shallow baking dish, stirring thoroughly. Add fillets and turn to coat with the liquid. Arrange in a single layer, skin side down. Place the tomato slices and artichokes on the fillets and sprinkle on the remaining oregano. Bake at 400° for 10-12 minutes or until fish flakes. Sprinkle with parsley and serve immediately.

Mrs. George L. Irvin, III

RED SNAPPER A LA FLORIDA

Serves 6
6 red snapper fillets
6 tablespoons butter
Salt and pepper to taste
8 tablespoons shallots, minced
7 tomatoes, peeled, seeded and chopped
3 cups dry white wine
2 cups heavy cream
3 tablespoons parsley, minced

In a baking dish, make a single layer of the fillets. Dot the fish with butter and season with salt and pepper. Sprinkle the shallots and 6 chopped tomatoes over the fillets, then add the wine. Bake at 350° for 15 minutes. Remove fish from oven and turn to broil. Drain off the cooking liquid to a sauce pan and over high heat, reduce the liquid to ½ cup. Lower heat and gradually add the cream, stirring constantly. Heat sauce, but do not boil. Add parsley and more salt and pepper, if necessary. Pour sauce over the fillets and garnish each fillet with the 1 remaining chopped tomato. Place under the broiler until the sauce is browned. Remove and serve immediately.
Mrs. John Renuart

RED SNAPPER WITH SOUR CREAM STUFFING

Serves 6
3-4 pound red snapper, cleaned with head removed
¾ cup celery, chopped
½ cup onion, chopped
¼ cup butter, melted
1 quart dry bread cubes
½ cup sour cream
¼ cup lemon, peeled and diced
2 tablespoons lemon rind, grated
1 teaspoon paprika
2½ teaspoons salt
2 tablespoons butter, melted

Sauté celery and onion in butter over medium heat until transparent. Remove from heat and add bread, sour cream, lemon, paprika and 1 teaspoon salt. Mix all the ingredients thoroughly and cool. Pat the fish dry on paper towels. Sprinkle the inside and outside with 1½ teaspoon salt. Stuff fish with cool stuffing and loosely close the opening with small skewers. Place fish in a well greased baking pan and brush with melted butter. Bake at 350° for 40-60 minutes or until fish flakes. Remove from oven, remove skewers and serve immediately.
Mrs. Karl Noonan

FILLETS OF SOLE WITH MUSHROOM FUMET SAUCE

Serves 6
¾ pound mushrooms
4 tablespoons butter
2 tablespoons vegetable oil
1 tablespoon shallots, minced
1 tablespoon lemon juice
2¾ pounds sole fillets
Salt to taste
Fresh ground pepper to taste
¾ cup dry white wine

Clean the mushrooms and remove the caps from 12. Slice the stems and the remaining whole mushrooms. In a small skillet melt 2 tablespoons butter with 1 tablespoon oil over medium heat. Toss the mushroom caps in the hot fat for 1-2 minutes or until golden brown. Remove from heat and set aside. In a large skillet melt remaining butter and oil over medium heat. Add the sliced mushrooms and cook for 2 minutes, stirring constantly. Add shallots and cook 1 minute; add lemon juice and remove from heat. Arrange folded fillets in a single layer in the bottom of a shallow, flame proof dish, greased with butter. Salt and pepper to taste. Spread the mushroom mixture over fillets, pour in the wine and marinate 30-60 minutes. Add enough water to cover the fish. On top of the stove, over medium low heat, bring liquid to simmer. Cover with buttered waxed paper and bake at 350° for 8-10 minutes or until done. Remove from oven and discard waxed paper. Using a bulb baster, draw up all of the liquid from the fish and strain into a sauce pan. Boil over high heat util the liquid is reduced to 1 cup. Pour over fish and garnish with mushroom caps. Add 1 tablespoon of flour kneaded with 1 tablespoon butter to sauce after it has been reduced for slightly thicker sauce.

Mrs. George Hero

FILLET OF SOLE

Serves 2
1 pound sole fillet
2 lemons
½ teaspoon garlic salt
½ teaspoon onion salt
Pepper to taste
½ cup dry white wine
1 cup sour cream
1 can cream of mushroom soup
1 bunch green seedless grapes

Pat fillets dry on paper towels. Squeeze lemon juice over fish. Sprinkle with garlic salt, onion salt and pepper. Roll fillets and placed in greased baking dish. Combine the wine, sour cream and soup in a small bowl. Arrange ½ the grapes around the fillets and pour the sauce over the fish and grapes. Bake at 350° for 30-40 minutes or until fish is tender and sauce bubbly. Garnish with remaining grapes and serve immediately.

Mrs. Jack Pfleger, Jr.

STONE CRABS

Serves 4
14 large stone crabs, cooked
1 cup butter
3 key limes, squeezed
1 clove garlic, crushed

Refrigerate the stone crabs until serving time. Ladies usually can eat 3 claws, men 4 claws. Melt the butter in a sauce pan over medium low heat, add the lime juice and garlic. Simmer at least 15 minutes before serving. Do not boil. Serve the stone crabs cold, in the cracked shell, with the melted butter sauce in a dish alongside.

L. D. Pankey

NUTTY YELLOWTAIL

Serves 4-6
2 pounds yellowtail cut into "fingers"
2 eggs
2 tablespoons milk
½ teaspoon salt
½ teaspoon freshly ground black pepper
½ cup flour
2 cups Macadamia nuts, minced in blender
4-6 tablespoons butter
2 tablespoons oil
2 key limes, quartered

Pat fish fingers dry with paper towel. Combine eggs and milk and whip with a whisk. Add salt and pepper to flour and mound on a sheet of waxed paper. Place nuts in a shallow dish. Roll the fish fingers in flour to coat. Dip in egg liquid, then into the nuts and place on a cake rack to dry for at least 30 minutes. Melt the butter and oil together in a heavy skillet over moderate heat. When butter becomes foamy, add the fish and cook 3-5 minutes on each side. Serve at once with key lime quarters.

Mrs. R.P. Martin

YELLOWTAIL MIAMI

Serves 6
1 pound shrimp, shelled and cleaned
4 tablespoons heavy cream
½ teaspoon salt
¼ teaspoon white pepper
2 egg whites, slightly beaten
2 cups heavy cream
12 fillets yellowtail
16 large shrimp
1 cup mushrooms, sliced
3 tablespoons butter, clarified
½ cup basic fish sauce (see Index)
Watercress
1 cup white wine

To make the filling, purée 1 pound of shrimp and 4 tablespoons heavy cream in a blender. Pour into a bowl, set in a bed of ice and using a wooden spoon, beat the purée until it is icy cold. Add the salt, pepper and egg whites and mix thoroughly. Add the 2 cups heavy cream gradually, beating until the mixture is a thick paste. Cover and refrigerate 2 hours. Trim the fillets into even pieces and cover with equal portions of the shrimp filling. Roll up the fillets and place in a buttered baking dish. Bring the wine to a boil, add 16 shrimp and turn to simmer for 5 minutes or until the shrimp turn pink. Drain the liquid and reserve. Peel and devein the shrimp and set aside. Pour the wine the shrimp were cooked in over the fillets. Cover the fillets with foil and bake at 350° for 20 minutes or until fish flakes when tested. Sauté mushrooms in clarified butter until tender. Remove fillets from oven and drain off liquid and strain through a fine sieve. Over high heat, boil the liquid and reduce to 1/3 cup. Add mushrooms and fish sauce, heat thoroughly and pour over yellowtail. Garnish with 16 large shrimp and watercress.

John Baratte

YELLOWTAIL A LA FLORENTINE

Serves 6
3 pounds yellowtail, fillets
Salt and white pepper to taste
2 pounds fresh spinach,
  trimmed and washed
1 teaspoon salt
8 tablespoons butter
2 tablespoons shallots, chopped
¼ cup fish stock
¼ cup dry white wine
Pinch of nutmeg
1 recipe Mornay sauce
  (see Index)
2 tablespoons Gruyere cheese,
  grated

Wash and trim fish into 6 equal fillets. Lightly pound fillets with the side of a knife to make uniform thickness. Pat dry with paper towels and season with salt and white pepper to taste and set aside. In a large pot, bring 3 quarts of water to boil. Add 1 teaspoon salt and spinach, return liquid to a boil and cook 4-5 minutes. Drain spinach. Butter a flame proof baking dish with 2 tablespoons butter. Sprinkle chopped shallots over the bottom of the pan. Fold the fillets in half and arrange 1 layer. Add fish stock and wine. Cover fish with a sheet of buttered waxed paper. Bring liquid to a simmer on top of the stove, then bake at 325° for 10-12 minutes or until fish flakes when tested. In another pan, add 6 tablespoons butter and spinach. Stir constantly for 1-2 minutes. Transfer spinach to large au gratin dish and spread it out evenly. Carefully arrange poached fillets on top of the spinach. Pour Mornay sauce over fillets and spinach and sprinkle the top with grated Gruyere cheese. Place under broiler for 30 seconds or until cheese is browned. Serve immediately.
Peggy Roberts

FILLETS DE YELLOWTAIL AUX BANANAS

Serves 2
1 pound yellowtail fillets,
** skinned and boned**
Salt and pepper to taste
1 cup flour
1 ripe banana
½ cup butter, melted
¼ cup vermouth

Wash fillets and pat dry with paper towels. Season with salt and pepper to taste. Dredge fillets in flour to cover. Place in a small buttered baking dish. Peel banana and cut in half or quarters. Place banana on top of each fillet. Melt butter and add vermouth and pour over fillets. Bake at 450° for 10-15 minutes or until fish flakes when tested. Baste frequently. Spoon pan juices over fillets when serving.

Mrs. Teri Tyson

TUNA TETRAZZINI

Serves 12
¼ cup olive oil
10 onions, sliced
2 green peppers, sliced
1 bunch celery, chopped
1 bunch parsley, chopped
2 big pinches marjoram
1 pinch thyme
1 pinch nutmeg
2 cans cream of mushroom soup
1 large can mushrooms, sliced
1 bottle green stuffed olives,
** sliced**
1 pint sour cream
Dash of Worcestershire sauce
Lemon
1 small package spaghetti,
** cooked**
4 cans white Albacore tuna,
** drained**
¼ cup Parmesan cheese
3 tablespoons butter
Tabasco, to taste

Sauté onions, green pepper, celery, parsley, marjoram and thyme in the olive oil over medium heat. Add more olive oil if skillet becomes dry or sticky. Combine the nutmeg, soup, mushrooms, olives, sour cream, salt, pepper and Worcestershire sauce with the sauteed vegetables. Stir in cooked spaghetti, then bite-sized pieces of tuna. Pour tetrazzini into a large casserole and sprinkle the top with Parmesan cheese. Dot with butter and bake at 350° for 30-40 minutes until brown and bubbly.

Mrs. Peter R. Harrison

Meats & Poultry

MEATS AND POULTRY

The City of Coral Gables obtained its name from the original name of this house, built in 1906 by city founder George E. Merrick. Later renamed Merrick Manor, the house is presently being preserved by the City. Pictured in the front yard is a Mexican Pre-Columbian male figure donated to the Lowe Art Museum by Mr. and Mrs. S.J. Levin.

BARBARA'S BRISKET

Serves 12
1 whole brisket, first cut and
well-trimmed of fat
1 package dry onion soup mix
¾ of medium size bottle of
ketchup
½ cup brown sugar
Pinch of garlic salt

Mix together the dry soup mix,
ketchup, brown sugar and garlic
salt. Spread over meat. Wrap
tightly in one or two sheets of
aluminum foil being careful to
prevent any juice from leaking
out. Bake at 325° for 2 hours, or
longer if desired. This makes its
own gravy and can be sliced like
London broil.

Mrs. Marcia Gonzalez

SHIRLEY'S BARBECUE

Serves 12 or more
1 Boston butt (3-4 pounds)
Salt
1 cup broth (or more if prefer
juicy)
2 tablespoons vinegar
2 tablespoons brown sugar
¼ cup lemon juice
1 cup ketchup
3 tablespoons Worcestershire
sauce
1 tablespoon mustard
Tabasco to taste
Salt and pepper to taste

Boil the Boston butt with some
salt for 3-5 hours. Cool and
remove from juice. Skim off
some of the fat from the broth
leaving a bit for flavor. Break
meat into medium large pieces
and set aside. Mix together the
broth, vinegar, brown sugar,
lemon juice, ketchup,
Worcestershire, mustard,
Tabasco and salt and pepper to
taste. Boil for 15 minutes. Add
meat to boiled mixture and cook
for 45 minutes. Serve over rice or
buns. This freezes nicely.

Mrs. John C. Sullivan, Jr.

POUPIETTES DE BOEUF

Serves 6-8

STUFFING:
1 large onion, minced
1 tablespoon butter
1/3 pound lean veal, ground
1/3 pound lean pork, ground
¼ pound fresh pork fat, diced
1 egg, lightly beaten
1 clove garlic
1/3 cup parsley, chopped
¼ teaspoon thyme
¼ teaspoon allspice
Salt and pepper to taste
BEEF:
2½ pound piece of lean beef,
   chuck, top round or sirloin
   sliced into 12-16 slices and
   flattened with mallet
String
2 tablespoons oil
1 tablespoon butter
1 large onion, sliced
1 carrot, sliced
1½ cups beef bouillon
1 cup dry vermouth
1 Bouquet Garni
1 tablespoon Dijon mustard
½ cup heavy cream
Parsley, chopped
BOUQUET GARNI:
10 sprigs parsley
Bay leaf
½ teaspoon thyme
3 garlic cloves

Stuffing:
Prepare stuffing by cooking
minced onion in butter until
tender. Mix onion with ground
meat and pork fat. Add egg and
seasoning. Combine thoroughly.
Salt and pepper to taste.
Set aside.

Beef:
Salt and pepper the flattened
pieces of beef and divide stuffing
between them. Roll up and tie
with string. Heat cooking oil with
butter and brown meat rolls.
Remove and add to same skillet
1 onion and 1 carrot, sliced, and
cook over low heat for 6 minutes
until they begin to brown. Add
bouillon, dry vermouth and
Bouquet Garni. Add poupiettes
and if needed, more bouillon to
cover meat. Bring to boil.
Transfer to preheated 300° oven
and bake 1 hour and 45 minutes.
Remove meat from oven; take off
strings. Strain sauce and skim off
fat. Reduce to 2 cups by boiling.
Add salt and pepper. Remove
from burner and stir in mustard
and cream. Reheat. Pour over
rolls and sprinkle with chopped
parsley.

Mrs. John Renuart

POT ROAST LATIMER

Serves 4-8 depending on size of
roast
3-6 pound chuck or California
style roast
2 tablespoons brown sugar
1/3 cup water
1/3 cup red wine vinegar
⅛ teaspoon cinnamon
¼ teaspoon allspice
2 onions, sliced
1 bay leaf
1 cup raisins
Salt and pepper to taste
¼ cup ginger snaps, crushed
1½ cups water

Place roast in pan and add brown sugar, water, vinegar, cinnamon, allspice, onion, bay leaf, raisins, salt and pepper on top of meat. Cover and roast at 350° for 2½ to 3 hours. Baste occasionally. Add a little water if necessary. Remove roast, when done, and put on heated platter. Add crushed ginger snaps and water to the pan and bring to a boil, stirring. Pour over roast and serve with noodles.

Mrs. W. Carroll Latimer

SWEET AND SOUR POT ROAST

Serves 6-8
3-4 pound chuck roast
2 tablespoons shortening
1 onion, chopped
1 bay leaf
1 teaspoon salt
¾ cup water
4 tablespoons brown sugar
3 tablespoons vinegar
3 tablespoons ketchup
½ cup raisins
1 cup cold water
1 tablespoon cornstarch

Brown pot roast in shortening in heavy pot. Add onion, bay leaf, water and salt. Simmer one hour. Mix together brown sugar, vinegar, ketchup and raisins. Add to meat. Cover and simmer for 1½-2 hours or until meat is tender. Remove meat to heated platter. Add water and cornstarch to sauce in pot and cook, stirring constantly, until gravy is thick and clear. Serve gravy over pot roast.

Mrs. Hugh T. Whitehead

LONDON BROILED STEAK

Serves 4-6
1 flank steak
½ cup lemon juice
¼ cup soy sauce
1 teaspoon dry ginger
1 tablespoon brown sugar
Coarsely ground pepper to taste

Place flank steak in shallow pan. Combine remaining ingredients and pour marinade over the meat. Marinate for 1-2 hours. Broil or charcoal grill.

Mrs. Edward F. Swenson, Jr.

STEAK DIANE

Serves 6 (do not increase)
6 fillet mignons, 1 inch thick
4 tablespoons butter
6 shallots, finely chopped
6 mushrooms, thinly sliced
4 tablespoons chives, minced
4 tablespoons parsley, minced
2 tablespoons Worcestershire
  sauce
Salt and pepper to taste
2 ounces brandy

Pound steaks until ½ inch thick. Sauté over high heat in 2 tablespoons foaming butter. In the meantime, in another pan, melt the other 2 tablespoons of butter and sauté the shallots and mushrooms. Add everything, except the brandy, and mix well. Put a little of this sauce mixture on top of each steak, cooking for 2 minutes (total cooking time for rare steaks should be 4-5 minutes). Warm brandy over direct heat. Touch brandy with a lighted match and pour flames over the steaks. Serve immediately.

Mrs. John Renuart

STEAK FRANÇAIS

Serves 4
Croûtes (bread, butter)
4 fillets of beef, 1½ inches thick
3½ tablespoons butter
1½ tablespoons shallots,
  minced
½ cup Burgundy or Madeira
1 teaspoon flour
2 teaspoons butter
1½ tablespoons wine

Sauté rounds of bread in about 2 tablespoons of hot butter until golden on both sides. Drain on absorbent paper. Hold in warm oven. In skillet, heat 1 tablespoon butter and cook fillets over high heat for about 4 minutes on each side. Remove to heated platter. Drain off fat and return skillet to medium heat. Add ½ tablespoon butter and 1½ tablespoons minced shallots and cook briefly. Add ½ cup wine and cook until reduced to about half. Stir in 1 teaspoon flour mixed to a paste with 1 teaspoon butter and cook for 30 seconds. Swirl in a bit of butter, about 1 teaspoon, and 1½ tablespoons of wine. Serve fillets on croûtes with sauce spooned over the top.

Mrs. John Renuart

MARINATED FLANK STEAK

Serves 6
1 tablespoon sugar
1 teaspoon cinnamon or ginger
1 clove garlic, minced
½ cup soy sauce
¾ cup port wine
1 flank steak

Mix all ingredients together and pour over meat. Allow to marinate at least 8 hours — preferably 24 hours, turning once. Charcoal grill or broil as desired.

Mrs. James A. Sawyer

SESAME STEAK

Serves 4
1 teaspoon lemon juice
1 tablespoon salad oil
¼ cup soy sauce
1 teaspoon brown sugar, (optional)
1 teaspoon onion powder
¼ teaspoon black pepper
¼ teaspoon garlic powder
¼ teaspoon ground ginger
1 tablespoon sesame seeds
1 flank steak

Mix ingredients and pour over steak. Allow to marinate at least 1 hour. Broil, or, for best flavor, charcoal grill.

Mrs. Fred E. Luhm

BARBECUE CUPS

Serves 10-12
1 pound ground beef
½ cup barbecue sauce (see Index)
2 tablespoons onions, chopped
1 tablespoon brown sugar
1 can refrigerated biscuits
¾ cup sharp Cheddar cheese, grated

Brown beef and drain off fat. Add sauce, onion and sugar. Roll each biscuit separately and press into muffin cups. Make sure dough reaches edges of cups. Spoon browned beef into dough cups and top with a sprinkle of cheese. Bake at 400° for 10-12 minutes.

Mrs. Karl Noonan

COMPANY CASSEROLE

Serves 4-6

8 ounce carton cottage cheese
8 ounce package cream cheese
1 cup sour cream
1 pound ground beef
16 ounces tomato sauce
1 tablespoon green pepper, diced
6 scallions, diced (or equal quantity of onion)
8 ounce package wide noodles

Have cheeses, sour cream, and vegetables at room temperature. Cream all of them together and let stand for several hours allowing flavors to blend. Brown ground beef; add tomato sauce. Cook noodles. Layer into greased casserole (first noodles, second cheese mixture, third more noodles, fourth meat and sauce). Bake at 350° for 35-45 minutes.

Mrs. James A. Wright, III

GROUND BEEF AND EGGPLANT

Serves 10

12 slices eggplant; peeled, ½ inch thick
2 pounds ground beef
3 tablespoons olive oil
¼ cup onion, chopped
¼ cup green pepper, chopped
2 tablespoons flour
2 teaspoons salt
¼ teaspoon fresh ground pepper
½ teaspoon oregano
2 cups tomato sauce
1½ cups Cheddar cheese, shredded

Cook peeled eggplant slices in salted water about 3-5 minutes. Brown meat in 2 tablespoons olive oil. Cook onion and green pepper in remaining oil until wilted. Combine meat with vegetables. Stir in flour, salt, pepper, oregano and tomato sauce. Cook until thickened. Arrange in layers in 2 quart shallow baking dish beginning with ½ of eggplant slices, ½ of meat mixture, and ½ of cheese. Repeat with other half of eggplant, meat, and cheese. Bake uncovered at 300° for 30 minutes.

Mrs. Jack Pfleger, Jr.

HAMBURGER QUICHE

Serves 6-8

1 unbaked pie shell (see Index)
½ pound ground beef
½ cup mayonnaise (see Index)
2 eggs
½ cup milk
1 tablespoon cornstarch
1½ cups grated Swiss or Cheddar cheese
1/3 cup sliced green onions
Dash of pepper

Brown meat in skillet; drain fat and set aside. Blend mayonnaise, eggs, milk and cornstarch until smooth. Stir in meat, cheese, onion and pepper. Turn into unbaked pastry shell. Bake at 350° for 35-40 minutes or until golden brown on top and knife inserted in center comes out clean.

Mrs. Richard R. Paige

MEAT LOAF WITH PIQUANT SAUCE

Serves 8-10
¾ cup dry bread crumbs or corn
flakes crumbs
1 cup milk
1½ pounds ground chuck
2 eggs, slightly beaten
¼ cup onion, grated or finely
chopped
1 teaspoon salt
⅛ teaspoon pepper
½ teaspoon sage
¼ cup ketchup
3 tablespoons brown sugar
¼ teaspoon nutmeg
1 teaspoon dry mustard

Soak crumbs in milk; add meat, eggs, onion, salt, pepper, sage and mix well. Shape into 2 loaves or 1 large loaf. Place in greased pan. Prepare piquant sauce by mixing together the ketchup, brown sugar, nutmeg and dry mustard. Pour mixture over meat loaves. Bake at 350° for 45 minutes, or 1 hour if large loaf.

Mrs. Karl Noonan

PICADILLO

Serves 6
2 onions, diced
2 green peppers, diced
4 tablespoons olive oil
1½ pounds ground beef
1 medium jar stuffed olives
1 small jar capers (optional)
½ box seedless raisins
12 ounce can tomato sauce
2 tablespoons Worcestershire
sauce
½ of juice from olive jar
¼ teaspoon oregano
½ teaspoon salt
¼ teaspoon pepper
½ teaspoon garlic powder or one
clove, crushed
½ teaspoon celery salt
¼ teaspoon paprika

Sauté onions and peppers in 2 tablespoons of the olive oil until softened and then set aside. Sauté beef in remaining 2 tablespoons of olive oil. Combine sautéed onions, peppers and beef in one large pan. Add olives, capers, raisins, tomato sauce and remaining seasonings, stirring to mix well. Cook covered for 40 minutes over low heat.

Mrs. Earl Becker
Mrs. Alan Greer

FILLED GROUND MEAT ROLL

Serves 10

2¼ pounds ground meat
   (any combination of pork,
   beef, veal, or lamb)

2 eggs, slightly beaten

1 cup light cream

½ cup milk

2 teaspoons salt

¾ teaspoon white pepper

1 tablespoon butter

¾ pound celery

Mushrooms and onions
   (optional)

½ package Boursin Fines Herbes
   Cheese

In large bowl, mix meat, spices, egg, milk and ¾ cup of the cream stirring gently. Cut celery in very thin slices. Divide meat onto greased or oiled waxed paper. Cover with the celery slices. Roll up jelly roll style. Do this with both so that you will have two rolls. If using mushrooms and onions, they can be included in the celery layer. Put both rolls in a large pan. Mix the cheese with the remaining ¼ cup cream and pour over the meat rolls. Bake at 325° for 1 hour, or until done.

Mrs. William Taylor

MEAT SAUCE FOR SPAGHETTI

½ slab of pork ribs or any cut
   of pork

Olive oil

1 onion, chopped

¼ teaspoon salt

⅛ teaspoon pepper

½ teaspoon basil leaves, minced

1 bay leaf

½ teaspoon oregano

4 ounce can tomato paste

2 15 ounce cans tomato pureé

2-3 cloves garlic

Cover bottom of sauce pan with oil and brown pork which has been cut up. Remove the pork and brown the onion and garlic. Add the tomato paste and equal amount of water. Add the spices and stir. Add the purée and an equal amount of water. Simmer for 1 hour, stirring often. Add the pork and simmer until oil has covered the surface. Skim off the oil. Cook over low heat. This recipe is doubled or tripled easily. This will make sufficient sauce for 2 pounds pasta. Extra sauce can be frozen if desired.

Vincent Gulla

SPAGHETTI WITH MEAT SAUCE

Serves 6
Cooking oil, to cover pan
1 onion, chopped
2 cloves garlic, minced or
　pressed
1 pound ground beef
1 teaspoon salt
1 bay leaf, crumbled
24 ounces tomato sauce
1½ cups water
1 pound box spaghetti
Parmesan cheese, grated

Cook onion and garlic in hot oil until soft. Add meat and brown. Drain if necessary. Sprinkle in seasonings. Stir in tomato sauce and water. Simmer for 45 minutes. Serve over hot spaghetti with grated cheese.

Mrs. Ray Fisher

BEEF BURGUNDY WITH OYSTERS

Serves 8-10
5 pounds sirloin or cross rib cut
　in 1 inch cubes
½ cup butter
1 pound fresh mushrooms,
　halved
½ cup onions, chopped
2 cups Burgundy or dry red wine
Pinch of salt, pepper, thyme,
　marjoram, tarragon, cayenne
1-2 pints fresh oysters or 2 cans
　oysters
3 tablespoons flour

Melt butter in a deep casserole, brown meat. Add mushrooms and onions and sauté. Add wine, seasonings and liquid from oysters. Cover and bake at 350° for 1 hour. Blend flour with little additional wine and stir into meat dish. Add oysters to meat dish and continue baking for about 10 minutes more. Serve with rice or noodles.

Mrs. Earl Becker

STEAK AU POIVRE

Serves 4
2½ pounds sirloin steak
4 tablespoons black
　peppercorns, smashed with
　hammer
1 tablespoon salt
3 tablespoons butter
2 tablespoons olive oil
½ cup brandy

Beat pepper and salt into both sides of steak. Sauté steak in hot oil and butter mixture until it reaches desired degree of doneness. Flame with warmed brandy. Serve at once.

Mrs. Hillard Willis

BEEF WITH PEPPERS

Serves 4-6
1½ tablespoons oil
1 clove garlic, crushed
1 pound beef, cut in thin pieces
　(round steak, flank, leftover
　sirloin or rib steak)
1 teaspoon salt
1 teaspoon pepper
1 cup beef bouillon or soup stock
2 tablespoons cornstarch
1 tablespoon soy sauce
2 tablespoons water
1 large green pepper, sliced
　lengthwise

In heated pan, brown the crushed garlic in oil. Remove garlic when brown and discard. Add the pieces of beef to the oil and fry. Season with salt and pepper. Add beef bouillon or soup stock and cook a few minutes longer. In the meantime make a mixture with the cornstarch, soy sauce and water. Add the cornstarch mixture to the beef, stirring carefully until liquid thickens. Add the green peppers and heat thoroughly.
Mrs. Manuel Carbonell

BEEF SHISH KABOBS

Serves 6-8
3 pounds sirloin tip, cubed
1 teaspoon tenderizer
2-3 whole Irish potatoes, 1 inch
　cubes and parboiled
2-3 whole onions, halved and
　parboiled, or sectioned
3-4 green peppers, quartered
1 large box cherry tomatoes
MARINADE:
2 tablespoons instant minced
　onion
2 teaspoons thyme
1 teaspoon marjoram
1 bay leaf, crushed
1 cup red wine vinegar
½ cup olive oil
3 tablespoons lime juice
¼ cup peppercorns, crushed

Tenderize beef cubes for 2 hours, then marinate beef in marinade for 8 hours *only*. Place on skewers, alternating beef, potatoes, onions, green peppers, and cherry tomatoes. Grill over charcoal.
Mrs. Joe Abrell

BARBECUED KABOBS

Serves 6
1 pound bacon sliced
1 pound sirloin steak, 1½ inch
  cubes
Cherry tomatoes
Sweet red peppers
Fresh mushrooms
Green peppers
MARINADE:
¼ cup salad oil
¼ cup ketchup
2 tablespoons vinegar
½ teaspoon salt
½ clove garlic, crushed

Place meat cubes in bowl. Blend marinade ingredients and pour over meat. Let stand 4 hours in refrigerator. Wrap beef in bacon slices and place on skewers, alternating with tomatoes, peppers, and mushrooms. Barbecue over grill, brushing with marinade several times.

Mrs. Earl Becker
Mrs. Charles K. Orr

TERIYAKI ROAST TENDERLOIN

Serves 6-8
½ cup dry sherry
¼ cup soy sauce
2 tablespoons dry onion soup
  mix
2 tablespoons brown sugar
2 pounds beef tenderloin
2 tablespoons water
Watercress and kumquats for
  garnishing

Combine dry sherry, soy sauce, dry onion soup mix and brown sugar. Place beef tenderloin in large clear plastic bag; set in deep bowl to steady roast. Pour in marinade and close bag tightly. Let stand 2 hours at room temperature or overnight in refrigerator. Occasionally press bag against meat in several places to distribute marinade evenly. Remove meat from marinade and place on rack in shallow roasting pan. Bake at 325° for 30-40 minutes, basting occasionally with about half of the marinade for medium rare. In small saucepan, heat the remaining marinade and the water until the mixture bubbles. Slice meat into ¼ inch slices and arrange on heated platter. Spoon wine sauce over slices of beef and serve, garnished with watercress sprigs and kumquats.

Mrs. Allen Bradford

LAMB CHOPS EN PAPILLOTE

Serves 6

6 rib lamb chops, 1¼-1½ inches thick, trimmed and French boned

Olive oil

2 cups Duxelles (see p. 275)

6 heart shaped pieces of cooking parchment paper 10 inches long by 13 inches wide

Butter

12 thin slices mildly smoked ham, cooked

Fresh parsley, minced

In skillet, brown fat edge of chops in 1 tablespoon olive oil. Lay chops flat and brown each side 2 minutes. Cut 6 heart shaped parchment papers, 10 inches long and 13 inches wide. Butter top side of papers. Fold hearts in half; open, put slice of ham along fold. Divide duxelles into 12 parts and top each slice of ham with one part. Lay a chop on top of duxelles on each heart, arranging it so that the straighter side of the bone is nearest the fold. Top each chop with 1 part duxelles and cover with ham slice. Fold paper over chops, starting at rounded edge top, crimp the edges tightly shut all the way around and twist the bottom tips. Oil a baking sheet lightly and put cases on it. Brush cases lightly with oil. Bake at 450° for 12-15 minutes until puffed and lightly browned. Remove from oven and carefully open by slitting with sharp knife. Sprinkle with chopped parsley and serve.

Mrs. Robert Hartnett

7 HOUR LAMB

Serves 8

½ pound salt pork

6 pound leg of lamb, boned

3 cloves garlic, sieved or crushed

2 cups beef stock

6 onions, sliced

6 carrots, sliced

1 celery top

1 sprig parsley

2 teaspoons salt

1 teaspoon thyme

¾ teaspoon pepper

Rinse salt pork; dice 2 slices and set aside remainder. Make slits in lamb at intervals and insert pork slivers and garlic. Roll and fasten lamb with skewers. Tie securely and remove skewers. In Dutch oven, add remaining ingredients and remainder of salt pork and bring to a boil. Place lamb in Dutch oven and simmer over very low heat or in a 200° oven for 7 hours. This is very paté-like at the end and can be cut and served with a spoon.

Mrs. John C. Sullivan, Jr.

ROAST LAMB WITH HERBS

Serves 8
6 pound leg of lamb
3 cloves garlic
1 teaspoon oregano
1 teaspoon rosemary
1 teaspoon thyme
2 teaspoons lemon juice
1 tablespoon olive oil
1 tablespoon salt
½ tablespoon black pepper

Lamb should not be boned; however, the skin should be removed. Cut garlic cloves into 2 or 3 slivers and insert in gashes cut into lamb at regular intervals. Combine remaining ingredients and rub all over outside of lamb. Use most of the mixture to coat the top well. Cover loosely with foil and allow to stand 2 hours at room temperature. Place lamb on rack in open roasting pan, without foil, and add 1 cup water to pan. Roast at 350°, allowing 20 minutes per pound for pink lamb and 25-30 minutes per pound for well done. When done, skim off fat, add a little more water to pan, bring to boil scraping up browned bits from bottom. Simmer until reduced by 1/3, season to taste. Serve sauce in heated sauceboat with lamb.

Tom Grant

CHOP SUEY

Serves 8
1½ pounds pork, cubed
1½ pounds veal, or chicken, cubed
2 bunches celery, finely chopped
2 pounds onions, finely chopped
1 small bottle soy sauce or 5½ ounces
2 cups water
2 tablespoons dark molasses
2 tablespoons dark brown sugar
2 tablespoons flour mixed in ¾ cup water
Pepper, to taste
No salt
Rice

Brown meat a little at a time in small amount of oil. Add vegetables, water, soy sauce and simmer 1 hour. Add molasses and brown sugar during final 20 minutes of cooking time. Add pepper and well-mixed flour and water mixture, simmering and stirring until somewhat thickened. Serve over hot fluffy rice.

Mrs. Denis Renuart

TOURTIERE MOTHER RENUART

"Tootsie-Eye" is a traditional dish to the French Canadian people. It is the specialty of the house at Christmas and New Year's.

Serves 35: 5 per pie
8 pounds fresh ham
2 cups water
4 onions, chopped
Salt and pepper to taste
4 cups soda crackers, crushed
Cloves, ground
Cinnamon, ground
All spice, ground
7 pie shells, unbaked
  (see Index)

Have butcher trim and grind the fresh ham. Place meat in a big pot and simmer with water. Add onion, salt and pepper. Simmer about 1 hour, stirring occasionally. Add a little water now and then if needed. When it is cooked, thicken with rolled cracker crumbs to desired consistency. Add spices to taste. Optional spices could include sage, garlic, cayenne or Tabasco. Fill pie shells and cover with a top layer of pastry which is pierced to allow steam to escape. Immediately bake at 375° for 10 minutes. Reduce heat to 325° and bake for additional 20-30 minutes. Remove when crust is golden brown. If desired they can be frozen and baked before serving. Serve with small whole pickled beets.

Mrs. John Renuart

CARVE DE VINLEO

Serves 6
3 pounds lean pork, ½ inch
  slices
1 cup dry white wine
3 tablespoons wine vinegar
2-3 cloves garlic, minced
1 bay leaf, crushed
3 tablespoons parsley, chopped
1½ teaspoons coarse black
  pepper
½ cup butter

Mix together wine, vinegar and seasonings and marinate pork at room temperature for 4 hours. Drain and dry pork, saving marinade. Heat butter until it sputters and quickly brown pork on both sides. Add half a cup of marinade, bring to boil, lower heat and simmer covered for 20-30 minutes or until tender. Serve with juice from pan.

Mrs. Hillard Willis

PORK IN BEER AND SOUR CREAM

Serves 6

3 onions, sliced

3 tablespoons butter

4 pounds lean pork loin, cut in 1 or 2 inch cubes

1 teaspoon salt

Pepper to taste

3-4 teaspoons paprika

1 tablespoon caraway seeds

1 can light beer

2 pounds mild sauerkraut, well drained

1 pint sour cream

Sauté onions in butter, add pork cubes, salt, pepper, paprika, and caraway seeds, stirring lightly to brown meat. Allow most of the juice to cook out and then add beer and simmer at least 1 hour over very low heat. Add sauerkraut; heat throughly. Add sour cream and warm through. Serve with big loaf of crusty rye bread.

Mrs. James Hauf

PORC À L'ORANGE

Serves 8

3-4 pound fillet of pork, boned and tied

4 tablespoons butter

4 carrots, cut in rounds

3 tablespoons cognac

1 cup dry white wine

1 bay leaf

Pinch of thyme

Salt and pepper to taste

1 orange

Brown pork in butter; add carrots. Pour on pre-heated cognac and wine. Add bay leaf, thyme, salt and pepper. Cover and cook slowly over low heat for 2 hours. Turn and spoon over sauce occasionally while cooking. Take pork out of pan and keep hot. Remove excess grease. Cut peel of orange into thin strips and blanch for 2 minutes in boiling water. Add strips to sauce along with juice of one orange. Simmer uncovered 10 minutes. Cut pork into slices and serve with sauce poured over it.

Mrs. Lawrence E. Lewis, II

PORK SATAY

Serves 5-6

1½ pounds pork tenderloin, sliced

8 Brazil nuts or walnuts, shelled

2 tablespoons coriander seeds or 1 tablespoon powdered coriander

⅛ teaspoon ground red pepper

¼ teaspoon black pepper

1 clove garlic, minced

2 tablespoons onion, minced

1 teaspoon salt

1 tablespoon brown sugar

3 tablespoons lemon juice

½ cup soy sauce

½ cup red wine

Grind nuts and coriander and mix with all other ingredients. Marinate pork tenderloin at room temperature for 2-3 hours. Broil or charcoal for about 45 minutes.

Mrs. Emory S. Lanier

ITALIAN SAUSAGE AND PEPPERS

Serves 4

2 cloves garlic

Fresh parsley

2 pounds Italian sausage

¼ cup olive oil

2 ounces salt pork

2 onions, sliced

6-8 green peppers, sliced

¼ pound Prosciutto, diced

16 ounces Spanish style tomato sauce

1 teaspoon rosemary

Black pepper

2 tablespoons ground beef

2 tablespoons tomato paste

Romano cheese, grated

Chop garlic and parsley together. Cut sausage in pieces. Combine olive oil and salt pork in saucepan and heat. Add onions and brown slowly. Add sausage and cook slowly for 20 minutes. Add green peppers, Prosciutto, tomato sauce, rosemary, pepper, garlic and parsley. Cook 10 minutes. Add ground meat and tomato paste to make a good sauce. Sprinkle Romano cheese over all when completed.

Michael Pirola

SAUERKRAUT AND SPARERIBS

Serves 12
3 large cans sauerkraut
4-5 pounds lean spareribs
Salt
Caraway seeds
1 apple

Layer the sauerkraut and the spareribs in a large kettle adding some salt and some caraway seeds after each layer. Do not drain sauerkraut and add a full can of water to the pot. Bring to a boil and simmer slowly for at least half a day. Place apple on top to keep down odor.

Mrs. F. E. Kitchens

HAM CREPES

Serves 10
20 crepes (see Index)
20 pieces baked ham, thinly sliced
1 cup Swiss cheese, grated
2 cups whipping cream
2 egg yolks

Place ham on crepes. Sprinkle with ½ cup cheese. Roll like a diploma. Place in shallow buttered baking dish (large enough to hold crepes flat). Beat cream until stiff. Stir in slightly beaten yolks and spoon over crepes. Sprinkle with remaining cheese. Bake at 450° for 15 minutes.

Mrs. Robert Ferrel

HAM AND CHEESE CREPES

Serves 6-10
CREPES:
⅞ cup flour
⅛ teaspoon salt
2 tablespoons butter
1½ cups milk
FILLING:
1½ cups thick white sauce (see Index)
Cayenne pepper
10 crepes
½ cup ham, diced or shredded
4 tablespoons butter, melted
½ cup Swiss cheese, grated
Parmesan cheese, grated

Sift flour and salt together. Beat with wire whisk. Add butter and milk one at a time. Let stand for two hours. Butter 5½ inch skillet. Over medium—low heat, pour 1 generous tablespoon of batter and rotate. Cook until bottom is brown. Turn. Slide on wire rack when done. To freeze, place sheets of waxed paper between crepes. Reheat at 250°.

Season white sauce highly with cayenne. Stir in ham and Swiss cheese. Mix well. Spread crepes with filling. Roll crepes. Arrange in leak proof serving dish. Pour butter over crepes. Dust with Parmesan. Bake at 400° until hot and bubbly. ½ cup beef or shrimp may be substituted for ham for variety.

Mrs. Charles Killingsworth

COUNTRY HAM

1 whole country ham

To prepare the Ham: With a ham saw remove the hock. Scrub ham thoroughly with a stiff brush to remove all mold and dirt. Soak in water 12 hours or overnight.

Barely Simmered Method:

Place ham in ham pot covered with water. Bring to a simmer but do not let water actually roll, just be on the verge of simmering and cook 18 minutes per pound. Remove from water to cool. If the little bone that protrudes from the end wiggles, it is done. If anything, cook slightly less than the required time.

Mrs. William Vass Shepherd

Foil Boat Method:
Place ham in boat shaped of heavy duty foil on a cookie sheet or broiling pan (a pan to catch liquid should the "boat" burst). Put 4 cups of water in boat around the ham. Take another piece of heavy duty foil and crimp edges around ham, making completely airtight. Place in oven at 400°. When oven reaches 400° bake for 20 minutes then turn the oven off for 3 hours. Turn oven back to 400° and when it reaches desired temperature, leave on for 20 minutes. Turn oven off and leave 6 to 8 hours longer. DO NOT OPEN OVEN during this process.
Mrs. Lawrence E. Lewis, II

Prepare for Glazing:
When ham has cooled cut off all excess fat and water leaving a nicely shaped layer of fat on top to score in symmetrical diamond pattern. Place whole cloves in corners of diamond pattern. Brush ham glaze (see Index) over ham and bake at 325° for 30 minutes.

SWEET AND SOUR PORK

Serves 4-6
¾ cup sugar
¼ cup soy sauce
1/3 cup vinegar
2/3 cup water
3 tablespoons cornstarch
2 pounds uncooked pork, 1 inch cubes
1 cup water
¼ cup onions, chopped
1 medium cucumber, sliced thin
2 tablespoons oil
2 tablespoons soy sauce
2 tablespoons cornstarch

Make the sweet and sour sauce in advance by combining the sugar, soy sauce, vinegar, water, and cornstarch, cooking over low heat until thick, stirring constantly. Set aside. Boil pork in water for 20 minutes. Pour out water and cool meat. Sauté onions and cucumbers in oil. To the cooled pork, add a mixture of 2 tablespoons soy sauce and 2 tablespoons cornstarch. Heat additional quantity of oil for deep fat frying, about 350°, and fry meat until crisp. Remove meat and drain. Combine meat with heated sauce and sautéed vegetables and serve.

Mrs. Manuel Carbonell

HAM LOAF

Serves 6
1 pound cured ham, ground
1 pound fresh pork, ground
2 eggs, slightly beaten
2/3 cup cracker crumbs or oatmeal
1/3 cup minute tapioca
1¼ cup milk
SAUCE:
1 clove garlic, crushed
¼ cup vinegar
½ cup water
½ cup brown sugar
1 tablespoon prepared mustard

Gently combine ham, pork, eggs, crumbs, tapioca and milk and shape into loaf in shallow baking pan. Combine sauce ingredients in a saucepan and boil for one minute, sitrring constantly. Pour boiled sauce over shaped meat loaf. Bake at 350° for 2 hours. Sauce should become thick and syrupy.

Mrs. C. A. Allen, Jr.
Mrs. Fred E. Luhm

HAM, RICE AND CHEESE

Serves 4-6
¾ cup long grain rice
1½ cups water
¼ cup onion, finely chopped
2 tablespoons soy sauce
1 medium clove garlic, minced
2 cups diced cooked ham
½ cup celery, chopped
½ cup mayonnaise (see Index)
1 tablespoon vinegar
1 cup Swiss cheese, grated

In skillet, cook rice over low heat until lightly browned. Add water, onion, soy sauce and garlic, mixing well. Cover and cook 20 minutes or until rice is tender and all of liquid is absorbed. Add ham and celery; heat through. Stir in mayonnaise, vinegar, Swiss cheese and heat until warm.
Mrs. Charles D. Hall

BEULAH'S VEAL PAPRIKA

Serves 6
¼ pound salt pork
3 pounds veal, boneless and cubed about 1½ inches
1 pound fresh mushrooms, sliced
1 cup onions, sliced
3 beef bouillon cubes
1½ cups hot water
1½ teaspoons salt
½ teaspoon pepper
2 tablespoons paprika
1 cup sour cream
Parsley, chopped
Cooked noodles

Render salt pork until all fat has been cooked out. Remove salt pork. Flour veal generously and brown in fat. Remove meat. Add mushrooms and onions, cover and cook slowly for 15 minutes, stirring occasionally. Add bouillon cubes which have been dissolved in hot water. Add salt, pepper, paprika and blend carefully. Pour all into 2½ quart casserole and bake at 350° for 1½ hours. Add sour cream in center of casserole and sprinkle with parsley. Serve with noodles.
Mrs. Henry H. Bryant, III

VEAL SCALLOPINE WITH MUSHROOMS

Serves 4
6 thin, even slices veal
Flour to dredge
Butter to sauté
½ cup dry white wine or vermouth
Fresh mushrooms

Sauté mushrooms in a little butter and set aside. Coat veal in flour and sauté in butter until browned. Pour wine and mushrooms over all and simmer covered for about 8 minutes. Place veal on heated serving platter. Continue cooking and stirring sauce in pan until thick. Pour mushroom sauce over veal and serve.
Mrs. Peter R. Harrison

VEAL SCALLOPINE WITH PARMESAN

Serves 4
6 thin, even slices veal
Flour
4 tablespoons butter
Parmesan cheese, grated
¼ cup water
1 bouillon cube
3 tablespoons sherry

Flour veal and sauté in hot butter. Sprinkle Parmesan cheese over each piece while frying, adding more butter as needed to keep from sticking, until each piece is browned and crusty. While browning, bring water to a boil and dissolve bouillon cube; add to skillet after removing meat; scrape well and stir until blended. Add sherry and return meat to pan; simmer for ½ hour, checking occasionally.

Mrs. David Wahlstad

VITELLO TONNATO

Serves 10-12
5 pounds lean veal
1 small can anchovies
3 stalks celery, chopped
2 carrots, sliced
1 onion, sliced
½ sour pickle (not dill, not sweet)
1 clove garlic
Parsley, chopped
1 can tuna in oil
Peppercorns
⅛ teaspoon thyme
2 cups chicken stock
2 cups dry white wine or if vermouth slightly less
1½ cups mayonnaise (see Index)
Salt, Tabasco and lemon juice to taste
Cold rice
Capers

Have butcher bone, roll and tie veal. Put meat in kettle. Add anchovies, celery, carrots, onion, pickle, garlic, parsley, tuna, peppercorns and thyme. Add chicken stock and wine and bring to a boil. Cover kettle, reducing heat, and simmer gently for 3-4 hours until veal is tender when tested with fork. Let meat cool in stock and chill overnight. Lift veal from stock and remove strings. Wrap in foil and refrigerate. Remove all solidified fat from stock. Cook stock until it is reduced to 2 cups. Strain and chill until it begins to thicken. Put mayonnaise in blender and gradually add enough of the chilled stock to make a smooth sauce. Season sauce with salt, little Tabasco and lemon juice, to taste. Carve veal into thin slices, arrange on platter of cold rice sprinkled with finely chopped parsley. Spoon some of the sauce over the veal and sprinkle with capers. Serve remaining sauce separately.

Mrs. John Renuart

ARROZ CON POLLO

Serves 6
3 whole chicken breasts
1/3 cup flour
1 teaspoon paprika
Salt and pepper to taste
5 tablespoons Wesson oil or
  olive oil
4 ounce can pimientos
1½ cup converted rice
1 medium onion, minced
½ green pepper, minced
2 cloves garlic, minced
2 medium pieces celery,
  chopped
24 ounces chicken broth
¼ teaspoon saffron
Juice of ½ lemon
2 large tomatoes, cut into wedges
  (optional)
10 ounce package frozen peas

Bone the chicken and cut each breast in half lengthwise. Cut crosswise into ¾ inch thick pieces. Place the chicken in a bag with flour, paprika, salt, and pepper. Shake well to coat the chicken. Remove from the bag and shake off excess flour. Heat 3 tablespoons of oil in a saucepan. Sauté chicken pieces until light brown. Remove from the pan. Cut pimientos in half lengthwise and then into ¼ inch strips. In a deep pot heat 2 tablespoons of oil. Add rice and cook over medium heat, stirring constantly until rice turns deep yellow. Add onion, green pepper, and celery and sauté 1 minute longer. Add chicken broth, saffron and lime juice. Bring to a boil. Add chicken, pimientos, and tomato wedges and stir well. Reduce heat as low as possible and cook covered, without stirring, until rice is tender, about 20 minutes. Cook peas, drain and add to cooked rice mixture. Toss lightly. Serve from covered casserole.

Mrs. Ray Fisher
Mrs. J. Michael Garner

CHICKEN WRAPPED IN BACON

Serves 8
4 chicken breasts, boned and
  split
Bacon strips for each piece, lean
1 cup sour cream
1 can mushroom soup
1 package dried smoked beef
  rounds

Wrap each piece of chicken in a strip of bacon. Combine sour cream and mushroom soup in a separate bowl. Line the sides and cover the bottom of a baking dish with dried smoked beef rounds. Place chicken in the baking dish and pour the soup-sour cream mixture over this. Bake at 300° for 2-3 hours. This can be covered until the last 30 minutes when it should be lightly browned.

Mrs. Andrea Ferguson
Mrs. John Patterson

CHICKEN WITH ASPARAGUS

Serves 4
4 chicken breasts, boned
2 eggs
2/3 cup milk
1 cup flour
Salt and pepper, to taste
¼ pound butter
Cream cheese (sliced to cover breast)
2 packages frozen asparagus, cooked
Sour cream (to cover each piece)
Parmesan cheese, grated

Dip breasts into eggs and milk mixture and then roll in flour, salt, and pepper. Brown in butter over low heat. Simmer for about 20 minutes. Remove from pan and place in casserole dish. Put slices of cream cheese on top of chicken and then lay cooked asparagus spears on top of cream cheese. Add a generous spoonful of sour cream to top it off. Sprinkle with Parmesan cheese and put under the broiler until slightly brown.

Mrs. Peter R. Harrison

CHICKEN WITH CUCUMBERS

Serves 6
1 large cucumber
½ cup chicken stock
½ cup vermouth
6 chicken breasts, halved
Salt and pepper to taste
6 tablespoons butter
2½ tablespoons brandy
½ cup whites of scallions, sliced
1½ cups heavy cream
Grated rind of ½ lemon

Peel cucumber, halve lengthwise, and remove seeds. Cut into thin slices and reserve ¾ of them. Combine the remaining ¼ with chicken stock and vermouth. Bring to a boil, remove from heat, and let steep for a few minutes. Drain this liquid, discarding the cucumber, and keep warm. Skin the breasts and season with salt and pepper. Heat butter and sauté the chicken for 5 minutes over low heat, turning often to prevent browning. Ignite the brandy and pour it over the chicken. When the flame dies remove the chicken from the skillet. Add scallions to the skillet and cook until tender. Return chicken to the skillet, cover, and cook for 6 minutes in the stock mixture. Remove the chicken to a serving dish. Cook skillet contents to almost a glaze, add heavy cream, lemon rind, and salt to taste. Add reserved cucumber slices. Heat through and pour sauce over chicken.

Mrs. John Renuart

CRAB-STUFFED CHICKEN BREASTS

Serves 6
6 boneless skinned chicken breasts
Salt and pepper to taste
½ cup onion, chopped
½ cup celery, chopped
3 tablespoons butter
3 tablespoons white wine
1 cup crabmeat, drained and flaked
½ cup herb seasoned stuffing mix
2 tablespoons flour
½ teaspoon paprika
6 tablespoons butter
1 recipe Hollandaise sauce (see Index)
2 tablespoons white wine
½ cup Swiss cheese, shredded

Pound chicken to flatten; sprinkle with salt and pepper. Cook onion and celery in butter until tender. Remove from the heat and add white wine, crabmeat, and stuffing mix. Toss to blend. Divide among the chicken breasts, roll up and secure. Combine flour and paprika and coat the chicken. Place in a baking dish and drizzle with melted butter. Bake uncovered in a 375° oven for 1 hour. Remove to a platter and keep warm. Add wine and Swiss cheese to Hollandaise sauce and pour over chicken. Serve at once.
Mrs. Richard R. Paige

CHICKEN DIVAN

Serves 8
4 large chicken breasts
Salt to taste
1 onion
1 celery stalk
2 packages frozen broccoli
1 can cream of celery soup
½ cup mayonnaise (see index)
½ cup heavy cream
1½ cup sharp cheese, grated
3 tablespoons sherry or lemon juice
1 teaspoon Worcestershire sauce (optional)
½ cup buttered bread crumbs
½ cup Parmesan cheese, grated

Boil chicken with salt, onion and celery until tender. Cook the broccoli in salt water until slightly tender. Arrange the broccoli in one layer in the bottom of a baking dish. Pull the chicken from the bones and place in a layer over the broccoli. Make a sauce with the soup, mayonnaise, cream, cheese, sherry and Worcestershire sauce. Pour the sauce over the chicken and broccoli and sprinkle the Parmesan cheese and bread crumbs over the top. Bake at 350° for 30 to 45 minutes.
Mrs. Bishop Davidson
Mary E. Kitchens
Mrs. Robert White

CHICKEN KIEV

Serves 8
8 supremes (4 whole chicken
   breasts boned)
Salt and pepper
STUFFING:
1½ sticks soft butter
1 teaspoon lemon juice
½ teaspoon salt
2 tablespoons parsley, minced
1 tablespoon chives, minced
Pepper to taste
1 cup flour
2 eggs
2 teaspoons water
1 teaspoon oil
2 cups bread crumbs
SAUCE SMITANE:
4 tablespoons sweet butter
2 shallots, chopped
1 clove garlic, minced
Bay leaf
4 tablespoons flour
½ cup vermouth
2 cups chicken broth
Salt and pepper to taste
1 teaspoon Worcestershire sauce
½ cup sour cream
¼ cup chives, chopped

Flatten the breasts, skin-side-down to about ¼ inch thick. Season with salt and pepper. Combine the next 6 remaining ingredients, beating until soft. Shape into a rectangle 3" x 4" on waxed paper and chill. Cut the butter into 8 lengths, place on the flattened meat and fold each meat piece around the piece of butter envelope style. Refrigerate for ½ hour. Dip in a plate of flour, then in another dish in which 2 eggs have been beaten with 2 teaspoons of water and 1 teaspoon of oil. Finally dip in 2 cups of fresh bread crumbs. Wrap in waxed paper and refrigerate for 1 hour before frying. Deep fat fry at 375°, 4 breasts at a time for 6 minutes.

Sauce:
Sauté shallots in butter with garlic and bay leaf. Add flour and cook for 2 minutes. Add chicken broth, salt, pepper and Worcestershire sauce. Bring to a boil and simmer for 10 minutes. Add sour cream and chives. Pour over the chicken.

Mrs. Jack Courtright

LEMON CHICKEN BREASTS

Serves 6
3 whole chicken breasts, split
½ cup flour
1½ teaspoons salt
¼ teaspoon pepper
½ cup butter
1/3 cup lemon juice
¼ cup parsley, chopped

Skin, bone and pound breasts. Dip them into mixture of flour, salt, and pepper. Shake off excess flour and chill. In a large skillet heat butter and sauté breasts 2-3 minutes per side. Drain on paper towel and keep warm until all are cooked. Stir lemon juice into drippings, heating but not boiling. Spoon pan juice over chicken, sprinkle with parsley and serve.

Mrs. Banning Lary

CHICKEN BREASTS IN MUSTARD SAUCE

Serves 6
2 tablespoons butter
1 small onion, chopped
1 tablespoons parsley, chopped
6 chicken breasts, skinned and
  boned
1 teaspoon salt
Pepper, to taste
MUSTARD SAUCE:
1 tablespoon butter
1 small onion, chopped
½ teaspoon oregano
1 tablespoon flour
½ cup light cream
½ tablespoon lemon juice
1 tablespoon prepared mustard
1 teaspoon dry mustard
½ teaspoon salt
½ cup chicken broth

Heat butter in large skillet and sauté onion and parsley for several minutes. Add chicken; sauté until nicely browned, about 10 minutes. Salt and pepper the chicken. Reduce heat and cook, covered, for 10 minutes longer.

Sauce:
Heat butter in a medium saucepan. Sauté the onion and oregano and remove from heat. Stir in flour. In a small bowl combine cream, lemon juice, both mustards, salt and chicken broth. Add this to the saucepan and cook over medium heat stirring for 3 minutes. Place chicken breasts in a shallow baking dish and pour the mustard sauce over the top. Place under the broiler for a few minutes to glaze the top. Serve with rice or noodles.

Mrs. James A. Sawyer

CHICKEN STROGANOFF

Serves 4
4 chicken breasts, split, boned,
  and skinned
Butter
1 onion, chopped
¼ cup parsley flakes
1 can cream of chicken soup
1 pint sour cream

Butter the insides of the chicken breasts and sprinkle them with onion and parsley. Roll them up and place in a greased casserole seam side down. Cover with soup and bake at 350° for 1½ hours. Remove the chicken to a serving dish. Stir sour cream into the soup in the casserole. Pour this over the chicken. Serve the chicken over noodles.

Mrs. William H. Walker

SUNSHINE CHICKEN

Serves 4
4 whole chicken breasts, boned
  and skinned
Butter, softened
Salt and pepper, to taste
2 cloves garlic, minced
2 teaspoons dried tarragon
1 package frozen asparagus,
  defrosted
SAUCE:
3 egg yolks
2 tablespoons fresh lemon juice
¼ teaspoon dry mustard
¼ teaspoon salt
½ cup butter, softened

Place each chicken breast between 2 pieces of waxed paper and pound thin. Spread the inside of each breast with butter. Sprinkle with salt, pepper, garlic, and finally tarragon. Place 5 asparagus stalks diagonally across each breast and roll up. Place seam side down in a shallow baking dish. Spread with more soft butter. Bake at 375° for 1 hour.

Sauce:
Combine egg yolks, lemon juice, dry mustard and salt in the top of a double boiler. Add butter. Place over hot, but not boiling, water and cook, stirring with a wire whisk, until sauce thickens. Remove from heat and spoon over the chicken breasts. Serve with rice and watercress.

Mrs. Taffy Gould Beber

CHICKEN WITH ARTICHOKES

Serves 6
3 pound chicken, cut up
1½ teaspoons salt
¼ teaspoon pepper
½ teaspoon paprika
6 tablespoons butter
½ pound mushrooms, cut in
  large pieces
2 tablespoons flour
1½ cup chicken consommé or
  bouillon
3 tablespoons sherry
12-15 ounce can artichoke hearts

Salt, pepper, and paprika the chicken. Brown in pieces in 4 tablespoons of the butter. Place chicken in a casserole dish. Add 2 tablespoons of butter to the pan in which the chicken was browned. Add the mushrooms and sauté for 5 minutes. Sprinkle flour over the mushrooms and stir in the consommé and sherry. Cook over medium heat for 5 minutes. Meanwhile, arrange the artichokes between the chicken pieces. Pour the mushroom-sherry sauce over them. cover and bake at 375° for 1-1½ hours. (This can be prepared the day ahead and baked just before serving.)

Mrs. Rodney G. Keep

CHICKEN WITH ORANGE AND LEMON

Serves 4
4 whole chicken breasts with wing bones
½ cup clarified butter
Juice of 1 orange
Juice of 1 lemon
1 teaspoon tarragon
1 teaspoon orange peel, grated
½ teaspoon lemon peel, grated
1 cup heavy cream
¼ cup Madeira wine
¼ cup Chablis wine
Salt, to taste
Pepper, to taste
Paprika
3 tablespoons Parmesan cheese, grated

Remove the skin and bones from whole chicken breasts, leaving the wing bones attached. In a large skillet sauté the chicken in butter over low heat until it is golden and almost cooked through. Remove the chicken from the skillet and keep it warm. To the butter remaining in the skillet add the juices, tarragon, and grated peels. Stir the mixture over low heat. Very gradually, add the cream, keeping the sauce bubbling constantly to prevent separation. Add Madeira and Chablis, salt and pepper. Sprinkle the sauce with paprika. Return the chicken to the skillet and cook over low heat, basting until it is cooked through. Arrange the chicken in a flame proof casserole dish, pour the sauce over it and sprinkle with Parmesan and a light dusting of paprika. Put under the broiler until glazed. Serve immediately. This is good with crusty French bread and a good white wine.

Francien Ruwitch

KEY WEST FRIED CHICKEN

Serves 6
2 fryers, cut up
2 cups key lime juice
1 cup water
1 cup vegetable oil
8 cloves garlic
2 teaspoons salt
¼ cup Worcestershire sauce
3 tablespoons sugar

Marinate chicken pieces for 8 hours in a mixture of the above ingredients. Remove chicken from marinade, dredge in flour, and deep fry in oil.

Mrs. Lester R. Johnson, Jr.

APRICOT CHICKEN

Serves 4
1 fryer, cut up
Flour
2 tablespoons vegetable oil
1/3 cup Teriyaki sauce
2 tablespoons apricot jam
1 tablespoon minced onion
1 tablespoon lime juice

Coat chicken with flour and brown slowly in hot oil. Combine remaining ingredients and pour evenly over the chicken. Cover. Simmer for 45 minutes turning once.

Mrs. Ray Fisher
Mrs. Jack Pfleger, Jr.

CHICKEN IN BLACK CHERRY SAUCE

Serves 6
1 frying chicken, 2½-3 pounds, cut in pieces
1 can bing cherries, pitted
1 cup red wine
2 tablespoons lemon juice
2 cloves garlic, minced
½ teaspoon ginger
½ teaspoon oregano
1 chicken bouillon cube
¼ cup corn starch
Salt and pepper, to taste
Fat or cooking oil

Drain the cherries, saving the juice. To the juice add wine, lemon juice, garlic, ginger and oregano. Marinate the chicken in this sauce overnight, refrigerated. Remove the chicken from the sauce (save sauce), and pat dry. Salt and pepper the chicken before browning in fat in a skillet. Pour sauce over chicken and add a bouillon cube. Cook over low heat for 30 minutes or until done. In a separate bowl dissolve cornstarch in water to form a paste. Add this to the chicken, stirring until smooth and thick. Finally add the cherries. Serve hot.

Mrs. Manuel Carbonell

CHICKEN À LA BORDELAISE

Serves 4
2 cups diced chicken
2 tablespoons butter
2 tablespoons flour
1 cup chicken stock
1 teaspoon Worcestershire sauce
1 clove garlic, mashed
Salt and pepper, to taste
12 mushroom caps
¼ cup sherry

Cook chicken in boiling water. Set aside one cup of stock. Bone and dice chicken. Melt butter and stir in flour. Cook for several minutes and add chicken stock, stirring until thick and smooth. Add Worcestershire sauce, garlic, salt and pepper. Fold in mushrooms and sherry. Simmer for 5 minutes before adding diced chicken. Serve hot over toast points. (This is also good with turkey.)

Mrs. William Harward

BUTTERMILK CHICKEN

Serves 8
2 fryers, cut in pieces
1 quart buttermilk
Garlic powder
2 tablespoons butter
2 onions, sliced
1 tablespoon curry
¼ teaspoon ginger
Cloves

Sprinkle chicken with garlic powder and marinate in buttermilk for 1½-2 hours in the refrigerator. In an electric frying pan sauté the onions in butter. Add spices. Finally add the chicken and buttermilk, and simmer for 1½ hours. Serve with rice and chutney.

Mrs. Jerry Marcus

CHICKEN CREPES

Serves 6-9
12-18 basic crepes (see Index)
6 tablespoons butter
1 cup fresh mushrooms, sliced
1 cup chicken, diced
3 hard cooked egg yolks, mashed
1/3 cup sour cream
1 tablespoon fresh parsley,
    chopped
¾ teaspoon salt
Pepper to taste
½ cup spinach, cooked and well
    drained
3 tablespoons Parmesan cheese,
    grated
Veloute sauce (see Index)

Melt ½ butter (3 tablespoons). Sauté mushrooms. Remove from heat. Mix in chicken, yolks, sour cream, parsley, salt, pepper and spinach. Fill crepes and roll tightly. Arranged in buttered baking dish. Sprinkle with cheese. Dot with remaining butter. Bake at 425° for 10-15 minutes or until done. Serve with Veloute sauce. Turkey may be substituted for the chicken.

Mrs. Robert Ferrel

CHICKEN DIABLE

Serves 4
1 fryer, cut up
½ stick butter
½ cup honey
¼ cup prepared mustard
1 teaspoon salt
1 clove garlic, minced
1 teaspoon curry powder

Melt butter in a shallow baking dish. Stir in remaining ingredients. Roll the chicken in butter mixture coating both sides. Arrange, skin-side-down, in a single layer in the same dish. Bake at 375° for 1 hour, basting every 15 minutes.

Mrs. Taffy Gould Beber

CHICKEN CURRY

Serves 6
3 cups chicken, cooked and
    diced
4 tablespoons butter
¼ cup onion, finely chopped
¼ cup apple, peeled and
    chopped
4 tablespoons flour
1 cup light cream
1 cup chicken broth
1-2 teaspoons curry powder
Salt and pepper to taste
3 tablespoons white raisins

Sauté the onion and apple in butter until tender. Stir in flour and blend. Gradually add cream and broth, stirring until the sauce thickens. Season with curry powder, salt and pepper. Add raisins and chicken. Serve over yellow rice.

Mrs. Tolson Meares

GLAZED CHICKEN WITH APPLES

Serves 4
3 pound chicken, split
1 teaspoon salt
¼ teaspoon pepper
¼ teaspoon nutmeg
¼ teaspoon ginger
3 large apples, peeled, cored and
    thickly sliced
¼ cup blond raisins
2 tablespoons sugar
¼ teaspoon apple pie spice or
    cinnamon
½ lime, juice and grated rind
2 tablespoons butter
¼ cup white dry wine
¼ cup orange marmalade
½ orange, juice and rind

Sprinkle chicken on both sides with salt, pepper, ginger and nutmeg. Set aside. Butter the bottom and sides of a baking dish. Place apple slices and raisins in the dish in a single layer. Sprinkle with sugar, spice, lime juice and rind, and dot with butter. Arrange chicken, skin-side-up, over apples. Bake at 325° uncovered for 1 hour. In a small sauce pan combine wine, orange juice and rind, and marmalade. Bring to a boil then simmer until thick, 10-15 minutes. Brush the top of the chicken from time to time with glaze as it cooks for 30 minutes longer. Serve with brown rice cooked in bouillon. Arrange chicken and fruit over rice.

Del Rubin

CHICKEN LYN

Serves 4
1 chicken, cut up
6 tablespoons flour
½ teaspoon salt
1 teaspoon ginger
2 tablespoons flour
6 tablespoons butter, melted
1 cup beef broth
1 onion, chopped
1 tablespoon curry
1 tablespoon sugar
2 tablespoons coconut
2 tablespoons applesauce
2 tablespoons ketchup
2 tablespoons lemon juice
2 tablespoons prune juice
½ cup almonds, slivered
1 cup mushrooms, sliced

Roll washed and dried chicken in the flour, salt and ginger mixture. Place in a baking dish. Combine all of the remaining ingredients and spoon over the chicken. Bake in a 325° oven for 1½-2 hours, basting occasionally.

Mrs. Sandy D'Alemberte

CHICKEN MARENGO

Serves 4
2½-3 pound frying chicken, cut up
1/3 cup flour
1 teaspoon salt
¼ teaspoon pepper
¼ cup olive oil
1 clove garlic, crushed
3 tablespoons onion, chopped
1 can tomatoes, 14½ ounce size
1 cup white wine
¼ teaspoon rosemary leaves
¼ teaspoon marjoram
1 cup mushrooms, sliced
½ cup green olives, sliced
½ cup consommé
2 tablespoons flour

Flour, salt, and pepper chicken. Brown in oil, adding garlic gradually. Add onion, tomatoes, wine and herbs. Cover and cook slowly for 30 minutes. Add mushrooms and olives. Make a paste of consommé and flour. Thicken the chicken mixture with this. Serve with rice.

Mrs. Henry H. Bryant, III

CHICKEN MEDLEY

Serves 4
1 large chicken, cut up
Salt and pepper
Cooking oil
1 large onion, cut in strips
4 small green peppers, seeded
    and cut in thin strips
Garlic, to taste
½ cup Serano ham, chopped
4-6 tomatoes, peeled, seeded
    and chopped
Ripe olives

Salt and pepper the chicken. Heat the cooking oil until a light haze forms over the top. Brown the chicken, turning often until golden brown in color. Remove the chicken. Add to the oil, onion, green peppers, garlic, and ham. Cook until tender 8-10 minutes. Add tomatoes, raise the heat, and cook until a sauce is formed. Stir, add chicken, reduce the heat, and continue stirring to cover the chicken. Cook 30-45 minutes, until chicken is tender but not falling off the bones. Add olives and serve with noodles.

Mrs. Reynolds Allen

OVERSTUFFED CHICKEN

Serves 8
2 chickens, whole
4 medium onions, sliced
3 cloves garlic, minced
½ cup pine nuts
½ cup sesame oil
1 box couscous
3 tablespoons cumin powder
1 can chickpeas
1 tablespoon salt
1 lemon

Sauté onions, garlic, and pine nuts in sesame oil until browned. Broil chicken in 2 quarts of water until half done. Remove chicken and add box of couscous to the broth. Stir once, turn heat down and let rise for about 15 minutes. Add cumin, chickpeas and salt to couscous along with ¾ of the sautéed mixture. Stuff chicken with this mixture. In an ovenproof platter arrange chicken on a bed of couscous mixture. Top chicken with remaining sauteed mixture. Bake for 20 minutes at 350°. Squeeze lemon over chicken before serving.

Carol Hotchkiss

SWISS CHICKEN

Serves 6
1 whole chicken
2 cups celery, diced
2 cups bread cubes, toasted
1 cup mayonnaise (see Index)
½ cup milk
½ cup onion, chopped
1 teaspoon salt
½ teaspoon pepper
12 ounces Swiss cheese, cut in
   slivers

Boil chicken in water until
tender. Cool, then take the meat
off the bones. In a 2 quart
casserole dish combine all of the
other ingredients. Add all of the
chicken to this. Cook at 350° for
about 30 minutes until hot and
bubbly.

Mrs. Robert Hays

TAFFY'S CHICKEN VERONIQUE

Serves 4
1 large frying chicken cut into
   8 pieces
3 tablespoons flour
Salt and pepper to taste
1 stick butter
2 cloves garlic minced
1 cup fresh mushrooms, sliced
½ cup walnut halves
½ cup dry vermouth
2 cups seedless green grapes

In a bag combine flour, salt, and
pepper. Shake the chicken in the
bag, a few pieces at a time, until
well coated. Melt butter in a large
skillet. Add garlic and chicken,
and sauté. Remove the chicken to
a platter and keep it warm. Add
mushrooms to the skillet and
sauté for 3 minutes. Add to the
chicken. Reduce the heat and
add vermouth to the skillet. Stir
to loosen crusty bits in the
bottom of the skillet and pour
into a small bowl. Return the
chicken, mushrooms and nuts to
the skillet. Sprinkle with grapes.
Pour the wine mixture over the
chicken. Cover and cook slowly
for 30 minutes. Serve with rice.

Mrs. Taffy Gould Beber

CHICKEN SALAD IN AVOCADO HALVES

Serves 8
6 chicken breasts, cooked,
    boned and chopped
1 cup celery, chopped
4 green onions, chopped
1 green pepper, chopped
3 tablespoons pimiento,
    chopped
5 tablespoons sweet pickle relish
1 medium sized tart apple,
    chopped
2 to 3 tablespoons fresh parsley,
    minced
Salt and pepper to taste
1 cup mayonnaise (see Index)
4 ripe avocados split, seeds
    removed
1 can Chinese noodles

Combine all ingredients except
noodles and avocados with
sufficient mayonnaise to
moisten. Add noodles just before
serving. Fill avocado shells with
salad and serve.
Mrs. Jacob Wilcox

CURRIED CHICKEN SALAD

Serves 4
4 pound roasting chicken
1 cup celery, diced
1 small crisp apple, diced
1 handful seedless grapes
½ sliced banana
1 cup mayonnaise (see Index)
3 to 4 tablespoons heavy cream
Imported curry powder
CONDIMENTS:
Hard boiled egg yolks (pushed
    through strainer)
Chopped egg whites
Toasted coconut
Raisins
Green onions, chopped
Cashew nuts, chopped
Bacon, crumbled
Mandarin oranges
Chutney (see Index)

Roast or boil chicken. Cool and
dice the meat. To 2 cups diced
meat add the above amount of
celery and fruit. To 1 cup
mayonnaise add 3 to 4
tablespoons cream and curry
powder to taste. Combine with
the chicken and fruit. Serve salad
on a bed of greens. Add dishes
from suggested condiment list.
Mrs. Edwin C. Lunsford, Jr.

HOT CHICKEN SALAD

Serves 6
2/3 cup mayonnaise
2 teaspoons vinegar
1 teaspoon salt
¼ teaspoon celery seed
2 cups cooked chicken, diced
1 cup celery, chopped
¼ cup slivered almonds
¼ cup candied dill strips or
   mango chutney
2 teaspoons minced onion
½ cup Cheddar cheese, grated

Blend mayonnaise, vinegar, salt, and celery seed. In a separate bowl combine the remaining ingredients. Toss all together. Place in a baking dish and sprinkle with cheddar cheese. Bake at 350° for 20 minutes.

Mrs. Sally Milledge

CHICKEN SALAD WITH A TWIST

Serves 8
6 ounce package of corkscrew
   macaroni
3 cups chicken, cooked and
   chopped
½ cup Italian dressing
½ cup mayonnaise
3 tablespoons lemon juice
1 tablespoon prepared mustard
1 medium onion, chopped
¾ cup ripe olive wedges
1 cup cucumber, diced
1 cup celery, diced
½ cup green pepper, diced
1 teaspoon pepper
Salt to taste
Lettuce
1 jar pimiento, diced

Cook macaroni following the package directions. Mix chicken and Italian dressing with hot macaroni. Cool. Blend mayonnaise, lemon juice, mustard and stir in onion, olives, cucumber, celery, and pepper. Add to macaroni mixture. Salt and pepper to taste. Mix well. Chill 2 or more hours to blend flavor. Before serving add a bit more mayonnaise to moisten. Serve in lettuce cups garnished with pimiento.

Mrs. Robert Kenworth

COLUMBUS CHICKEN SALAD

Serves 12
1 large chicken, boiled, and the meat chopped
1½ tablespoons gelatin
1½ cups chicken stock
2 cups celery, chopped
1 pint mayonnaise (see Index)
2 cups English peas
1 cup almonds, chopped
1 tablespoon capers
Salt and pepper to taste

Boil, bone and chop chicken, setting aside the stock. Soften gelatin in ½ cup of the stock. Add 1 cup of stock to this, and bring to a boil stirring until dissolved. Remove from the heat. In a bowl combine all of the remaining ingredients, adding the chicken and gelatin mixture and mixing well. Pour into a loaf pan or a mold and chill for several hours. Unmold on a platter bordered with lettuce. (Curry or Tabasco can be added according to taste.)

Mrs. Tom Huston

CORNISH HENS WITH MUSTARD SAUCE

Serves 4
2 Cornish hens
2 tablespoons butter
1 tablespoon Dijon mustard
½ teaspoon salt
¼ teaspoon pepper
1 recipe thick white sauce, bechamel (see Index)

Make a paste of the butter, mustard, salt and pepper. Spread this over the breast, wings and legs of the birds. Place in a buttered roasting pan and bake in a preheated 400° oven for 1 hour, basting with the pan juices. Let hens cool; cut in halves and arrange, bone-side-down, in a casserole. Cover hens with bechamel sauce and heat at 350° for 30 minutes before serving.

Mrs. John Renuart

ROASTED WILD FLORIDA DUCK

Serves 4
4 wild ducks
Salt and pepper, to taste
2 sticks of celery, with leaves
2 apples, cored and sliced
2 oranges, sliced
2 lemons, sliced
2 cups white wine
1 tablespoon Worcestershire sauce

Wash ducks. Salt and pepper the cavities and fill with celery and apple slices. Arrange ducks in a roasting pan. Surround with apples, oranges, lemons, and celery leaves. Pour wine over the ducks and add Worcestershire sauce. Bake ducks covered with foil in a 325° oven for 1½ hours. Uncover and cook for 30 minutes longer. Serve with wild rice.

Mrs. Vincent Damian

DUCKLING, ORANGE

Serves 8
2 dressed ducklings 5 pounds
  each
Juice of 2 lemons
4 bay leaves
½ cup honey
1 cup chicken stock
½ cup port wine
¼ cup red wine vinegar
2 garlic cloves, crushed
½ teaspoon tarragon
⅛ teaspoon rosemary
1 cup bitter orange marmalade
GARNISH:
Orange halves and kumquats

Wipe the ducklings with a damp cloth and sprinkle with lemon juice. Put 2 bay leaves in each cavity. Roast at 350° ½ hour or until the ducklings are golden. Pour off the fat, cool and quarter. Discard bay leaves and return to the roaster cut-side-down. Combine all of the remaining ingredients except the garnish and cook in a sauce pan over medium heat until well blended. Pour over the ducklings, cover the roaster, and bake at 300° for 1 hour. Uncover and baste. Bake for 15 minutes longer continuing to baste. Garnish with orange halves and kumquats.

Mrs. George L. Irvin, III

PHEASANT

Serves 4
2 pheasants
¼ cup flour
½ teaspoon salt
¼ teaspoon pepper
¼ cup cooking oil
1½ cups sherry
1 pound fresh mushrooms,
  sliced in half

Split the pheasant. In a bag combine flour, salt and pepper, and shake the pheasants in this. Brown pheasants in oil in a skillet. Remove and place in a roaster to which sherry has been added. Add fresh mushrooms, cover, and bake at 325° for 2 to 3 hours.

Mrs. John C. Sullivan, Jr.

Vegetables

VEGETABLES

Indian baskets from the Lowe Art Museum's large collection are filled with summer vegetables. Pictured here are a selection of Southwest American Indian and Northwest Coast Indian baskets. The fountain is part of the elaborate entrance gates to Country Club Prado in Coral Gables.

ARTICHOKE HEARTS IN PARMESAN CUSTARD

Serves 8
18 ounces frozen artichoke hearts
½ cup tomatoes, drained and chopped
1 teaspoon salt
¼ teaspoon pepper
¼ teaspoon garlic salt
2 teaspoons parsley, chopped
½ cup Parmesan cheese, grated
¾ cup water
¼ cup olive oil
6 eggs, beaten

Place the unthawed artichokes in the bottom of a greased 2-quart casserole. Sprinkle with tomatoes, salt, pepper, garlic salt, parsley and cheese. Pour in water and oil. Bake covered for 1 hour at 350°. Pour beaten eggs over casserole and bake uncovered for 15 to 20 minutes until eggs set.

Mrs. Julian Arnold

ARTICHOKES ITALIAN

Serves 15
7 cans marinated artichoke hearts
1 can chick peas, drained
1 pound fresh mushrooms, sliced lengthwise
4-ounce jar pimientos
1 pinch oregano
1 cup white wine
1 large bottle Italian dressing

Put ingredients in large bowl. Mix with 1 large bottle Italian dressing. Marinate in the refrigerator for at least two hours. Serve with a pierced serving spoon.

Mrs. Robert Vale

GINNY'S ASPARAGUS

Serves 6
2 cans asparagus spears
¼ cup butter
¼ cup flour
½ teaspoon salt
⅛ teaspoon pepper
1 cup sharp Cheddar cheese, grated
1/3 cup almonds, slivered

Reserve juice from asparagus. Melt butter in pan and add flour. Pour in a little asparagus juice at a time, making a cream sauce. Add seasonings. Place ½ of the asparagus in an 8" square pan with a layer of cheese and almonds and sauce. Repeat layers. Bake at 350° for 15 to 20 minutes until bubbling.

Mrs. Peter R. Harrison

FAMOUS BAKED BEANS

Most of all, never, never look down on the baked bean again!

Serves a bunch

2 #10 cans pork and beans, drained

2/3 stick of pepperoni, chopped

2 large green peppers, slivered

6 small white onions, chopped

16 ounces tomato sauce

1 tablespoon coarse ground pepper

1 tablespoon sage

1 teaspoon thyme

1 tablespoon oregano

2/3 of box of dark brown sugar

4 tablespoons allspice

2 cups burgundy wine

¼ cup Worcestershire sauce

2 tablespoons sweet basil

Bacon strips (optional)

Toss all ingredients in large roaster. Stir well, being sure sugar is dissolved. Let stand overnight, stirring occasionally if you feel like getting up, otherwise don't worry. Add bacon strips if you like. Bake for about 2 hours at 325° with pan covered or until thoroughly bubbly. Cook without the lid until a perfect crust forms, but *not* until beans dry out (the worst that can happen). Under *no circumstances* should beans be stirred while cooking. It can't help the delicate flavor and they'll look messy. Don't rush around at the last minutes to get it all together — the marinating is important.

Paul E. Thompson

SPICED BEANS

Serves 8

2 cans Bluelake beans

2 onions, sliced thin

2 tablespoons olive oil

4 tablespoons vinegar

¼ teaspoon salt

Dash pepper

1/3 cup mayonnaise (see Index)

½ pint sour cream

⅛ teaspoon dry mustard

1 tablespoon lemon juice

Blend beans, onions, olive oil, vinegar, salt and pepper. Marinate in refrigerator at least 2 hours. Add the remaining ingredients and serve cold. Will keep almost a week.

Mrs. Emory Lanier

BLACK BEANS HAVANA STYLE

Serves 30

12 cups black beans, dried
5 quarts water
10 onions, chopped
3 bunches celery hearts,
  chopped coarsely
3 large green peppers, sliced
10 cloves garlic, minced
1/2 cup olive oil
8 ham hocks
6 bay leaves
4 cloves
6 teaspoons chili powder
Tabasco, Worcestershire, salt
  and pepper to taste
1 large jar mango chutney
  (optional)
2 cans consommé (optional)
CONDIMENTS:
olive oil
Garlic wine vinegar
Scallions, finely chopped
Tabasco
Salt
Pepper mill

Soak dried beans in water overnight. Drain in morning. Sauté onion, celery, green pepper and garlic in olive oil until limp. Add to beans and water in roasting pan which can be covered tightly. (Electric roaster is also good.) Add ham hocks, bay leaves, cloves, chili powder and seasonings. Cook 1 hour at 300° reducing to 275° for 5 hours or until beans are tender. Thin with consommé if necessary. Serve with white or yellow rice and condiment tray.

Mrs. Hillard Willis

SWEET AND SOUR GREEN BEANS

Serves 8

1 quart fresh green beans,
  cooked
1 medium onion, chopped
8 slices bacon, fried crisp and
  crumbled
1/2 cup vinegar
1/2 cup sugar
1/2 cup bacon grease

Place a layer of cooked beans in a slightly greased flat casserole, then a layer of onion and a layer of bacon. Repeat layers. Pour sauce of vinegar, sugar and bacon grease over casserole. Cook uncovered at 350° for 30 minutes.

Mrs. Allen Bradford

SWISS BEANS

Serves 6
2 tablespoons butter
2 tablespoons flour
1 teaspoon salt
1 teaspoon sugar
¼ teaspoon pepper
½ cup onion, grated
1 cup sour cream
4 cups French style green beans,
  drained
½ pound processed Swiss
  cheese
TOPPING:
2 tablespoons butter, melted
½ cup corn flake crumbs

Melt butter, stir in flour, salt, sugar, pepper and onion. Add sour cream gradually, stirring constantly. Cook until thickened. Fold in beans and heat thoroughly. Pour into a greased 1½ quart casserole. Grate cheese over top. Combine butter and crumbs and sprinkle over cheese. Bake in 400° oven for 20 minutes.

Mrs. Boyce Ezell, III

HERBED BEANS IN FOIL

Good and easy for outdoor cooking.

Serves 8
20 ounces frozen green beans
Salt and pepper to taste
1 tablespoon lemon juice
3 tablespoons butter, melted
Dash paprika
Dash rosemary or marjoram

Place frozen vegetables on large square of heavy duty foil. Add remaining ingredients. Bring edges of foil up and fold, leaving space for steam expansion. Seal tightly. Cook over hot coals for 40 minutes turning frequently. If using a gas grill, cook 50 minutes without lid or 30 minutes with lid closed.

Mrs. James A. Sawyer

BROCCOLI CASSEROLE I

Serves 8
2 tablespoons butter, melted
2 tablespoons flour
3-ounce package cream cheese
1½ ounces blue cheese
1 cup milk
20 ounces chopped frozen
  broccoli
1/3 cup cracker crumbs

In a saucepan over medium heat, blend butter, flour, and cheeses. Add milk to make a sauce. When thickened, add broccoli which has been cooked and drained. Place in greased 1-quart shallow casserole. Top with crumbs. Bake for 30 minutes at 350°.

Mrs. Geoffrey Hill

BROCCOLI CASSEROLE II

Serves 8

2 packages frozen chopped broccoli or 1 large bunch fresh broccoli

1 cup sharp Cheddar cheese, grated

2 tablespoons onion, minced (optional)

1 cup mayonnaise

1 cup cream of mushroom soup, undiluted

2 eggs, well beaten

Cook and drain broccoli. Mix all ingredients together lightly. Bake in a casserole at 350° for 30 minutes. (For a puffier dish, use 4 eggs.)

Mrs. Banning Lary
Mrs. Phillipe Moore

BROCCOLI-RICE CASSEROLE

Serves 6

2 packages frozen chopped broccoli

1 cup rice, cooked

1 medium onion, chopped

8 tablespoons butter

1 can water chestnuts, slivered

1 can mushroom soup, undiluted

Parmesan or Romano cheese (optional)

Bread crumbs (optional)

Cook and drain broccoli according to package directions. Sauté onion in the butter until tender. Mix all ingredients and place in casserole. If desired, top with grated cheese and bread crumbs. Bake at 350° for 20-30 minutes or until heated through.

Mrs. Bishop Davidson

BROCCOLI WITH SOUR CREAM

Serves 8

20 ounces frozen chopped broccoli

8 ounces sour cream

2 tablespoons chives, chopped

1 can cream of celery soup

½ cup Cheddar cheese, grated

Cook and drain broccoli according to package directions. Mix with sour cream, chives, and soup. Place in casserole, and sprinkle cheese on top. Bake at 350° for ½ hour.

Variation:

Add ½ teaspoon grated lemon rind and 1 tablespoon lemon juice to sauce and sprinkle top of casserole with ¼ cup slivered almonds.

Mrs. Donald Boerema
Mrs. David Blount

CHEESE-BROCCOLI STRATA

Serves 6

20 ounces frozen, chopped broccoli or 1 bunch fresh broccoli, chopped

12 slices white bread, crusts removed

¾ pound sharp cheese, sliced

8 eggs, slightly beaten

3½ cups milk

½ teaspoon salt

2 tablespoons onion, minced

¼ teaspoon dry mustard

Cook and drain broccoli. With a doughnut cutter or small size glass cut 12 circles of bread from which the crusts have been removed. Fit leftover bread scraps into the bottom of a 13"x 9" baking pan. Layer the cheese and broccoli, and arrange the bread circles over the top. Combine the remaining ingredients and pour over the strata. Refrigerate overnight or at least 6 hours. Bake uncovered in a 325° oven for 55 minutes or until a knife comes out clean.

Mrs. Jay Van Vechten

MARINATED CARROTS

Serves 8

2 pounds carrots, peeled

1 can tomato soup, undiluted

1 medium onion, diced

1 cup sugar

¾ cup salad oil

¾ cup vinegar

1 tablespoon Worcestershire sauce

1 teaspoon prepared mustard

Salt and pepper to taste

Cook whole carrots until tender. Drain and slice. Return to pan and add all other ingredients. Bring to a boil. Store in refrigerator overnight. Serve either hot or cold.

Mrs. Boyce Ezell, III

AGNES NEWTON'S CARROT RING

Serves 6

1½ tablespoons butter

2½ cups carrots, freshly grated

2 eggs, beaten

1 can evaporated milk

½ teaspoon salt

½ teaspoon pepper

½ teaspoon sugar

½ cup blanched whole almonds

Melt butter in ring mold. Mix carrots, eggs, milk, seasonings and the almonds together. Fill mold with the mixture. Set in pan of water in very moderate oven, approximately 350°, and bake 1 hour or until set.

Mrs. George W. Cornell

CARROTS VICHY

Serves 8
3 bunches carrots, scraped
2/3 stick butter
½ cup Vichy water or chicken
  broth
1 teaspoon sugar
½ teaspoon salt
Pepper to taste
Parsley, minced

Slice carrots into thin rounds. In a saucepan blanch in boiling salted water for 3 minutes. Drain and refresh under cold running water. In a skillet toss the carrots with butter until well coated. Add the Vichy water or chicken broth, sugar, salt and pepper. Cook mixture tossing carrots occasionally until liquid evaporates and carrots are glazed. Reseason if necessary and sprinkle carrots with minced parsley before serving.

Mrs. Robert Hartnett

THREE C's CASSEROLE

Serves 12
4 cups celery, sliced
4 cups cabbage, diced
½ teaspoon salt
¼ teaspoon pepper
½ teaspoon oregano
SAUCE:
3 teaspoons butter
2 teaspoons flour
½ cup milk
1 can cream of celery soup
½ cup sharp Cheddar cheese,
  shredded
¼ teaspoon paprika

Cook celery and cabbage in boiling water for 10 minutes. Drain and add salt, pepper and oregano. Turn into buttered 2 quart casserole dish. Prepare sauce by melting butter. Slowly add flour to make a smooth paste. Add milk gradually and stir over low heat until mixture thickens. Stir in soup. Add cheese and paprika. Pour this sauce over casserole. Bake 15 minutes at 350°.

Variation:
For a main dish add 2 cups of diced chicken breasts.

Mrs. Jack Turner

FRENCH FRIED EGGPLANT

Serves 6
1 eggplant
2 eggs, beaten
2 tablespoons milk
1 cup dry bread crumbs
8 tablespoons Parmesan cheese, grated
3 teaspoons salt
¼ teaspoon ground pepper
Cooking oil
Celery salt

Peel and cut eggplant like French fried potatoes or in ½ slices if you prefer. Soak 15 minutes in water. Beat eggs with milk. Set aside. Combine bread crumbs, cheese, salt and pepper. Dip eggplant in egg mixture, roll in crumbs and fry in deep fat. Drain on paper towels and sprinkle with celery salt before serving.

Mrs. Tom Pennekamp

GRANDMOTHER'S EGGPLANT

Serves 6
2 medium eggplants, peeled
1 large onion, diced
2 medium fresh tomatoes, diced
Salt and pepper to taste
4 tablespoons butter, softened
1 egg
¾ cup bread crumbs
6-7 tablespoons butter, melted

Peel eggplant and boil in salted water 10-15 minutes or until tender. Drain and add to onion, tomatoes, seasonings and the softened butter. Mix well. Add the unbeaten egg and stir. Place in a buttered 1½ quart casserole. Sauté the bread crumbs in the melted butter until slightly bubbly and put on top of casserole. Bake in 325° oven for 35-40 minutes. (If making ahead, don't add topping until just before placing in oven.)

Mrs. Douglas Johnson

EGGPLANT WITH SHRIMP

Serves 10
1 large eggplant
½ cup water
8 tablespoons butter
1 egg, beaten
2 cups cracker crumbs
1 pound shrimp, chopped
16-ounce can stewed tomatoes
Salt and pepper to taste
Dash of Tabasco

Peel and slice eggplant. Add water and butter and cook until tender. Add egg, cracker crumbs, chopped shrimp, tomatoes, and season with salt, pepper and dash of Tabasco. Put ingredients in 1½ quart casserole and warm in oven for about 30 minutes at 350°.

Mrs. Tom Huston, Jr.

MUSHROOMS FLORENTINE

Serves 8
1 pound fresh mushrooms
3 tablespoons butter, melted
1½ pounds fresh spinach or 2 packages frozen leaf spinach
1 teaspoon salt
¼ cup chopped onion
¼ cup butter, melted
1 cup Cheddar cheese, grated
Garlic salt

Wash and dry mushrooms and spinach. Slice and sauté mushrooms in butter. Line a casserole with the spinach which has been seasoned with salt, onion and butter. Sprinkle with ½ cup Cheddar cheese. Place the sautéed mushrooms over the spinach and season with garlic salt. Cover with remaining cheese. Bake at 350° for 20 minutes.

Mrs. Paul Gimbel

HELEN COLE'S OKRA AND TOMATOES

Serves 8
¼ pound bacon
1 large package fresh okra, sliced
1 small onion, finely chopped
1 large can tomatoes
Salt and pepper to taste

Sauté bacon until done. Remove from pan and drain. When cool, chop into fine pieces. Divide the bacon and drippings in half. Sauté okra over high heat in half of bacon drippings and remove from pan. Add remaining bacon fat and sauté onion over medium heat until transparent. Add sautéed okra, tomatoes and seasonings. Cover and simmer over medium heat for 30 minutes.

Mrs. Carlton Cole

CHILLED PEAS

Serves 8
2 packages frozen peas
1 cup sour cream
Salt to taste
Pepper, freshly ground
Paprika
1 Spanish onion, thinly sliced

Cook peas approximately ½ of suggested cooking time. Drain thoroughly and cool slightly. Mix gently with sour cream; salt and pepper to taste. Place in serving dish and sprinkle top with paprika. Arrange onion rings over top and refrigerate several hours before serving.

Variation:
Omit the onions and add 3 diced raw carrots to the peas and sour cream mixture before garnishing with paprika.

Mrs. Kenneth Ryskamp
Robert Hartnett

JUNE'S CREAMED PEAS

Serves 6
10 ounce package frozen peas
1 medium size onion, grated
1 large lettuce leaf
2 tablespoons butter
½ teaspoon curry powder
1 can condensed cream of
  mushroom soup

Place peas in 4-cup casserole. Spread grated onion over peas and cover with lettuce leaf. Bake in 350° oven for 45 minutes. Remove lettuce. Mix in butter and curry powder and then stir in soup. Return to oven and bake 15 minutes longer or until bubbly hot.

Mrs. John Kelso

BAKED POTATOES

Serves 6
8 medium potatoes
Salt to taste
3 tablespoons butter
4 tablespoons grated cheese of
  your choice
1 tablespoon bread crumbs

Peel potatoes and put them in cold water. Slice almost through in very thin slices. Put them back in the water until baking time. Arrange in buttered shallow baking dish. Sprinkle with salt and divide the butter in dabs on top of the potatoes. Bake for 25 minutes at 375° basting often. Sprinkle with cheese and bread crumbs. Bake 20 minutes longer or until done and brown. Do not baste after the cheese and crumbs are added.

Mrs. William Taylor

CHEESE MASHED POTATOES

Serves 6
6 medium potatoes, cooked
8 ounce carton cottage cheese
8 ounce carton sour cream
1 small onion
Salt and pepper to taste
Butter
Slivered almonds

Mash potatoes. Mix the cheeses, onion and seasoning together in a blender. Add blended ingredients to potatoes. Place in buttered casserole. Dot with butter and bake covered at 350° for 25 minutes. Remove cover, sprinkle with slivered almonds and put under broiler until almonds are lightly browned.

Mrs. Robert Kaplan

KUGELIS

Serves 12
1 onion, diced
½ pound bacon, diced
½ cup water
½ cup butter
1 slice bread
1 small can evaporated milk
5 pounds potatoes, peeled and
    grated
2 eggs, beaten
Salt and pepper to taste

Finely dice onion and bacon and sauté in ½ cup water until water evaporates. Stir in butter. Soak break in milk, stirring to break up. Set aside. Grate potatoes and combine with all ingredients. Pour into well greased casserole and bake 10 minutes at 400°. Lower temperature to 350° and bake for 1 hour and 15 minutes.

Mrs. Emory Lanier

SALLY'S POTATO SOUFFLÉ

Serves 8
2 cups mashed potatoes
¼ cup pimiento, chopped
¼ cup green onion, chopped
1 clove garlic, minced
1 teaspoon salt
2 cups cottage cheese
1 cup sour cream
3 eggs, separated

Mash the potatoes and add pimiento, onion, garlic, salt, cottage cheese and sour cream. Separate eggs and add yolks to the potato mixture, blending thoroughly. Beat egg whites until stiff...fold into the potato mixture. Bake in greased pan at 350° approximately 30 minutes or until brown on top.

Mrs. Kenneth Ryskamp

POMMES DE TERRE DUCHESS

Serves 4
4 large potatoes
⅛ pound butter
½ teaspoon salt
White pepper to taste
3 egg yolks, slightly beaten

Peel and boil potatoes. Drain and place in bowl. Add butter, salt, pepper and slightly beaten egg yolks. Beat mixture well. Use pastry bag to make fancy border around a main dish. Place under broiler to brown for a few minutes. Serve immediately.

Mrs. Richard Dennis

POMMES DE TERRE MARTINIQUE

Serves 4
4 baking potatoes
1½ tablespoons butter
3 tablespoons fresh cream
1 egg, separated
Pinch of salt, pepper and
   nutmeg

Bake potatoes for 1 hour. Cut in half and empty center. Pass through sieve. In the top of a double boiler add the butter, cream, egg yolk and seasonings to the potatoes. Cook 3 minutes, stirring constantly. Add firmly beaten egg white. Place on buttered flat pan in egg shaped forms. Bake at 400° until brown.

Mrs. Richard Dennis

SWEET POTATO BALLS

Serves 6
6 slices of canned pineapple
4 tablespoons butter
6 medium sweet potatoes, baked
1 teaspoon salt
½ teaspoon orange rind, grated
1 tablespoon brown sugar
1 teaspoon cinnamon
1 cup coconut, shredded
½ cup pecans, finely chopped

Brush pineapple slices with 1 tablespoon of melted butter. Brown in oven for 10 minutes and set aside. Remove skin from baked sweet potatoes and beat pulp with an electric mixer. Add salt, orange rind, brown sugar, 2 tablespoons butter and cinnamon. Remove any strings from mashed potatoes and shape into 6 balls. Roll balls in coconut and pecans into which 1 tablespoon butter has been added. Place potato balls on top of each browned pineapple slice and cook 15 minutes at 350°. If made ahead and refrigerated, increase cooking time 10 minutes.

Mrs. Joe Subers

HAWAIIAN SWEET POTATOES

Serves 8

1 can (8½ ounce) crushed
   pineapple
2 cans (1 pound 2 ounces) sweet
   potatoes
½ cup butter, melted
1 teaspoon cinnamon
½ cup pecans, chopped
1/3 cup light brown sugar
¼ cup butter, melted

Drain pineapple, reserving liquid. In a large bowl, combine potatoes, pineapple, ½ cup butter and cinnamon. Beat until well blended and creamy. Fold in pecans. Add ¼ cup reserved pineapple syrup. Place potato mixture in a 2-quart casserole. Sprinkle the top with brown sugar and drizzle with melted butter. Bake at 375° for 20 mintues or until bubbling hot.

Variation:
Cover top of casserole with a layer of tiny marshmallows.

Mrs. Tolson Meares

RATATOUILLE

Serves 8

1 medium eggplant, peeled and
   diced
2 medium zucchini, peeled and
   diced
2 teaspoons salt
½ cup olive oil
2 medium onions, chopped
2 green peppers, chopped
2 cloves garlic, minced
3 tomatoes, cut up
¼ cup parsley, minced
¼ teaspoon pepper
1 cup pimiento olives

Toss cut up eggplant and zucchini in 1 teaspoon salt. Let stand one hour. Drain on paper towels. Sauté in ¼ cup of olive oil. In remaining ¼ cup of olive oil, sauté the onions, green peppers, and tomatoes. Combine the two mixtures and stir in the garlic. Cook over medium heat for 20 minutes, covered. Sprinkle with 1 teaspoon salt, parsley, pepper and olives and cook additional 5 minutes, uncovered, basting with juices from bottom of pan. Serve immediately.

Mrs. Jay Van Vechten

ELEGANT SPINACH

Serves 8

4 cups fresh spinach, chopped, or 2 packages frozen chopped spinach

½ cup butter, melted

8 ounces cream cheese, softened

3 lemons, squeezed

1 package frozen artichoke hearts

½ cup Parmesan cheese, grated

Paprika (optional)

Cook the fresh spinach until done and drain, or cook the frozen spinach according to package directions and drain. Add the hot butter to the soft cream cheese and beat until blended throughly. Add the drained spinach, mix well, and then add the lemon juice and mix to blend all of the flavors. Grease a baking dish with butter and layer the bottom with the artichoke hearts, cut side down. Pour the spinach mixture over the artichokes. Sprinkle the cheese and paprika over the spinach and bake at 350° for 30 minutes.

Mrs. John Klein

HERBED SPINACH AND RICE

Serves 6

1 10-ounce package frozen chopped spinach

1 cup rice, cooked

1 cup Cheddar cheese, shredded

2 eggs, slightly beaten

2 tablespoons butter, softened

1/3 cup milk

2 tablespoons onion, finely chopped

1 teaspoon Worcestershire sauce

1 teaspoon salt

¼ teaspoon rosemary or thyme, crushed

Cook and drain spinach. Mix with rice, cheese, eggs and remaining ingredients. Pour mixture into 10 x 6 x 1½ inch baking dish. Bake at 350° for 25 minutes or until set. Cut into squares.

Mrs. Fred E. Luhm

SPINACH PIQUANTE

Serves 8

2 packages frozen chopped spinach or equivalent fresh spinach

8-ounce package whipped cream cheese

Juice of ½ large lemon

Salt to taste

Generous dash of nutmeg

Tabasco to taste

½ teaspoon garlic salt (optional)

Cook spinach according to directions on package. Drain all liquid. Put in top of double boiler with remaining ingredients. Heat over boiling water before serving.

Mrs. Hillard Willis

VARIATION: Zucchini stuffed with Spinach Piquant

Scrub and par-boil 8 medium zucchini until just tender. Cut zucchini in half, lengthwise, and scoop out all the seeds. Spoon spinach piquant into the center of each zucchini half. Place in greased baking pan and bake at 325° for 10-15 minutes.

Mrs. William Mooney

SPINACH SOUFFLÉ

Serves 8

1 10-ounce package frozen chopped spinach

6 slices bacon, crumbled

¼ cup butter

¼ cup flour

¾ cup milk

½ pound sharp Cheddar cheese, cubed

¼ teaspoon pepper

1 tablespoon onion, minced

4 eggs, separated

Prepare spinach according to package instructions and drain. Sauté bacon, crumble and set aside. Make white sauce with butter, flour, milk, cheese and pepper. Stir until cheese is melted. Remove from heat. Stir in spinach, bacon and onion. Gradually add slightly beaten egg yolks and cool slightly. Fold in stiffly beaten egg whites and pour into 1½ quart soufflé dish. Bake 45 minutes at 350°.

Mrs. William Atwill

SQUASH PUDDING

Serves 6
3 pounds yellow squash or zucchini
½ cup bread crumbs
½ cup onions, minced
2 eggs, lightly beaten
¼ cup butter, melted
1 tablespoon sugar
1 teaspoon salt
½ teaspoon pepper
Tabasco to taste
¼ cup butter, melted
½ cup bread crumbs

Wash squash, trim ends and cut into 1-inch pieces. Cook squash in boiling salted water to cover 10 minutes or until tender. Drain and mash or puree coarsley in blender. In a bowl combine squash with bread crumbs, onion, eggs, butter, sugar, salt, pepper, and Tabasco. Transfer mixture to lightly buttered casserole. Pour melted butter over top and sprinkle with bread crumbs. Bake in pre-heated 375° oven for 45 to 60 minutes or until puffed and crumbs browned.

Variation 1:
For cheese pudding, omit bread crumbs and onion. Make a cheese sauce (see Index) and combine with squash and seasonings. Pour into baking dish and sprinkle ½ cup grated cheese over top. Bake as directed.

Variation 2:
Use wheat germ instead of bread crumbs.

Mrs. William Atwill
Mrs. Jack Beckwith
Mrs. Jack Courtright
Mrs. Linda Zack

STUFFED SQUASH

Serves 8
8 small yellow squash
½ cup sharp Cheddar cheese, grated
3-4 tablespoons Worcestershire sauce
Salt and pepper to taste
2 tablespoons onion, diced
¾ cup bread crumbs or stuffing mix
Butter

Boil squash until almost done and fork tender. Cut squash in half lengthwise and scoop out pulp. While warm, add cheese, Worcestershire, salt, pepper, onion and mix well. Spoon pulp mixture back into shells and top with a mound of buttered crumbs which have been sautéed in enough butter to make them moist. Place in a lightly buttered dish and put in 300-350° oven for 15-20 minutes. Crumbs should be lightly browned and squash piping hot.

Mrs. Alvah H. Chapman

DOT'S TOMATO PIE

Serves 8

Pastry for 1 pie shell (see Index)

5 medium tomatoes, peeled and sliced

½ cup mayonnaise (see Index)

½ cup Parmesan cheese, grated

1 garlic clove, put through press

Bake pie shell unfilled for 5 minutes, pricking first with fork to prevent puffing. Slice tomatoes and arrange in bottom of cooked shell. Mix other ingredients and pour over tomatoes. Return to 300° oven and bake for 45 minutes. Serve hot.

Mrs. John Patterson

SWEDISH SUMMER VEGETABLES

Serves 4

2-3 onions, chopped

2-3 tablespoons butter

½ cup fresh parsley, minced

½ of a red pepper, cut into strips

½ of a green pepper, cut into strips

1-2 parsnips, sliced

1 cucumber or zucchini, sliced

6 tomatoes and ¼ cup water or 1 large can whole tomatoes

1 tablespoon tomato paste

¼ teaspoon thyme

Salt and pepper to taste

Cook onions and parsley in the butter until soft and golden. Add peppers and parsnips to the onion mixture and cook a while longer. Add the remaining vegetables and tomato paste. Season and let cook, covered, about 20 minutes. Especially good with pork, ham or fish.

Mrs. William Taylor

CHEESE ZUCCHINI

Great for cookout with steak.

Serves 8

6 zucchini, washed and sliced

3 ripe tomatoes, sliced

2 onions, sliced

10 slices sharp American cheese

10 slices bacon

Salt and pepper to taste

Garlic salt to taste

Pinch of dried oregano

In 15 x 8 x 2 inch pan, layer ingredients in order given. Season each layer with the salt, garlic salt, pepper and oregano. Begin with zucchini, end with bacon. Bake at 350° for 45 minutes.

Mrs. John C. Sullivan Jr.

APPLES FLAMBÉ

Serves 8
1½ cups sugar or enough to make apples sweet
Water
8 apples peeled and cut into eighths
Juice of 2 lemons
½ small bottle maraschino cherries
¼ cup brandy or bourbon

Combine sugar and water and let it come to a hard boil. Drop apples in and add lemon juice. Cook 10-15 minutes until apples are tender. Do not stir. Before serving put in 1½ quart casserole. Add cherries. Place in 375° oven until sizzling hot. Remove and pour brandy or bourbon over. Flame the brandy and serve immediately.

Variation:
Use both red and green cherries to make dish look festive, especially for Christmas.

Mrs. Boyce Ezell, III

HOT CURRIED FRUIT

Serves 12
1 can cling peach halves
1 can pineapple, sliced
1 can pear halves
1 can apricots, optional
1 small bottle maraschino cherries
1/3 cup butter
¾ cup light brown sugar
2-4 teaspoons curry powder

Drain the fruit and pat dry with paper towels. Arrange fruit in layers in a large casserole dish. Melt the butter in a saucepan over low heat. Add sugar and curry powder to butter and stir to blend thoroughly. Pour butter sauce over the fruit and bake uncovered at 325° for 1 hour. Serve hot. Fruit can be baked ahead, refrigerated and reheated at serving time.

Mrs. Robert Bartelt
Mrs. Earl Becker
Mrs. Fred E. Luhm
Mrs. James A. Sawyer
Mrs. Thomas P. Wenzel, Jr.

HOT PINEAPPLE CASSEROLE

Good with baked ham.

Serves 6
½ cup butter
8 slices white bread, crusts removed and crumbled
1 large can crushed pineapple
¾ cup sugar
4 eggs, beaten

Combine ingredients in casserole and bake at 350° for 35-40 minutes. Serve piping hot!

Mrs. Robert Bartelt

Salads,
Salad Dressings,
& Sauces

SALADS, SALAD DRESSINGS AND SAUCES

A Gandharan head of Buddha, donated to the Lowe Art Museum by Mr. and Mrs. C. Ruxton Love, is pictured in the gardens of El Jardin. Built in 1918, El Jardin is considered a superb example of Spanish Renaissance architecture. It is listed on the National Register of Historic Places and is now the home of Carrollton School.

MARINATED ARTICHOKE SALAD

Serves 16-18
7 cans artichoke hearts, drained, left whole or halved
1 can chick peas, drained
1 pound mushrooms, sliced or left whole
1 jar pimiento, sliced
Pinch oregano
Salt and pepper to taste
1 cup white wine
1 pint Italian dressing
Parmesan cheese, freshly grated

Mix together and chill. Sprinkle with cheese just before serving.
Mrs. Robert Vale

ARTICHOKE AND RICE SALAD

Serves 8
1 package chicken flavored rice mix
4 green onions, thinly sliced
4 green onions, thinly sliced
½ green pepper, chopped finely
12 pimiento olives, sliced
1 small can sliced mushrooms, drained
12 ounces marinated artichoke hearts
¾ teaspoon curry powder
1/3 cup mayonnaise (see Index)
Salt and pepper to taste

Cook rice, leaving out butter. Cool in bowl and add onion, pepper, olives and mushrooms. Drain artichoke hearts saving marinade. Cut hearts in half. Add curry powder and marinade to the dressing and combine thoroughly. Add artichokes to the rice mixture. Mix in the dressing and chill for several hours before serving.
Mrs. Kenneth Ryskamp

ASPARAGUS SALAD

Serves 10
1 cup sugar
1 cup water
½ cup white vinegar
2 packages unflavored gelatin
½ cup water
Juice of 1 lemon
1 cup celery, diced
8 stuffed olives, sliced (optional)
1 small can pimientos
1 small can asparagus, drained*
½ cup pecans, chopped
¼ cup Bermuda onion, chopped
   fine
Mayonnaise (see Index)
Lettuce

Combine first three ingredients in a saucepan and bring to a boil. Add gelatin that has been dissolved in ½ cup water. Let cook, then add remaining ingredients. Pour in medium mold or 9" x 12" dish. Refrigerate. Serve on lettuce and garnish with a dab of mayonnaise.

*Fresh asparagus may be used when in season.

Mrs. John Patterson
Mrs. Dwight Plyler, Jr.
Mrs. William H. Walker

AVOCADO MOUSSE

Serves 8
1 tablespoon unflavored gelatin
   dissolved in 2 tablespoons
   cold water
1 small package lime Jello
2 cups hot water
1 cup mashed avocado, very ripe
½ cup mayonnaise (see Index)
1 tablespoon lime juice
   (optional)
½ cup whipping cream, slightly
   whipped
Salt and cayenne to taste

Dissolve gelatin in cold water. Dissolve lime Jello in hot water. Combine, stirring until clear. Add avocado and mayonnaise (and optional lime juice) and mix well. Add whipping cream. Pour into mayonnaise-greased mold and refrigerate overnight.

Mrs. Charles Sansone

AVOCADO ROQUEFORT

Serves 6
3 avocados, ripe
3 to 4 ounces Roquefort cheese
3 to 4 tablespoons lager beer
3 to 4 tablespoons French
   dressing
Black pepper, freshly ground
Salt to taste

Split avocados in half lengthwise. Remove the stones. Mash cheese till smooth with the beer. Fill avocados with this mixture. Drizzle with freshly ground pepper and salt to taste. May be served as a first course or as a salad.

Mrs. Reynolds Allen

NAPLES AVOCADO SALAD

Serves 12
1 clove garlic, crushed
¼ cup mayonnaise (see Index)
½ cup sour cream
2 tablespoons milk
Pinch oregano
Pinch of thyme
Pinch of bay leaf
Salt and pepper to taste
3 medium avocados
Lime juice
3 medium zucchini, sliced thin
Lettuce leaves

In large bowl crush garlic and rub around bowl. Add mayonnaise, sour cream, milk and seasonings. Mix well. Cut avocados into small bite-sized pieces. Squeeze lime juice over them, to keep from discoloring. Cut zucchini in thin slices. Add vegetables to cream mixture. Toss and refrigerate 1 hour before serving. Serve on lettuce leaves.

Mrs. Lindsey D. Pankey, Jr.

AVOCADO-SHRIMP SALAD MOLD

Serves 8
2 envelopes unflavored gelatin
1½ cups water
1½ teaspoon salt
⅛ teaspoon curry powder
2 teaspoons Worcestershire
    sauce
1 tablespoon lemon juice
1½ tablespoons chives, chopped
¼ cup onions, minced
2 cups avocado, mashed with
    silver fork
2 pounds shrimp, cooked and
    cleaned
¾ cup heavy cream, whipped
¾ cup mayonnaise (see Index)
1 recipe cucumber sauce (see
    Index)

Soften gelatin in ½ cup cold water. Add 1 cup boiling water and stir until dissolved; cool. Add salt, curry powder, Worcestershire, lemon juice, chives, onions and mashed avocado to gelatin and blend thoroughly. Add shrimp and chill until the consistency of thick egg whites. Fold in cream and mayonnaise. Refrigerate until firm. Serve cold with cucumber sauce.

Mrs. W. Carroll Latimer

GREEN BEAN AND ARTICHOKE SALAD
Good and easy, for a "bring along" dinner!

Serves 4

2 cans Italian green beans, drained

1 can artichoke hearts, drained

DRESSING:

¼ cup red wine

1 teaspoon onion juice

¼ cup pimiento, diced

½ cup olive oil

½ teaspoon salt

½ teaspoon powdered oregano

¼ teaspoon crushed rosemary

½ teaspoon cracked pepper

Shake dressing in a jar and pour over vegetables. Marinate at least overnight.

Mrs. Frank C. Sargent, III

SUMMER SALAD

Serves 8

1 pound green beans, cut in 1½ inch pieces

1 pound wax beans, cut in 1½ inch pieces

1 pound can kidney beans

22 ounces mandarin oranges, drained

½ red onion, minced

1 bunch scallions, chopped

Whites of 2 hard-boiled eggs, chopped

1 cup summer salad dressing (see Index)

Cook green beans in salted, boiling water until just tender, about six minutes, drain. If fresh wax beans are used cook them the same way. Combine all beans, oranges and onions. Add eggs whites to dressing and pour over beans. Toss and chill before serving.

Mrs. Timothy Howe

VARIATION: Calico Bean Salad

Add to beans one pound of sliced mushrooms, 1 green pepper, 1 onion thinly sliced, 1 can pitted black olives. Dress with vegetable oil, red wine, vinegar, basil, parsley, sugar and salt, to taste.

Mrs. Harold Neas

SLUMGULLIAN SALAD

Luncheon salad on board a boat or great for a picnic.

Serves 6

3 cans assorted drained beans such as green, wax, kidney, garbanzo

1 package frozen beans, cut or Italian style

2 cups cabbage, finely shredded

3 cups of beef, julienne strips

10 radishes, sliced

6 tomatoes, cut in wedges and seeded

3 hard boiled eggs, sliced

DRESSING:

1 cup mayonnaise (see Index)

¾ cup sour cream

3 tablespoons vinegar

1 onion, shredded-squeeze juices out

½ tablespoon sugar

Salt and pepper to taste

Drain salad ingredients *thoroughly* and mix (success depends on dryness). Combine dressing ingredients separately and pour over salad. Serve in individual containers for picnic.

Mrs. Edward Weed

JELLIED BEETS

Serves 6

1 envelope unflavored gelatin

¼ cup cold water

1 cup bouillon

¼ cup lemon juice

¾ cup cole slaw dressing

¾ cup celery, chopped

1 cup beets, chopped

Salt and pepper to taste

Lettuce

Mayonnaise (see Index)

Parsley sprigs

Soften gelatin in cold water. Heat bouillon. Add to gelatin and stir until dissolved. Add lemon juice and cole slaw dressing. Cool until gelatin begins to set. Mix in celery and beets. Pour into individual molds and chill. To serve, unmold on crisp lettuce leaves, garnish with a dollop of mayonnaise and a sprig of parsley.

Josephine McNair Schutt

CAESAR SALAD

Serves 10
¼ cup olive oil
¾ cup salad oil
1 clove garlic, mashed
½ teaspoon dry mustard
½ teaspoon cracked pepper
4 anchovies, cut up
1 tablespoon Worcestershire
  sauce
¼ teaspoon Tabasco
3 cups bread, cubed
Olive oil
2 garlic cloves
2 heads Romaine lettuce
2 eggs, coddled
Lemon
Parmesan cheese, grated

Prepare oil base. In a jar mix oils, mashed garlic, mustard, pepper, anchovies, Worcestershire and Tabasco. Refrigerate overnight. Prepare 3 cups croutons by frying bread cubes over a low flame in olive oil flavored with a split clove of garlic. Rub a wooden bowl with another garlic clove. Fill with chilled, washed and dried Romaine which is torn or cut into bite-sized pieces. Pour the dressing over the lettuce leaves and toss to coat evenly. Break 2 coddled eggs, boiled for 1½ minutes, over the greens and toss thoroughly, but gently. Add the juice of at least 1 lemon and ½ cup freshly grated Parmesan cheese and toss again. Add the croutons last to prevent from getting soggy and toss once more. Serve at once.

Mrs. Kermyt W. Callahan, Jr.

CAMLIS SALAD

Serves 8
1 cup garlic olive oil
1 teaspoon ground pepper
½ teaspoon salt
2 pinches oregano
2 heads Romaine lettuce
2 tomatoes, cut in wedges
½ pound bacon, rendered and
  finely chopped
½ cup fresh Romano cheese,
  grated
½ bunch scallions, chopped
1 coddled egg, room temperature
Juice of 1 lemon
1 cup croutons

Cut 2 cloves garlic and let sit in oil at least 2 hours. Sauté 1 cup cubed bread in oil till crisp and golden. Reserve, draining on brown paper bag. Render bacon. Reserve. Grate cheese. Reserve. Coddle egg and bring to room temperature. Tear chilled, washed and dried Romaine into bite-sized pieces and place in salad bowl. Add salt, pepper and oregano and toss with oil until well-coated. Add scallions. Break coddled egg over lettuce and sprinkle with lemon juice. Toss to mix evenly. Add grated cheese, bacon and croutons, tossing again. Serve at once.

Mrs. James Hauf

CRANBERRY-APPLE SALAD

Nice with baked chicken salad.

Serves 6
1 envelope unflavored gelatin
¼ cup cold water
1 pound jellied cranberry sauce
¼ lemon, minced
1 apple, minced

Soften gelatin in cold water 2 minutes and dissolve over hot water. Crush the canned cranberry sauce with a fork and add dissolved gelatin. Chill. Coarsely grind lemon and apple in a food grinder. When gelatin mixture begins to gel, stir in lemon and apple. Pour into mold and serve cold.

Mrs. James A. Wright, III

CRANBERRY-RASPBERRY MOLD

Serves 12
8¼ ounce can pineapple, crushed
1¼ cups orange sections, fresh or mandarin, drained
½ cup orange juice
3 ounce package raspberry gelatin
1 package unflavored gelatin
16 ounce can whole cranberry sauce
1 teaspoon grated orange peel
1 cup whipping cream, whipped

Drain and reserve pineapple; to syrup, add enough boiling water to make 1 cup. Add ½ cup orange juice. Dissolve gelatins. Stir in cranberry sauce and orange peel. Chill till thickened. Fold in oranges and pineapple. Fold whipped cream into mixture. Pour into 6-cup mold and chill at least 4 hours.

Mrs. Maurice Harrison, Jr.

CUCUMBER RING

Serves 8
1 envelope unflavored gelatin
½ cup cold water
½ teaspoon salt
1½ cups cucumber, seeded and shredded
6 ounces cream cheese
24 ounces cream style cottage cheese
1 tablespoon grated onion
½ cup celery, finely chopped
½ cup mayonnaise (see Index)

Soften gelatin in water. Add salt. Stir over low heat until gelatin dissolves. Halve cucumbers and scrape out seeds. Shred and drain before measuring. Beat cheeses together until well-blended. Stir in gelatin. Add cucumber and remaining ingredients. Pour in 6-cup ring mold. Chill 6-7 hours. Unmold on bed of lettuce or on thin, scored slices of cucumber.

Mrs. Geoffrey Hill

CUCUMBERS IN SOUR CREAM

Serves 6
2 large cucumbers, peeled and
    thinly sliced
1½ teaspoons salt
1 cup sour cream
1 tablespoon onion, minced
2 tablespoons lemon juice
¼ teaspoon sugar
Dash pepper
5 radishes, thinly sliced
Lettuce leaves
1 teaspoon parsley, finely
    chopped

Toss cucumbers with 1 teaspoon salt and refrigerate until well chilled. Combine sour cream with ½ teaspoon salt, lemon juice, sugar, pepper and radishes. Reserve ½ sour cream mixture for garnish. Toss cucumbers with remaining sour cream mixture and refrigerate. To serve, arrange cucumbers in sour cream on a bed of lettuce leaves, garnish with reserved sour cream mixture, and sprinkle with parsley.

Mrs. Charles Miller

FLORIDA FRUIT SALAD

Serves 8
3 grapefruit, peeled and
    sectioned
3 oranges, peeled and sectioned
2 bananas, sliced
2 cups honeydew or cantaloupe
    balls
1 cup watermelon balls
1 cup plain yogurt
½ to 1 teaspoon lime juice
1 teaspoon sugar or to taste
White port wine

Combine all fruit in large bowl and chill. Make dressing with yogurt, lime juice and sugar, mixing well. Spoon fruit into individual compotes over ice and sprinkle with 1 teaspoon white port. Add 2 tablespoons of dressing or pass in serving bowl.

Mrs. Lindsey D. Pankey, Jr.

HEAVENLY FLORIDA AMBROSIA

Serves 6 or more
1 cup heavy cream
½ cup sour cream
1 cup small marshmallows
2 cups freshly sliced orange
    sections
1 cup freshly sliced grapefruit
    sections
1 cup flaked coconut, preferably
    fresh

Whip cream and fold in sour cream. Fold in fruit sections. Add marshmallows and coconut. Chill overnight. Serve over lettuce or with plain cake if used as dessert.

Mary E. Kitchens

GRANNY WILLIS' FRUIT SALAD

Serves 12

3 bananas, cut into bite-sized pieces

3 apples, cut into bite-sized pieces

4 oranges, sectioned and peeled

2 grapefruit, sectioned and peeled

1 cup raisins

1 cup pecan pieces

2 cups miniature marshmallows

1 pint cooked salad dressing (see Index)

1 pint whipped cream

Boston lettuce

Combine fruit. Add raisins, pecans and marshmallows. Combine salad dressing and whipping cream by folding gently together and then into the fruit. Serve in cups of Boston lettuce leaves.

Mrs. John Renuart

GAZPACHO SALAD I

Serves 8

2 envelopes unflavored gelatin

34-ounce can tomato juice

½ cup garlic red wine vinegar

1 teaspoon salt

Tabasco to taste, lots is good

2 tomatoes, peeled and diced

1 cup cucumber, peeled and finely diced

½ cup green pepper, finely diced

½ to 1 cup sweet onion, minced

1 tablespoon chives, minced or scallion tops

In medium sized pan sprinkle gelatin over ¾ of tomato to soften. Place over low heat stirring constantly until dissolved. Stir in remaining juice, vinegar, salt and Tabasco. Set in a bowl of ice. Stir constantly till unbeaten egg white consistency, about 15 minutes. Fold in vegetables. Combine carefully. Pour into 1½ quart mold rinsed in cold water. Refrigerate until firm. Unmold by running spatula around mold and set briefly in cold water. Garnish with watercress. Serve with a bowl of avocado dressing (see Index).

Mrs. George Hero

GAZPACHO SALAD II

Serves 4
Hardtack or 4 Matzo crackers
2 tomatoes cut in wedges, seeded
1 cucumber, sliced thinly
1 small green pepper, thinly
   sliced
1 medium onion, finely chopped
1 clove garlic, mashed
1 heaping cup mayonnaise
   seasoned with:
2 tablespoons lemon
Worcestershire to taste
Cayenne to taste
Salt and pepper to taste

Soak hardtack in cold water until soft; a couple of hours. (Do not soak the matzos.) Squeeze out water and allow to drain in a colander, as dry as possible. Add vegetables and dried hardtack to seasoned mayonnaise. Let stand in refrigerator overnight. Keeps 10 days.

Mrs. Hagood Clarke

SNAPPY TOM ASPIC

Serves 8
3 cans Snappy Tom mix
1½ packages unflavored gelatin
2 teaspoons onion, grated
1 tablespoon lemon juice
Ice water
¼ small cabbage, shredded
1 cucumber, seeded and
   chopped
½ green pepper, chopped
1 carrot, shredded
½ cup celery, chopped
Salt, pepper, Worcestershire
   sauce, and Tabasco to taste

Heat Snappy Tom to a slow boil; add onion and lemon juice. Dissolve gelatin in a small amount of ice water. Add to heated mixture and stir until dissolved. Cool. Combine all ingredients and pour in a lightly oiled loaf or mold pan. Chill at least 8 hours.

Mrs. Harry Taylor

BRANDIED GREEN GRAPES

Serves 4
2½ cups seedless green grapes;
   slice in half lengthwise if
   desired
1 teaspoon lemon juice
¼ cup honey
2 tablespoons brandy
½ cup sour cream

Clean grapes. Mix all ingredients together and pour over grapes in 8″ glass dish. Cover, refrigerate and marinate overnight or 8 hours. At serving time use slotted spoon and divide on lettuce leaves. Top with additional sour cream, if desired.

Mrs. Bill Vessels

GRAPEFRUIT SALAD

Serves 6
2 to 3 heads of Bibb lettuce
2 cups grapefruit sections
Dry vermouth
Paprika
French dressing
1½ pints heavy cream
¼ cup lemon juice
Salt and pepper to taste
4 tablespoons chopped chives or
  minced scallion tops

Wash and pat lettuce leaves dry. Refrigerate. Marinate grapefruit, in enough vermouth to cover, for a few hours. Arrange sections on lettuce leaves and sprinkle with paprika. Accompany with French dressing and cream dressing made by adding lemon juice, salt, pepper, and chopped chives to the heavy cream.

Mrs. Kermyt W. Callahan, Jr.

MIAMI BEACH COMPOTE

Serves 6
3 large grapefruit
1 large avocado, diced
2 tablespoons sugar
2 tablespoons white port
1 teaspoon key lime juice
¼ cup chopped almonds

Peel, seed, and cut the grapefruit into sections. Mix with remaining ingredients. Refrigerate for at least 2 hours. Serve in individual compotes over ice as first course.

John Baratte

GRAPEFRUIT-SPINACH SALAD

Serves 6
10 ounces fresh spinach, washed
  and drained
6-8 slices bacon, crisply cooked
¼ pound fresh mushrooms,
  sliced
2 Florida grapefruit, peeled and
  sectioned or diced
DRESSING:
¼ cup salad oil
2 tablespoons vinegar
2 tablespoons grapefruit juice
1 tablespoon soy sauce
¼ teaspoon Tabasco
¼ teaspoon salt
¼ teaspoon dry mustard

Coarsely tear spinach into large salad bowl. Add bacon, mushrooms, and grapefruit sections. Blend oil, vinegar and grapefruit juice with the rest of the dressing ingredients. Toss with spinach, crumbled bacon, mushrooms and grapefruit.

Mrs. John Patterson

GREEN GODDESS SALAD

Serves 8-10

1-1/3 cups mayonnaise (see Index)

½ cup cream or sour cream

2 tablespoons green onions, chopped

2 tablespoons parsley, chopped

1 peeled clove garlic, mashed

½ tube anchovy paste

3 tablespoons tarragon vinegar

1 teaspoon salt

½ teaspoon powdered mustard

Tabasco to taste

Worcestershire sauce to taste

Ground pepper to taste

Salad greens, endive, Romaine, Boston, etc.

2 hard boiled eggs, sliced

Combine ingredients. Mix thoroughly. Let stand several hours to season, and chill. If more green is desired add additional parsley, scallion greens, and fresh dill minced in equal proportions. Prepare salad greens by washing, drying carefully, and tearing into bite-sized pieces. Chill. Place in large bowl at serving time. Add eggs and enough dressing to coat greens. Toss lightly. Serve at once.

Mrs. Banning Lary

WILTED LETTUCE

5 strips bacon, fried and crumbled

1 large head Boston lettuce

¼ cup bacon fat

¼ cup wine vinegar

1 teaspoon dry mustard

1½ teaspoons sugar

⅛ teaspoon garlic powder (optional)

¼ teaspoon salt

¼ teaspoon pepper

2 eggs, hard boiled and chopped (optional)

Fry bacon until crisp. Remove, drain and crumble when cool. Return ¼ cup fat to skillet, and add vinegar and seasonings. Bring to a boil, stirring. Combine lettuce, scallions, and crumbled bacon in a salad bowl and pour dressing over salad. Toss to mix, sprinkle with eggs and serve at once.

Mrs. Philippe Moore
Mrs. Kenneth Claussen

MUSHROOM SALAD

Serves 8
2 pounds firm white mushrooms
¾ cup of French dressing (see Index)
¼ cup scallion tops, minced
2 to 3 heads Bibb lettuce, washed and dried
Salt and pepper to taste

Thinly slice mushrooms. Combine with dressing and green scallion tops. Add ¼ teaspoon salt and a large pinch of cracked black pepper. Toss and serve on crisp lettuce leaves which have been lightly dressed. Serve on chilled plates.

Mrs. John Renuart

SALADE BALLADE

Serves 4
1 pound mushrooms, thinly sliced
Onion rings, thinly sliced
2 ounces wine vinegar
¼ cup olive oil
Salt and pepper to taste
½ cup blue cheese, crumbled
½ cup stuffed olives, sliced
Lettuce leaves, washed, patted dry and refrigerated

Combine oil, vinegar, and salt and pepper to taste. Pour over rest of ingredients and mix. Serve on crisp lettuce leaves.

Mrs. Arthur Weller

COOL SALAD

Serves 6
1 bunch watercress, washed, picked over, patted dry and chilled
2 endive, washed, dried, cut and chilled
2 cans mandarin oranges, chilled and drained
Poppy Seed dressing (see Index)

Put chilled ingredients in a salad bowl. Toss ingredients with poppy seed dressing. Serve on chilled plates.

Mrs. Edward F. Swenson, Jr.

GOLD COAST SALAD

Serves 2
1 cup oranges, sliced
Cointreau to taste
½ cup sour cream
Dash of nutmeg
Lettuce leaves

Marinate orange slices in Cointreau to cover. Mix sour cream and nutmeg with oranges. Chill and serve on lettuce leaves.

Mrs. Arthur Weller

AMELIA'S HOT GERMAN POTATO SALAD

Amelia was Mrs. Ezell's great aunt's cook.

Serves 8-10
8 slices bacon
¼ cup onion, chopped
3 tablespoons flour
2/3 cup white vinegar
2/3 cup water
½ cup sugar
4 teaspoons salt
½ teaspoon ground pepper
1 teaspoon dry mustard
2 quarts potatoes, peeled, cooked and diced
¼ cup fresh parsley, chopped

Fry bacon. Remove from pan, dry and crumble. Add onions to fat. Cook until soft. Add flour, stirring well until smooth. Add vinegar, water, sugar and spices. Cook until medium thick. Add to hot potatoes. Toss parsley in and stir in crumbled bacon. Mix very carefully. Serve while warm. If made ahead, refrigerate and reheat at 350° until hot.

Mrs. Boyce Ezell, III

HOT POTATO SALAD

Serves 8
6 slices bacon
½ cup onion, chopped
2 tablespoons green pepper, chopped
1/3 cup Italian dressing
4 cups potatoes, sliced and cooked
1 tablespoon vinegar
1 teaspoon sugar
½ teaspoon celery seed
Salt and pepper to taste

Cook bacon crisp and drain. Cook onion and pepper in Italian dressing until tender. Add potatoes and rest of ingredients. Toss to blend. Heat thoroughly. Correct seasoning.

Mrs. Fred E. Luhm

GERMAN POTATO SALAD

Serves 6
8 potatoes
½ pound bacon
2 tablespoons onion, finely chopped
¾ cup bouillon
¾ cup cider vinegar
Salt and pepper to taste

Boil potatoes in their jackets. Peel and slice them while hot. Fry bacon and break into small pieces. Sauté onions in bacon fat. Add bouillon and vinegar, salt and pepper to taste. Bring mixture to a boil and pour over hot potatoes and crumbled bacon. Serve at once.

Mrs. William Harward

PAPAS A LA JUANCAINA

*This Peruvian dish may be served as salad,
first course, or for luncheon.*

Serves 8

8 medium yellow potatoes
4 hard boiled eggs, or more,
   halved
1 medium onion, sliced
½ cup lemon juice
Salt and pepper to taste
Pinch of chili powder
Cottage cheese, large container,
   large curd
2 hot peppers
½ teaspoon turmeric
1/3 cup milk
1 cup oil
1 clove garlic
Lettuce leaves
8 black olives, or more

Boil potatoes until done. Peel when cool, cut in half or quarters, and refrigerate. Hard boil eggs and reserve them. Slice onion and pickle in lemon juice; cover with salt and pepper and a pinch of chili powder. Make sauce in blender: cottage cheese, hot peppers, turmeric, milk, oil, garlic, salt and juice of 1 lemon. Pour over chilled potatoes on lettuce leaves. Garnish with hard boiled egg halves, black olives, and pickled onion slices.

Ramijia, Peruvian cook
The Loyal Domning Family

CRISP GARDEN SLAW

Serves 8

8 cups cabbage, shredded
2 carrots, grated
1 green pepper, thinly sliced or
   chopped
½ cup onion, minced
¾ cup cold water
1 small jar of pimiento, chopped
   (optional)
1 envelope unflavored gelatin
½ cup sugar
2/3 cup vinegar
2 teaspoons celery seed
1½ teaspoons salt
¼ teaspoon black pepper
1 teaspoon mustard powder
2/3 cup salad oil

Mix cabbage, carrots, green pepper, onion, pimiento, and ½ cup water. Chill. Soften gelatin in ¼ cup cold water. Combine sugar, vinegar, celery seed, salt, pepper, and mustard in saucepan and bring to a boil. Add gelatin and stir until completely dissolved. Cool until slightly thickened and beat. Gradually beat in salad oil. Dry vegetables thoroughly. Add dressing and mix. Chill. Should keep well for over a week. (Gelatin is ingredient that preserves crispness. It is not meant to be molded.)

Mrs. Julian Arnold
Mrs. Jay Van Vechten

MOLDED COLE SLAW

Serves 8
1 package lemon Jello
1 tablespoon sugar
1 teaspoon salt
2 tablespoons lemon juice
1 cup hot water
½ cup sour cream
½ cup mayonnaise (see Index)
1 tablespoon mustard
1 cup cabbage, shredded
1 cup celery, diced
½ cup carrot, grated
2 tablespoons onion, grated

Mix first five ingredients together, stirring until gelatin dissolves. Cool for a moment in the refrigerator. Mix next three ingredients together and add to the gelatin mixture. Add the vegetables. Pour into a greased mold. Sliced avocados may be added. Celery seed may be substituted for a part of the celery (1 teaspoon). Recipe doubles easily.

Mrs. Hagood Clarke

SPINACH SALADS

Serves 6
SALAD:
1 pound fresh spinach
6 green onions, thinly sliced
4 eggs, hard-boiled and coarsely chopped
8 bacon slices, crisply cooked and crumbled
Dash pepper, freshly ground

Wash spinach, remove stems, break leaves into bite-sized pieces. In a salad bowl, lightly toss spinach with onions, eggs, bacon and pepper. Refrigerate covered about 2 hours. Combine dressing ingredients, mix well, pour dressing over salad and toss to coat the spinach evenly. Serve at once.

Mrs. Charles Miller

VARIATIONS: To 1 pound spinach add:
I. 2 red apples chopped, 3 hard-boiled eggs chopped, 1 large onion thinly sliced, and 4 ounces blue cheese, crumbled. Dress with ½ cup mayonnaise,

DRESSING:
1 clove garlic, crushed
½ cup olive oil
½ teaspoon salt
3 tablespoons lemon juice
¼ cup cider vinegar

½ cup sour cream and 1 teaspoon lemon juice.
Mrs. Steve Pease
II. 1 handful bean sprouts, 1 can fried onion rings, asparagus spears cooked and cut in pieces, artichoke hearts marinated in oil, 2 eggs chopped, ½ pound mushrooms, sliced, ¼ cup freshly grated Parmesan. Dress with ¼ cup tarragon vinegar, 1 teaspoon dry mustard powder, pinch of sugar, juice of key lime, and oil from the artichokes.
Mrs. Frank de Robertis
III. 5 strips bacon, crumbled, 2 tomatoes cut in small wedges, ¼ pound mushrooms halved, 1 egg chopped finely. Marinate

Continued

Continued

tomatoes and mushrooms in dressing of 4 tablespoons tarragon vinegar and 6 tablespoons bacon drippings (oil to make balance), salt, pepper and 2 tablespoons prepared mustard. Combine vegetables and dressing with spinach. Top with eggs.

Mrs. Robert Vale

IV. ½ head Iceberg lettuce, ½ pound bacon crisply fried. Dress with 1 cup salad oil, 1/3 cup vinegar, 1 tablespoon onion juice, 1 teaspoon dry mustard, ¼ cup sugar, 1 teaspoon salt, and 1 tablespoon poppy seeds (optional) which have been well combined first.

Mrs. R. Thomas Fairar

SPINACH SALAD ORIENTAL

Serves 4
1 pound spinach, cleaned
5 slices bacon, cooked and
  crumbled
1 cup water chestnuts, sliced
1 cup bean sprouts (optional)
1-2 eggs, hard boiled and sliced
DRESSING:
1 cup salad oil
¼ cup sugar
¼ cup white vinegar (do not use
  wine vinegar)
1/3 cup ketchup
1 onion, grated
1 teaspoon salt

Combine ingredients for salad and for dressing separately. Marinate salad with part of dressing one hour before serving. This amount of dressing will be enough for 3 pounds of spinach. Dressing refrigerates well. The salad will wilt to about half the original amount.

Mrs. Don Shoemaker
Mrs. Robert White

MOLDED SPINACH SALAD

Serves 10
2 packages frozen spinach,
  chopped (broccoli or
  asparagus, chopped, may be
  substituted)
3 eggs, hard-boiled and chopped
1¾ teaspoons salt
¾ cup mayonnaise (see Index)
1½ envelopes gelatin
¼ cup water, cold
1 cup beef consommé
4 teaspoons Worcestershire
  sauce
2 teaspoons lemon juice
Dash of Tabasco
1 heaping teaspoon horseradish
1 tablespoon vinegar
1 onion, grated

Cook frozen spinach without any additional water adding salt. Drain very well. Combine spinach with egg and mayonnaise. Soak gelatin in cold water and dissolve in hot consommé. Add consommé to the vegetable mixture. Add seasonings and pour into a mold. Refrigerate at least 4 hours.

Mrs. Tom Pennekamp

TOMATO COUPE

Serves 6
6 medium tomatoes
2 large avocados
5 tablespoons vinaigrette (see Index)
Lime juice
Salt and pepper to taste
6 slices bacon, cooked crisply and drained
Lettuce leaves

Cut off tomato tops. Scoop out, drain, and dice pulp. Invert shells to drain. Toss diced avocado, which has been liberally sprinkled with lime juice, with tomato pulp and dressing. Season to taste. Chill several hours. Fill tomato shells and garnish with crumbled bacon, sprinkled on top. Arrange on lettuce leaves and serve cold.

Mrs. Hillard Willis

TOMATOES FILLED WITH PESTO

Pesto is also good used as a sauce for pasta.

Serves 6
6 medium size ripe tomatoes
French dressing (see Index)
PESTO:
1 cup fresh basil leaves or ¾ cup dried and ¼ cup more parsley
1 cup fresh parsley
2 garlic cloves
¼ cup Parmesan cheese
½ cup olive oil
Salt and pepper to taste
¼ cup pine nuts, finely chopped

Loosen skins of tomatoes by placing in boiling water for a few seconds. Peel tomatoes. Cut a slice off the stem end and make sure there is a good opening and that tomato is well cored. Marinate the cases by spooning some French dressing into the tomato openings and chilling for several hours. Drain and fill with the pesto. To make pesto remove basil leaves from stems, combine basil leaves, parsley leaves, garlic, cheese and oil in blender. This should make a thick sauce. Add salt and pepper and stir in nuts. Divide sauce between tomatoes. Cover and chill.

Mrs. John Renuart

TOMATOES VINAIGRETTE

Serves 6
12 tomato slices, from firm large
  tomatoes
1 cup olive oil
1/3 cup wine vinegar
2 teaspoons oregano leaves,
  crushed
1 teaspoon salt
½ teaspoon pepper
½ teaspoon dry mustard
2 cloves garlic, crushed
6 cups Bibb lettuce
Minced scallions
Minced parsley

Arrange slices of tomatoes in a square baking dish, 8″ x 8″ x 2″. Combine oil, vinegar, oregano, salt, pepper, mustard and garlic in a jar with a top. Shake vigorously and spoon over tomatoes. Chill 3 hours or more, spooning liquid over tomatoes occasionally. To serve, arrange 2 slices on each lettuce cup and sprinkle with scallions and parsley. Drizzle each salad with a little dressing.

Mrs. Robert Freyer

SWEET-SOUR TOMATO SLICES

Serves 4-6
2 green onions, sliced thinly
½ cup salad oil
½ cup vinegar
¼ to ½ cup water
½ tablespoon sugar
1 teaspoon sweet basil
½ teaspoon salt
¼ teaspoon pepper
4 tablespoons parsley, minced
6 firm ripe tomatoes, sliced ½
  inch thick

Combine all ingredients, except tomatoes, in a jar. Place cover on tightly and shake until well blended. Pour over sliced tomatoes. Chill.

Mrs. Timi Nichols

PARMESAN-VEGETABLE SALAD
Great for picnics and boating!

3 medium zucchini, bias-sliced
  ¼ inch thick, about 4 cups
2 medium tomatoes, cut in
  wedges and seeded
1 small head cauliflower, broken
  into small buds
½ cup salad oil
1/3 cup vinegar
1-ounce envelope Italian cheese
  salad dressing mix

In large bowl combine zucchini, tomatoes, and cauliflower. In screw top jar combine oil, vinegar, and mix. Cover and shake to blend. Pour dressing over vegetables, stirring gently. Cover and refrigerate at least 4 hours before serving. Drain to serve.

Mrs. Kenneth Claussen

PICNIC SALAD

Serves 8-10

VINAIGRETTE SAUCE:

6 tablespoons olive oil

2 tablespoons wine vinegar

1 teaspoon salt

12 grinds of pepper mill

SALAD:

4 cups rice, cooked firmly

½ cup onion or scallions, chopped

½ cup celery, chopped

½ cup cucumber, seeded and chopped

½ cup green pepper, minced (optional)

Fresh parsley, chopped

Fresh tarragon, chopped

Blend all ingredients together for sauce. Combine rice, vegetables, dressing and herbs and toss well. Adjust seasonings. Sprinkle with more chopped parsley.

Mrs. Karl Noonan

SHIPBOARD SALAD

Serves 8

1 large head of lettuce, cut in chunks and well drained

1 cucumber, medium to large, shredded

2 celery stalks, medium to large, shredded

1 can water chestnuts, thinly sliced

1 package uncooked frozen peas, thawed and well drained

1 large onion, thinly sliced

Hellman's Mayonnaise

1/3 cup Parmesan cheese

6-8 slices bacon, fried and crumbled

Cherry tomatoes

Make the day before. Layer in order listed. Spread mayonnaise over top of salad, covering completely. Sprinkle Parmesan cheese over top, cover and refrigerate. Before serving, sprinkle on crumbled bacon, halve the cherry tomatoes and arrange around edge of salad. *(Warning: The success of this salad depends on the dryness of its ingredients.)*

Mrs. Kenneth Ryskamp

WALDORF SALAD

Serves 6

6 tart red apples, diced
2 tablespoons lemon juice
1 cup celery, diced
1/3 cup seedless raisins
1 cup tiny marshmallows
  (optional)
¼ cup mayonnaise (see Index)
¼ cup heavy cream, whipped
½ cup California walnuts,
  coarsely broken
6 lettuce cups

Core tart apples and dice fine. Sprinkle with lemon juice. Combine apples, celery, raisins, marshmallows and mayonnaise. Fold in whipped cream. Just before serving, add nuts. Put in individual lettuce cups and serve cold.

Mrs. Philippe Moore

FROZEN WALDORF SALAD

Serves 6-8

2 eggs, slightly beaten
½ cup sugar
½ cup pineapple juice
¼ cup lemon juice
⅛ teaspoon salt
½ cup celery, diced
½ cup pineapple, crushed
2 tart apples, diced
¾ cup nuts, chopped
½ cup heavy cream, whipped
Lettuce leaves

Combine first five ingredients in a saucepan. Cook over low heat until thick, stirring constantly. Cool. Add celery, pineapple, apples and nuts. Mix thoroughly. Fold in whipped cream. Pour into individual molds and freeze. Serve on lettuce leaf.

Mrs. Jack Turner

AVOCADO DRESSING

1 large ripe avocado, peeled and
  seeded
½ cup sour cream
½ cup light cream
1 tablespoon onion, grated
1½ teaspoons salt
Dash cayenne
⅛ teaspoon sugar
1 clove garlic, crushed
2 tablespoons lemon juice

Mix all ingredients in a blender. Refrigerate for several hours before use. Cover by placing a piece of plastic-wrap directly on surface of sauce in order to prevent discoloration. Cover container carefully, as well.

Mrs. John Miller

BLUE CHEESE DRESSING

Makes 1 quart
4-ounce package blue cheese or
    Roquefort
1 cup mayonnaise (see Index)
1 cup yogurt or sour cream
1 tablespoon wine vinegar
¼ teaspoon monosodium
    glutamate
¼ teaspoon dill weed, crushed
¼ teaspoon Tabasco
½ teaspoon Worcestershire
    sauce
¼ teaspoon thyme, crushed
¼ teaspoon onion salt
1 teaspoon salt
Milk

Combine all ingredients except blue cheese and milk in a blender. Add cheese and blend at medium speed for 5 seconds. Add milk to thin to desired consistency. This will keep in refrigerator for several weeks.

Mrs. Douglas Oppenheimer

CELERY SEED FRUIT DRESSING

Makes 1½ cups
½ cup sugar
1 teaspoon dry mustard
1½ teaspoons onion, grated
2 tablespoons vinegar
1 cup oil
1 tablespoon celery seed
2 tablespoons vinegar

Combine first 4 ingredients in an electric mixer. Add 1 cup salad oil slowly, beating constantly. Add last 2 tablespoons vinegar, then celery seed and continue beating until thick. Good with avocado, grapefruit or any fruits.

Mrs. Conway Hamilton

EGG DRESSING

Serves 4
1 large egg
¼ cup vegetable oil
20 drops white vinegar
Salt and cayenne to taste
1-2 scallions, minced

Boil egg 3 to 4 minutes. Scoop out in a glass bowl. Whip with a fork and add some salt. Add oil a little at a time. Dressing should blend together. Add about ¼ cup oil in all. Finally, add 20 or so drops of vinegar, half at a time. Add a sprinkling of cayenne. This dressing is good with Boston, Bibb or iceberg lettuce. Be sure to add 1 or 2 scallions, minced.

Mrs. Denis Renuart

FRENCH SALAD DRESSING

2 egg yolks
1 tablespoon lemon juice
1 tablespoon sugar
1 tablespoon salt
½ teaspoon white pepper
½ teaspoon granulated garlic
2 tablespoons paprika
1 cup peanut oil
½ cup wine vinegar

Beat egg yolks. Add seasonings. Add oil slowly, alternating with portions of vinegar. Keep refrigerated.

Mrs. Richard Dennis

JO'S FRENCH DRESSING

2 cups good olive oil
2/3 cup garlic wine vinegar, red
Large pinch oregano
Salt and ground pepper to taste

Mix ingredients thoroughly in a large jar with a tight fitting top. Shake thoroughly when making and again before using. Gauge 1 tablespoon of dressing per handful of lettuce leaves. One large handful should be enough for each person. Do not use more than 2 greens, 1 is sufficient. Bibb is my choice. Optional additions are capers, well drained, or sliced scallions. Store in refrigerator.

Mrs. Hillard Willis

VINAIGRETTE SAUCE

2 cups good olive oil
1 cup garlic wine vinegar, red
Salt to taste
Oregano leaves
Hand-ground pepper

Combine ingredients as above. Shake vigorously and refrigerate. This is good as a marinade for peeled, whole tomatoes and for slightly cooked fresh vegetables such as green beans, broccoli and asparagus. Arrange vegetables in pyrex dishes for refrigeration. Salt and pepper vegetables. Pour generous amount of sauce over all. Snipped parsley, dill and scallion ends may be added. Shake well before using.

Warning: Tomatoes make dressing watery.

Mrs. Hillard Willis

GRAPEFRUIT SALAD DRESSING
Unusual, but makes a good combination.

Serves 12 or more
1 cup vegetable oil
1 cup ketchup
1 cup pecans, chopped
1 bottle small pearl onions, drained
1 teaspoon salt
1 teaspoon vinegar, or to taste
2-3 hard-boiled eggs, mashed fine

Mix all ingredients in the listed order. Refrigerate. Arrange sectioned grapefruit, and avocado if desired, on lettuce leaf for individual servings. Spoon dressing over top. Dressing can be kept refrigerated for 3 weeks.
Mrs. John Aurell

BLENDER MAYONNAISE

Makes 3 cups
2 egg yolks
1½ teaspoons salt
1¼ teaspoons dry mustard
½ teaspoon paprika
2 tablespoons vinegar
2 tablespoons lemon juice
2 cups salad oil

Put eggs and seasonings in container of blender. Mix at high speed until blended. Stop and with a rubber spatula push ingredients on side of blender into eggs. Add the lemon juice and start at high speed. Remove middle cap in the lid and very slowly pour in half of the salad oil. Add half of the vinegar and the rest of the oil. Work the ingredients down in the well. Add rest of vinegar while blending.
Mrs. Kermyt W. Callahan, Jr.

MAYONNAISE A L'AIL
Mayonnaise and garlic dressing.

3 egg yolks
½ cup white vinegar
¼ teaspoon sugar
1 teaspoon salt
¼ teaspoon Accent
¼ teaspoon white pepper
2 cloves garlic, crushed
1 cup oil

Beat egg yolks. Add seasoning and garlic. Add oil slowly, alternating with vinegar. Beat a *long, long* time until white. Keep refrigerated.
Mrs. Richard Dennis

DIVINE MAYONNAISE COTTEN SHEPHERD

Makes 1½ cups
2 egg yolks
1 cup oil, not olive oil
1 teaspoon powdered mustard
2 tablespoons lime juice
Large pinch cayenne or to taste
½ teaspoon salt
2 large pinches fine grind black
    pepper or to taste

Beat yolks with an electric beater or mix master, *not blender,* on low speed. Add one teaspoon mustard powder, beat until well combined. Add two tablespoons lime juice. Add ¼ cup oil a few drops at a time. Be sure each addition of oil is well combined before adding the next. Add ¼ cup of oil in a very thin stream. Make sure it is well incorporated before more is added. Add seasoning to taste. I recommend ½ teaspoon salt and very liberal sprinkling of cayenne and a more liberal one of black pepper. (Some prefer white pepper because of color. I find it tasteless, and like this colorful spicy version.) Beat again on low and add the last half cup of oil no more than ¼ cup at a time in a *thin* steady stream. Make sure each addition is well incorporated. Finish with lemon drops to taste and more seasoning if desired.

Variation:
Add curry to make curry sauce for cold artichokes, extra powdered mustard for sauce for stone crabs, etc.

Mrs. John Renuart

SUMMER SALAD DRESSING

Makes 3 cups
2¼ cups oil, olive or vegetable
¾ cup tarragon or wine vinegar
6 shallots, finely chopped, or
    small onion may be
    substituted
1/3 cup parsley, chopped
Snipped fresh dill to taste
Salt and pepper to taste
⅛ teaspoon Tabasco

Put everything in a glass jar and shake.

Mrs. Timothy Howe

POPPY SEED DRESSING

An old recipe especially good over all fresh fruit.

Makes about 1 quart
1½ cups sugar
2 teaspoons dry mustard
2 teaspoons salt
¾ cup white vinegar
3 tablespoons onion juice
2 cups vegetable oil
3 tablespoons poppy seeds

Mix sugar, mustard, salt and vinegar. Obtain onion juice by grating a large sweet onion on the fine side of a grater. Strain for onion juice. Add onion juice and stir it in thoroughly. Add oil slowly, beating constantly using a medium speed on electric mixer. Continue to beat until thick, 20-30 minutes. Add poppy seeds and beat a few minutes longer. Store in refrigerator, away from freezing compartment. Keeps about 3 weeks.

Mrs. Alan Greer
Mrs. Fred E. Luhm

COOKED SALAD DRESSING

Serves 6-8
2 tablespoons flour
½ teaspoon dry mustard
Cayenne to taste
2-3 teaspoons sugar
1 teaspoon salt
2 egg yolks
¾ cup milk
2 tablespoons butter
¼ cup vinegar
1 teaspoon celery seed (optional)

Sift together flour, mustard, pepper, sugar, salt and add egg yolks and milk. Cook in double boiler over boiling water until mixture begins to thicken. Add the butter and slowly add the vinegar. Add celery seed, if desired. Good with fresh tomatoes.

Mrs. Dwight Plyler, Jr.

AUNT JULIE'S DRESSING

Makes 5 cups
2 cups vegetable oil
1 cup ketchup
1 cup vinegar
1 cup sugar
1 teaspoon Worcestershire sauce
1 onion, grated
1 garlic clove, crushed
Salt and pepper to taste

Mix ingredients and refrigerate. As dressing stands it improves. Keeps 3 weeks.

Mrs. John Courtright

C. K.'s SALAD DRESSING

Makes 1 quart
2½ cups mayonnaise (see Index)
¾ cup sour cream
1 tablespoon dill, minced
1 tablespoon parsley, minced
2 tablespoons Parmesan cheese
2 teaspoons cracked black
   pepper
Juice of ½ lemon
1 tablespoon Worcestershire
   sauce
2 teaspoons onion, grated

Blend all the ingredients and chill before serving.

Mrs. George W. Cornell

SPLENDID SALAD DRESSING

Makes 1½ pints
1 cup mayonnaise (see Index)
1 cup buttermilk
1½ teaspoons prepared Dijon
   mustard
2 cloves garlic, crushed
¼ teaspoon thyme
1 teaspoon Accent
1 teaspoon Beau Monde
½ teaspoon fine herbs
1 teaspoon dill, minced
Salt and pepper to taste
½ cup Roquefort (optional)

Combine ingredients with a spoon or whip. *Do not* put in a blender or electric mixer. Refrigerate.

Mrs. Clarke Jones

VINAIGRETTE AU ROQUEFORT

Makes 1½ cups
½ cup olive oil
¼ cup red wine vinegar
2 tablespoons lemon juice
1 teaspoon salt
½ teaspoon black pepper
¼ teaspoon sugar
1 egg
¼ cup Roquefort cheese,
   crumbled
1 teaspoon onion juice

Place everything in jar. Shake well. Refrigerate. Shake well before using.

Mrs. Richard Dennis

BARBECUE SAUCE

Makes 2 cups
¼ cup onion, chopped
1 tablespoon drippings or oil
½ cup water
2 tablespoons vinegar
1 tablespoon Worcestershire
   sauce
¼ cup lemon juice
4 tablespoons brown sugar
1 cup chili sauce (or ketchup
   with extra Tabasco)
½ teaspoon salt
¼ teaspoon paprika
2 shakes liquid smoke
¼ cup parsley, chopped
Tabasco (optional)

Sauté onion in drippings until brown. Add all of the other ingredients and simmer for 20 minutes.

Mrs. Hugh T. Whitehead

ADMIRAL PARSON'S BARBECUE SAUCE

Makes 3 cups
1 cup water
½ cup vinegar
¼ pound butter
4 tablespoons brown sugar
4 tablespoons hot mustard
4 teaspoons salt
1 large bay leaf
¼ teaspoon cayenne
1 teaspoon Tabasco
½ teaspoon mustard seed
1 large onion, grated
2 large cloves garlic, grated
½ lemon, juice and grated rind
⅛ teaspoon rosemary
4 teaspoons parsley, chopped
1 teaspoon black pepper
¼ teaspoon coriander, ground
½ teaspoon liquid smoke
1 cup ketchup
4 tablespoons Worcestershire
   sauce

Combine water and vinegar. Add butter and melt slowly. Add everything but the ketchup and Worcestershire. Bring to a boil and simmer 20 minutes. Add the ketchup and Worcestershire and simmer 10 minutes. Keep refrigerated

Mrs. James D. Brock

BARBECUE SAUCE WITH BEER

Makes 2 cups
1/2 cup brown sugar
1/4 cup prepared mustard
1/2 cup ketchup
1 teaspoon Worcestershire sauce
1/2 cup onion, finely chopped
1/2 teaspoon salt
1/4 teaspoon black pepper
1/2 cup beer

Combine all ingredients in saucepan. Bring to a boil. Simmer for 5 minutes. This is a sweet sauce and goes especially well with hamburgers, hot dogs and pork.

Mrs. Robert Hance

BARBECUE SAUCE FOR SHRIMP

Sauce for 80 shrimp
1 pound butter
1 bottle horseradish, 5 ounces
1/2 bottle ketchup, 16 ounce size
4 tablespoons Tabasco
4 tablespoons salt
1 cup vinegar
6 lemons
2 tablespoons Worcestershire
　sauce
Fresh ground pepper to taste

Melt butter, then add all the other ingredients, blending thoroughly. Allow 8 jumbo shrimp for men, 6 jumbo shrimp for women. Clean, peel and devein shrimp. Marinate shrimp for at least 8 hours. Cook on skewers over low fire, turning and basting frequently. Do not overcook.

Mrs. John Renuart

BARBECUE MARINADE

Makes 3 1/2 cups
1 1/2 cups salad oil
3/4 cups soy sauce
2 tablespoons dry mustard
2 1/2 teaspoons salt
1 tablespoon pepper
1/2 cup wine vinegar
2 tablespoons parsley, minced
4 cloves garlic, crushed
1/2 cup fresh lemon juice
Pinch basil
Pinch oregano
Pinch tarragon
Pinch Italian seasoning
Pinch Season-All

Place all ingredients in a large jar and mix well. Marinate meat or chicken 4 hours or more.

Mrs. Robert Ferrel

CLEAR BROWN STOCK

Makes 8 quarts
4 pounds beef stew meat, lean
4 pounds veal stew meat, lean
2 pounds beef bones, cracked
2 pounds veal bones, cracked
4 tablespoons butter
4 carrots, sliced
2 onions, large, sliced
1 cup celery, diced
2 tablespoons salt
Bouquet Garni

Brown the meat and bones in butter. Place in soup pot with about 8 quarts of water, or enough to cover all ingredients by 2 inches, and add remaining ingredients. Cover and simmer for 6 hours. Skim off fat periodically. Strain and refrigerate. When cold, lift off the layer of fat before using stock.
John Baratte

BASIC BROWN SAUCE

1 large carrot, chopped
1 medium onion, chopped fine
1 tablespoon parsley, chopped fine
1 clove garlic, minced
6 small mushrooms, chopped fine
1¼ cups butter
¼ teaspoon powdered bay leaf
1 tablespoon thyme
¼ teaspoon salt
¼ teaspoon pepper
½ cup flour
6 cups clear brown stock (see Index)
½ cup tomato purée

Cook vegetables in butter with the seasonings until soft and brown. Mash into a paste and combine with the flour. Cook in large saucepan over low heat for 10 minutes, stirring constantly. Add the brown stock, which has been heated, and the tomato purée and simmer the sauce until it is reduced by half.
John Baratte

CHEESE SAUCE

Makes 1½ cups
1 cup medium white sauce (see Index)
1 cup Cheddar cheese, grated
½ teaspoon dry mustard
¼ teaspoon paprika
Dash of cayenne

Make white sauce with ½ cup of chicken stock and ½ cup milk, if desired. Add cheese and seasonings to the hot sauce. Stir constantly until the cheese melts and the sauce is smooth.
Mrs. Lindsey D. Pankey, Jr.

BASIC FISH SAUCE

6 cups clear fish stock (see Index)
12 tablespoons butter
9 tablespoons flour
Salt and pepper to taste

Boil stock until it reduces to 2/3 the amount (4 cups). Mix butter and flour together thoroughly and add to the stock. Add salt and pepper to taste. Cook, stirring constantly, with a wire whisk until it is a medium thick sauce.

John Baratte

HOLLANDAISE

Makes 1 cup
1 cup sweet butter, softened
4 egg yolks
3 teaspoons lemon juice
Pinch salt
Few drops Tabasco

Divide soft butter into 4 parts. In the top of a double boiler over hot (not boiling) water, put the egg yolks and 1 part of the butter. Stir constantly with a whisk until the butter is incorporated. Add each portion of the butter in the same manner. Do not let the water come to a boil at any time. Remove saucepan from the heat and beat for 2 minutes with a whisk. Add the lemon juice and seasoning. Replace over the hot water and beat 2 minutes longer. If it curdles, immediately beat in 1 to 2 tablespoons of boiling water.

Mousseline Sauce:
Add 1 cup of whipping cream, which has been whipped with a smidgeon of salt, to the above recipe for hollandaise. The result is a lighter, not rich, sauce. Excellent with poached salmon.

Mrs. John Renuart

MARCHAND DE VIN SAUCE
Serve with Eggs Hussarde

Makes 2 cups
1/3 cup mushrooms, finely
 chopped
1/2 cup boiled ham, finely
 chopped
1/3 cup shallots, finely chopped
1/2 cup onion, finely chopped
2 tablespoons garlic, minced
1/2 teaspoon salt
Cayenne to taste
3/4 cup butter
2 tablespoons flour
3/4 cup consommé
1/2 cup red wine

Brown vegetables in butter until golden brown. Add the flour and seasonings. Brown well, 7-10 minutes. This must be done slowly or it will scorch. Add the consommé and wine. Simmer 35 to 45 minutes. Pour sauce into a blender and blend until the mixture is just puréed. Sauce should be thick, and ingredients unrecognizable.

Mrs. George W. Cornell

MORNAY SAUCE

Makes 1¼ cups
1 cup medium white sauce (see
 Index)
1 egg yolk
2 tablespoons light cream
2 tablespoons Parmesan cheese,
 grated
2 tablespoons Gruyere cheese,
 grated

Add a little white sauce to egg yolk and cream and stir until thoroughly blended. Add to rest of white sauce and cook until hot, do not boil, stirring constantly. Keep stirring and add the Parmesan and Gruyere cheeses and continue stirring until cheeses melt and sauce thickens. Pour sauce over desired food and brown in oven before serving.

Mrs. Lindsey D. Pankey, Jr.

VELOUTE SAUCE

Makes 1½ cups
2 tablespoons butter
2 tablespoons flour
2 cups chicken stock
¼ cup mushrooms, minced
Pinch of nutmeg
Salt and white pepper to taste

Melt butter in top of double boiler (not aluminum) and stir in flour. When blended, slowly add stock and cook, stirring until thickened. Add mushrooms and simmer, in double boiler, for about 1 hour. Add nutmeg and season to taste.

Mrs. Frank Marston

WHITE SAUCES

Makes 1 cup
THIN WHITE SAUCE:
1½ tablespoons butter
1½ tablespoons flour
½ teaspoon salt
Dash of white pepper
Sprinkle of nutmeg
1 cup milk
MEDIUM WHITE SAUCE:
2½ tablespoons butter
2½ tablespoons flour
Repeat same ingredients as
above, starting with salt
THICK WHITE SAUCE:
4 tablespoons butter
4 tablespoons flour
Repeat same ingredients as
above, starting with salt

Melt the butter in a saucepan over moderate heat. Stir in the flour and blend with a wire whisk until thoroughly blended. Add the seasonings, continue stirring and add the milk. Stir continuously until the sauce thickens and is smooth.

Mrs. Karl Noonan

REMOULADE SAUCE

Sauce for 4 pounds shrimp
1 teaspoon dill, chopped
1 teaspoon parsley, chopped
2 teaspoons horseradish
1 teaspoon Dijon mustard
½ teaspoon dry mustard
1 teaspoon curry powder
⅛ teaspoon cayenne
1 teaspoon chili powder
1 teaspoon salt
Freshly ground pepper
2 eggs, hard boiled and pushed
through sieve
1½ cups sour cream
1½ cups mayonnaise (see Index)
½ leek, chopped or 2 spring
onions, chopped
1 clove garlic, minced

Mix all ingredients together thoroughly. To serve, either marinate cooked and cleaned shrimp in sauce over night or use as a sauce poured over the shrimp. Both the shrimp and sauce should be served cold.

Mrs. William Mooney

HAM GLAZE

Whole cloves
2 tablespoons honey
1½ cups brown sugar, light
1 tablespoon dry mustard
1 tablespoon white vinegar
Few tablespoons pineapple juice

Decorate ham with cloves. Mix glaze and put on ham during last 45 minutes of cooking.

Mrs. Don Shoemaker

MUSTARD SAUCE FOR HAM

Serves 12 or more
1 cup sugar
1 pint heavy cream
4 tablespoons dry mustard
1 pinch salt
2 egg yolks

Heat cream in double boiler. Mix mustard, sugar, and salt and add to the beaten egg yolk. Pour over heated cream and mix. Cook until it thickens, slightly. Can be made ahead of time and reheated, but will be thicker and might lump. If it lumps, put it in the blender.

Mrs. Don Shoemaker

QUICK MADEIRA SAUCE

Serves 4 to 6
1 package frozen mushrooms
   (6 ounces whole mushrooms
   in butter)
1 tablespoon chives, chopped
1 package dry mushroom gravy
   mix (or onion mix)
½ cup Madeira
1 cup water

In a saucepan melt mushrooms and add chives. Stir in mushroom gravy mix and water. Add Madeira wine. Simmer until thickened. May add more water if too thick.

Mrs. Charles K. Orr

ANCHOVY SAUCE

Accompaniment for chilled, baked or poached salmon.

1 cup sour cream
3 teaspoons anchovy paste
1½ tablespoons grated lemon
   rind
1½ tablespoons parsley, minced
½ teaspoon lemon juice
Dash Tabasco

Combine all the ingredients and serve chilled.

Mrs. Hillard Willis

CUCUMBER SAUCE
Good on chilled salmon.

3 large cucumbers, peeled,
seeded, and coarsely grated
2 pints sour cream
1 pint mayonnaise (see Index)
½ cup fresh dill, minced
Salt and pepper to taste
2 tablespoons lemon juice

Blend sour cream and
mayonnaise. Fold in cucumber
and seasoning. Serve chilled.

Francien Ruwitch
Mrs. W. Carroll Latimer

EGG SAUCE FOR POACHED SALMON

1-1/3 cups water in which
salmon is poached (fish stock)
4 tablespoons butter
4 tablespoons flour
1-1/3 cups heavy cream
3 egg yolks
3 hard cooked eggs
3 tablespoons parsley, chopped
Salt and cayenne pepper to taste
Tabasco to taste

Strain stock. Melt butter, stir in
the flour and cook several
minutes. Stir in stock. Cook until
thickened. Mix cream and egg
yolks and slowly stir mixture into
fish sauce. Heat, stirring
constantly, until thickened. Do
not let boil. Fold in coarsely
chopped hard-boiled eggs and
parsley. Season to taste with salt,
cayenne, or Tabasco.

Mrs. John Renuart

LEMON HERB SAUCE FOR FISH

1 recipe medium white sauce
(see Index)
½ cup cottage cheese or yogurt
2 tablespoons lemon juice
¼ teaspoon dill weed
½ teaspoon marjoram
½ cup Parmesan cheese, grated
2 tablespoons white wine

Add all of the ingredients to the
white sauce and put in blender
for a few seconds. Pour over
cooked fish fillet and broil about
3 minutes.

Mrs. Larry Stewart

OLD SOUR
Use on meats, fish, almost anything but ice cream!

1 cup key lime juice
1 tablespoon salt

Mix salt and lime juice. Fill glass bottle and cork tightly. Let stand in cool place until fermentation stops (about a week).
Tom Pennekamp

TOMATO SAUCE FOR CANNELLONI

1 cup onion, chopped
1 clove garlic, crushed
¼ cup olive oil
1 can Italian tomatoes
1 can tomato paste
1 tablespoon salt
1 teaspoon sugar
1 teaspoon oregano
½ teaspoon basil
¼ teaspoon pepper
2 tablespoons parsley, minced

Brown onion and garlic in oil. Add tomatoes and tomato paste and the seasonings. Cover and simmer 1 hour.
Mrs. Jack Courtright

CORN RELISH

1 dozen ears of corn
1 large cabbage
1 dozen onions
6 green peppers
6 red peppers (or pimientos)
2 hot peppers
1½ pints vinegar
2 cups sugar
½ cup salt
4 tablespoons mustard
2 tablespoons celery seeds
2 tablespoons turmeric

Cut corn off the cob. Put cabbage, onions and peppers through a food grinder using the coarse blade. Combine everything in a large kettle. Cook over medium heat, stirring occassionally, 1 hour. Seal in hot sterile jars.
Mrs. Dwight Plyler, Jr.

GUAVA SHELLS

Makes 7 pints
4 dozen ripe guavas
2 cups sugar
3 cups water
½ cup lime juice

Wash guavas and cut out stem end. Trim any blemishes. Slice in half and remove seedy center. Combine sugar, water, and lime juice and boil for a minute or two. Add guavas. Cook until tender (5-10 minutes). Fill sterile jars and seal.

Mrs. Orin Ford Pearson

MANGO HALVES IN GINGER SYRUP

1 pound mango sections
¼ cup lime juice
2 cups granulated sugar
2 cups water
1 piece ginger root

Select fruit that is beginning to show color. Peel, cut in sections, and add lime juice. Cook in sugar syrup until tender. Let stand until cold. Pack the fruit in the jars. Add ginger root to syrup and boil until thick. Pour boiling syrup over the fruit. (Process pint jars 20 minutes in boiling water bath.)

Mrs. Orin Ford Pearson

FLORIDA MANGO CHUTNEY

3¼ cups mangoes, peeled and
   thinly sliced
2½ cups sugar
1 cup brown sugar
1 cup cider vinegar
½ cup raisins
¼ cup ginger, finely chopped
2 tablespoons garlic, minced
2 tablespoons salt
1 teaspoon ground cloves
2 small hot peppers, chopped

Put mangoes in large glass bowl with both plain sugar and brown sugar. Cover the bowl and place in ice box overnight. Drain the liquid into a large pan reserving the mango slices. Add the vinegar, raisins, ginger, garlic, salt and cloves. Remove seeds from the hot peppers, cut them into very thin slices cross-wise, and add them to the mixture. Simmer, stirring often, for 60 minutes. Add mango slices and simmer 30 minutes longer. Pour into hot sterilized jars. Cover tightly.

Mrs. Charles K. Orr

MILD MANGO CHUTNEY

Makes 4 quarts
1¼ quarts green mangoes, sliced
3 green bell peppers, finely
  chopped
1 large Spanish onion, chopped
1 clove garlic, minced
1 tablespoon salt
1 pound dark brown sugar
1 tablespoon white mustard seed
2 teaspoons allspice
2 teaspoons cinnamon
2 teaspoons ground cloves
1 pound raisins (or half raisins
  and half currants)
1 cup vinegar
1 cup grapefruit juice
Candied ginger, finely chopped
1 package slivered almonds

Combine first five ingredients.
Let stand 1 hour and drain. Heat
next 8 ingredients. Add mango
mixture and boil 30 minutes,
covered. Add ginger and
almonds and cook 5 to 10
minutes more, uncovered. Pour
into prepared jars and seal while
hot.

Variation:
If a hotter chutney is desired add
2 minced hot peppers to the
mango mixture at the beginning
of the recipe.

Mrs. Lyle Roberts

MANGO CHUTNEY

8-10 large hard green mangoes
2 tablespoons salt
4 cups brown sugar
2 cups malt or wine vinegar
2 oranges, peeled and cut into
  small pieces
1 orange peel (thinnest layer of
  outer skin)
2 tablespoons crystallized
  ginger, minced
1 teaspoon allspice
Large pinch cayenne
1 cup white seedless raisins
½ cup rum
2/3 cup pecans, finely crushed

Peel mangoes. Cut into 1" x 2"
pieces. Place in a bowl and
sprinkle with salt. Cover with
cold water and let stand 30
minutes. Drain well. Place
mangoes in pot. Add the brown
sugar and vinegar. Add the small
pieces of oranges, the orange
peel, which has been minced,
and cook for 10 minutes over
medium heat, stirring
frequently. Add ginger, allspice
and cayenne. Soak raisins in the
rum while chutney cooks 30
minutes or more, until syrup has
thickened. Add raisins and rum
and cook 5 more minutes. The
syrup should be the thickness of
honey. Add the pecans. Pour
chutney into sterilized glass jars.
Seal and store at room
temperature. Serve with curry or
with roasts.

Mrs. Fred E. Luhm

HOT PEPPER JELLY

Makes 6 pints
2 bell peppers
6 banana peppers
7 jalapeño peppers
8½ cups sugar
2 cups red vinegar
2 bottles Certo
Green food coloring

Cap peppers and grind, fine seed included. Dissolve sugar and vinegar and bring to a boil. Add peppers and boil for one minute. Set aside and cool for 1 minute. Add Certo and desired amount of color. Fill sterilized jars. To serve, spread on bed of cream cheese as an appetizer. Accompany with crackers.

Mrs. Lyn Brooks Howle

PEPPER JELLY

Makes 7 half-pint jars
¾ cup jalapeño peppers, chopped
¾ cup green bell peppers, chopped
1½ cups vinegar
6½ cups sugar
6 ounce bottle Certo
Green food coloring
6 drops Tabasco (optional)

Put vinegar and seeded peppers in the blender and blend until finely minced. Pour peppers and vinegar into a heavy saucepan and cook over medium heat until mixture comes to a boil. Add sugar and stir until dissolved. Remove from heat and let sit for 5 minutes. Add Certo and 6 drops of Tabasco. Pour into sterilized jars. Serve with whipped cream cheese and crackers. (As the jelly ages it gets milder if Tabasco is not used.)

Mrs. Lindsey D. Pankey, Jr.

GUAVA JELLY

Makes 4 cups
2 cups guava juice
2 cups sugar
1-2 tablespoons lime juice

Use firm ripe guavas and a few slightly green ones to make the guava juice. Slice guavas into the kettle and add 2 cups of water for each 4 cups of fruit. Boil rapidly 15 to 20 minutes until soft. Stir occasionally. Strain through a jelly bag. Measure the juice. Add an equal amount of sugar. Add lime juice if guavas have a mild sweet taste. Cook until the mixture reaches the jelly stage. The slower the cooking the darker the jelly.

Mrs. Orin Ford Pearson

TROPICAL MANGO JAM

Makes 6 half pints
3 cups mangoes, ground
2 tablespoons lime juice or to taste
1 package of pectin, powdered
4-5 cups sugar

Grind the mangoes in a food grinder or blender. Pour the mango pulp and the lime juice into a large saucepan and stir in the pectin. Bring the mixture to a boil, stirring often, and add the sugar. Stir to dissolve the sugar and let the mixture come to a boil again. Boil for 1 minute and remove from the heat. Continue stirring and skim off the foam for 5 minutes more. Ladle the hot fruit into sterilized jars leaving ½ inch space at the top. Seal with paraffin.

Mrs. Robert Hays

FROSTED GRAPES

Grapes will sparkle as though made of crystal.

Large cluster green grapes
Large cluster red grapes
1 egg white
½ cup sugar, granulated

Rinse grapes and break into small clusters. Dry thoroughly. Beat 1 egg white until foamy. Brush egg foam all over grapes. Roll grapes at once in sugar. Set on waxed paper to dry for 1 hour. Use as garnish. This is pretty on a silver platter with Christmas turkey or around a cheese platter.

Mrs. Robert Hartnett

QUINCE JAM AND QUINCE JELLY

6 large quinces
Sugar
Water

Peel and quarter quinces. Wash the peel and seeds with cold water. Put them into a large kettle. Cover with water and boil until the water is half gone. Put the liquid aside to make the jelly.

To Make Jam:
Put remaining parts of quince which have been cut into small pieces in another pot. Cover with cold water. Cook until soft. Measure a cup of sugar for every cup of quince mixture. Add sugar to quince and cook over low heat stirring constantly until the sugar is dissolved. Cook until quince turns dark red. Stir frequently. Cook over low heat 1 to 2 hours until the syrup is thick. Fill sterile glasses and seal.

To Make Jelly:
Take cooled reserved liquid from the peel and seed and strain through 2 layers of cheese cloth. Again measure liquid and add 1 cup sugar for every 1 cup liquid. Stir and cook over low heat until the sugar dissolves and the liquid turns red. Fill sterile glasses and seal.

Mrs. Robert S. Jones

GREEN TOMATO RELISH

Makes 3 quarts
12 large green tomatoes
3 large onions
3 green peppers
1 red sweet pepper
2½ cups sugar
2½ cups cider vinegar
1 teaspoon salt
2 tablespoons pickling spices
1 teaspoon mustard seeds
1 teaspoon celery seed
Hot, sterilized quart jars

Put all vegetables through the food chopper and drain. Combine vinegar, sugar, salt and spice bag in a large kettle. Add vegetables and boil down for 20 or 30 minutes. Spoon into hot jars and seal. Cool before storing. This will keep unrefrigerated for up to a year. (Old stockings make good spice bags.)

Mrs. Robert Hance

GREEN TOMATO PICKLE

7 pounds very green tomatoes
3 cups building or slaked lime
(available at a building
supply store)
2 gallons water
1 tablespoon cloves
1 tablespoon white mustard seed
1 tablespoon allspice
1 tablespoon mace
5 pounds sugar
3 pints vinegar
Green food coloring

Slice tomatoes ⅛ inch thick. Soak for 24 hours in lime water (3 cups lime to 2 gallons water.*) Drain and soak in cold water for 4 hours. Change the water each hour. Put whole spices in a bag which can be made from an old stocking. Make a syrup of the sugar and vinegar. Pour over the tomatoes and let stand overnight. Boil tomatoes in syrup with spices for ½ hour. Add green food coloring until the desired color is reached. Be sure to remove the spice bag or the tomatoes will darken. Pour into sterile jars and seal.

*Weight tomatoes down so none float to the surface in the lime water.

Mrs. Park Dallis
Mrs. Peter Ray

WATERMELON PICKLE

10 pounds watermelon
10 pounds sugar
4 quarts white vinegar
1 tube Lillys' lime, available at
pharmacy
Sea salt to taste
½ box whole cloves
½ box cinnamon sticks
½ box whole allspice
Green food coloring

Prepare watermelon rind by peeling away dark green skin and all pink fruit. Cut into 2 inch fingers. (Look for a "thick rind" watermelon.) Barely cover fruit with lime and water in a large pan and let sit overnight. Drain and rinse. Cover with water and salt. Bring to a boil and boil 20 minutes. Drain. Cover with fresh water. Bring to a boil and boil 20 minutes. Drain. Make a syrup of sugar and vinegar. When sugar is dissolved add fruit, spices which have been tied in a muslin bag, and a few drops of green food coloring. Cook until the fruit begins to look clear, about 1¾ hours. Stir occasionally to prevent sticking to the bottom.

Mrs. Malcolm D. McNaughton

Breads

BREADS

A nineteenth century American wool coverlet completes arrangements for a seaside picnic. The blue and white coverlet was donated to the Lowe Art Museum by Mr. B.W. Brenning. Matheson Hammock Park is the picnic site; the roots seen in the picture are those of the aquatic mangrove tree.

BANANA BREAD

Makes 1 loaf
¼ cup butter
1 cup sugar
2 eggs, beaten
1½ cups mashed banana, very ripe
1½ cups flour
½ teaspoon baking soda
½ teaspoon salt
½ cup walnuts or pecans, chopped

Cream butter and sugar. Blend in eggs and banana. Add sifted dry ingredients and nuts. Bake in a greased loaf pan for 45 minutes to 1 hour at 350°.

Mrs. Tom Pennekamp

BAKING POWDER BISCUITS

Makes 10-12 biscuits
2 cups all-purpose flour
2 teaspoons baking powder
1 teaspoon salt
8 tablespoons butter, cut into bits
2/3 cup milk

Preheat oven to 400°. Grease a baking sheet with butter. Combine the dry ingredients and sift into a deep bowl. Add butter and mix with the dry ingredients until the consistency is coarse and flakey. Add milk and mix until the dough will form a compact ball. Roll out and cut biscuits. Arrange on the baking sheet and bake at 400° for about 20 minutes or until golden.

Mrs. George L. Irvin, III

BUTTERMILK BISCUITS

Makes 12 large biscuits
2 cups flour
3 teaspoons baking powder
¾ teaspoon salt
¼ teaspoon baking soda
1/3 cup shortening
¾ cup buttermilk, approximately

Sift together dry ingredients. Cut in shortening until particles are fine. Add milk to make a soft dough. Knead lightly until you can pick up. Roll on floured surface keeping dough rather thick, ¾ inch, and cut with floured cutter. Bake at 450° for 12 minutes.

Mrs. C. C. Jones

ANN'S BOSTON BROWN BREAD

Serves 8 to 10
1 cup Kellogg's All Bran
1 cup sour milk (add 1
    tablespoon vinegar to
    sweet milk)
½ cup raisins
4 tablespoons molasses
¼ cup sugar
1 teaspoon baking soda
¼ teaspoon salt
1 cup flour

Mix together bran, sour milk, and raisins. Add molasses. Sift dry ingredients and combine. Put mixture in a greased, one pound coffee can. Cover tightly with foil. Steam for 3 hours; or, in pressure cooker, steam 15 minutes with steam escaping, then cook at 10 pound pressure for 1 hour.

Mrs. Ann Wood

HEATH BAR COFFEE CAKE

Serves 12 to 15
2 cups flour
¼ pound butter
1 cup brown sugar, light
½ cup white sugar
1 cup buttermilk
1 teaspoon soda
1 egg
1 teaspoon vanilla
6 Heath candy bars
¼ cup pecans

Blend flour, butter, and sugars. Set aside ½ cup of this mixture. To the rest add buttermilk, soda, egg, and vanilla. Pour into a greased and floured 10"x14" pan. Crush Heath bars and pecans. Add this to the mixture previously set aside. Sprinkle over the top of the batter and bake at 350° for 30 minutes.

Mrs. William H. Walker

SOUR CREAM COFFEE CAKE

Serves 12 to 16
CAKE:
½ cup butter
1 cup sugar
2 eggs
2 cups flour
1 tablespoon baking powder
1 teaspoon baking soda
¼ teaspoon salt
1 cup sour cream
1 teaspoon vanilla
TOPPING:
½ cup chopped nuts
1 teaspoon cinnamon
½ cup sugar or brown sugar

Mix butter and sugar together. Add eggs, beat well. Sift dry ingredients together. Add to the egg mixture. Mix in sour cream and vanilla. Pour half of batter into greased and floured 10" tube pan. Cover with half of nut topping. Add rest of batter, cover with topping. Bake at 350° for 45 minutes. Keeps indefinitely in plastic bag or wrapped in foil for several days in refrigerator.

Mrs. Hagood Clarke
Mrs. James A. Wright, III
Mrs. Linda Zack

CORN BREAD SUPREME

Serves 6
1 cup self-rising white corn meal
8¾-ounce can corn, cream style
½ cup cooking oil
1 cup sour cream
3 eggs, beaten

Combine all of the ingredients. Pour into greased cake pan or skillet. Bake at 400° until brown. Serve hot.

Mrs. Tom Huston

GEORGIA CORN BREAD

Serves 6
¼ cup vegetable shortening, or bacon drippings
2 cups white corn meal
2 tablespoons flour
2 tablespoons double acting baking powder
1 teaspoon baking soda
1 teaspoon salt
1 egg
2 cups buttermilk

Melt shortening in a 9" iron skillet over medium heat, brushing the sides with oil. Sift together dry ingredients. Combine egg and buttermilk and stir into the dry ingredients. Add the melted shortening. Pour into the hot skillet and bake at 450° for 20 to 25 minutes.

Mrs. Dwight Plyler, Jr.

CRANBERRY CITRUS NUT BREAD

Makes 2 loaves
2 cups all purpose flour, sifted
1 cup sugar
1½ teaspoons baking powder
1 teaspoon salt
½ teaspoon baking soda
¼ cup butter
1 teaspoon orange peel, grated
½ cup orange juice
¼ cup lime juice
1 egg, beaten
1 cup fresh cranberries, chopped
½ cup pecans, chopped

Sift together dry ingredients. Cut in butter. Combine peel, juice and egg. Add this to dry ingredients, mixing just to moisten. Fold in berries and nuts. Pour into 2 greased 6" x 3" x 2" pans and bake at 350° for 1 hour.

Mrs. Robert Hartnett

CRANBERRY CAKE

Serves 6-8
2 cups cranberries
½ cup sugar
½ cup nuts
2 eggs, beaten
1 cup sugar
1 cup flour
¾ cup butter, melted

Mix berries, sugar and nuts and pour in well-buttered pan, preferably a spring form pan. Beat eggs and sugar and blend carefully with flour and butter. Pour over berries. Bake at 350° for about 45 minutes. Remove from pan and sprinkle top with powdered sugar.

Mrs. William Taylor

BASIC CREPES

Serves 15; 30 crepes
6 eggs
1 cup plus 2 tablespoons flour
1½ tablespoons sugar
½ teaspoon salt
3 cups milk
¼ pound or less butter

Beat eggs. Add flour, sugar, and salt. Beat until smooth. Gradually add milk, beating constantly. Melt 1 teaspoon butter in 7" skillet. Add 2 tablespoons batter to cover bottom of skillet. Cook bottom until golden brown. Turn with spatula and cook other side until light brown. Transfer each crepe to waxed paper. Repeat for each crepe. To Freeze: Separate each crepe with a piece of waxed paper and put in air tight container.

Mrs. Robert Ferrel

DATE NUT LOAF CAKE

1¼ cups flour
½ teaspoon double acting
    baking powder
½ teaspoon salt
¼ cup bourbon
½ teaspoon rose water (optional)
1 pound dates, stoned and cut in
    large pieces
3 cups walnuts, broken
¼ cup flour
½ cup butter
1 cup sugar
2 eggs

Sift flour, baking powder, and salt together and mix alternately with the bourbon and rose water. Mix dates, walnuts and ¼ cup flour. Add this to above mixture. Cream butter and sugar until light and then add eggs, one at a time, beating thoroughly. Combine both mixtures and turn into one 9" x 5" or two 7" x 3" loaf pans greased and lined with paper. Bake at 300° for 1½ hours. Put pan of water in the bottom of the oven during baking.

Mrs. Josephine M. Schutt

DILL BREAD

Makes 1 loaf
¼ cup warm water
1 package dry yeast
2 tablespoons butter
1 tablespoon onion, finely chopped
1 egg
1 cup cottage cheese, room temperature
2 teaspoons dill weed
1 teaspoon salt
1¼ teaspoon soda
2½ cups flour

Sprinkle yeast in warm water and stir until dissolved. Mix in the remaining ingredients thoroughly, adding the flour last. Cover the bowl, place in a warm spot and let rise for 1½-2 hours. Stir down and put dough into a greased loaf pan. Let dough rise again. Bake at 350° for 40 minutes.

Mrs. Steve Pease

FRENCH BREAD

Makes 2 loaves
1 cup milk
1 tablespoon butter
1 tablespoon sugar
2 teaspoons salt
1 cup hot water
1 package yeast, dissolved in ½ cup warm water
6 cups white flour, more or less

Scald milk and stir in butter, sugar, and salt and hot water. Cool. Add yeast mixture to the milk mixture. Add flour to form a soft dough. Knead on a lightly floured board until the dough blisters, and then place in a greased bowl. Let the dough rise until double, punch down, knead 5 minutes and let rise again. After rising again, punch down, divide dough in half, knead and shape into 2 long loaves. Place on a greased cookie sheet that has been sprinkled with corn meal. Brush warm water on the loaves and dust the top with cornmeal. Let bread rise until almost double again and bake at 375° for 30 minutes. Take from the oven, cover generously with stiffly beaten egg whites and continue to bake for another 10 minutes.

Mrs. George L. Irvin, III

COUNTRY CORN FRITTERS

Serves 12
1 cup flour, self rising
1 teaspoon salt
½ teaspoon pepper
1 teaspoon sugar
2 eggs, beaten
1½ cup whole kernel corn
½ cup milk
2 teaspoons salad oil
Hot shortening

Blend together flour, salt, pepper and sugar. Mix eggs, corn, milk and salad oil and add to dry ingredients. Beat with mixer until smooth. Drop by spoonfuls into deep hot shortening until brown.
Mrs. Geoffrey Hill

DINAH'S GARLIC BREAD

Makes 1 loaf
¼ cup milk
1 tablespoon butter
1 tablespoon garlic powder
French or Italian bread
Parmesan cheese

Heat ¼ cup of milk and add butter and garlic powder, stirring over heat until blended. Sprinkle Parmesan cheese on waxed paper. Dip sliced bread in liquid mixture and turn in the Parmesan cheese with tongs. Place on greased cookie sheet. Bake at 400° for 5 to 10 minutes.
Mrs. Barbara Bachmann

HOLIDAY FRUIT BREAD

Makes 2 loaves
1½ cups milk
4 tablespoons butter
4 tablespoons sugar
1½ teaspoons salt
2 packages yeast, dissolved in
**   ½ cup warm water**
2 cups whole wheat flour
1 egg, beaten
1 cup dried apricots, peaches or
**   apples, or combination,**
**   chopped**
3 cups white flour

Scald milk and mix with butter, sugar, and salt. Cool. Stir yeast mixture into milk mixture. Blend in whole wheat flour, egg, and fruit. Add the white flour until the mixture is dough. Knead and let rise. Knead again and shape into 2 loaves. Let rise and bake at 350° for about 35 minutes.

Glaze:
If you wish to glaze the bread, mix lemon juice and powdered sugar to a spreading consistency and brush on the bread just as you take it from the oven.
Mrs. George L. Irvin, III

HUSH PUPPIES

Serves 6
1 cup self-rising flour
1 cup self-rising meal
1 egg
1 cup milk, approximately
1 large onion, chopped
Deep fat for frying

Sift together flour and meal. In a separate bowl beat egg, add milk and onion. The batter should not be thick. When fat reaches 380°, drop by teaspoonfuls into fat. Turn once. Drain well on absorbent paper.

Mrs. Peter Ray

LEMON BREAD

Makes 1 loaf
6 tablespoons butter
1-1/3 cups sugar
2 eggs, beaten
½ cup milk
Grated rind of 1 lemon
Juice of one lemon
1½ cups flour
1 teaspoon baking powder
¼ teaspoon salt
½ cup walnuts, chopped

Cream butter and one cup of the sugar. Mix eggs with milk and lemon rind. Combine flour, baking powder, salt and nuts. Mix all of these with hand mixer until smooth. Pour into loaf pan lined with foil. Bake at 350° for 1 hour. After removing from oven, while still hot, pour mixture of 1/3 cup sugar and lemon juice over the loaf.

Mrs. Philippe Moore

MANGO BREAD

Makes 2 loaves
2 eggs
1¼ cups sugar
½ cup vegetable oil
¼ cup honey
2 cups mango, slightly mashed
2 cups all-purpose flour
2 teaspoons cinnamon
2 teaspoons baking soda
½ teaspoon salt
½ teaspoon vanilla
½ cup walnuts, chopped
½ cup raisins

Beat eggs until fluffy. Beat in sugar, oil, and gradually add honey. Blend in mango. Combine dry ingredients and add very gradually to the mixture. Stir in vanilla, walnuts, and raisins. Pour into greased and floured bread pans. Let stand for 20 minutes. Bake at 350° for 50 to 60 minutes. Frozen mango can be used.

Mrs. Robert Hays

EASY BRAN MUFFINS

Makes 50 muffins
15-ounce box raisin bran
5 cups flour
3 cups sugar
5 teaspoons baking soda
2 teaspoons salt
4 eggs
1 quart buttermilk
1 cup oil

In a large bowl mix raisin bran, flour, sugar, soda, and salt. Mix eggs, buttermilk and oil separately and combine. Bake at 425° in lined muffin tins for 15 minutes. Batter may be covered and refrigerated for six weeks, and used as needed.

Mrs. D. Robert Graham

OATMEAL MUFFINS

Makes 24 muffins
1 cup quick oats
1 cup buttermilk
1 egg, beaten
½ cup dark brown sugar
½ cup cooking oil
1 cup flour
½ teaspoon salt
1 teaspoon baking powder
½ teaspoon soda

Soak oats in buttermilk for 1 hour. Add beaten egg and blend thoroughly. Add sugar and oil. Sift dry ingredients together. Add to oats mixture and mix lightly. Fill greased tins 2/3 full. Bake in a 400° oven for 15 to 20 minutes. These will freeze nicely.

Mrs. Geoffrey Hill

AUNT JULIE'S ORANGE BREAD

Makes 1 loaf
2 tablespoons butter
1 cup sugar
1 egg, beaten
¾ cup orange juice
2 tablespoons orange rind, grated
½ cup dates, chopped
½ cup nuts, chopped
½ teaspoon baking soda
1 teaspoon baking powder
¼ teaspoon salt
2 cups flour

Cream butter and sugar. Add the next five ingredients. Sift the dry ingredients and add to the mixture. Bake in a greased loaf pan for 1 hour or longer at 325°.

Mrs. Jack Courtright

PUMPKIN BREAD

Makes 1 loaf
2 cups sugar
1½ cups vegetable oil
4 eggs
2 cups pumpkin
3 cups flour, sifted
2 teaspoons baking soda
2 teaspoons baking powder
2 teaspoons cinnamon
2 teaspoons allspice
¼ teaspoon salt
1 cup nuts, chopped

Cream sugar and oil together. Beat at a slow speed adding the eggs one at a time. Add pumpkin and dry ingredients, continuing to beat. Fold in the nuts, and pour into a greased and floured loaf pan filling ½ to ¾ full. Bake at 350° for 50 minutes or until bread tests done.

Mrs. Frank C. Sargent, III

SAFFRON BUNS

Makes 3 dozen buns
2-4 bags saffron
1 cup butter
2½ cups milk
¼ pound cake yeast
1 cup sugar
1 egg
1 teaspoon salt
7-8 cups flour

Chop saffron and set aside. Melt butter, add milk and heat to 98°. Crumble yeast in a large bowl and stir until dissolved with a little of the warm liquid. Add the remaining liquid, saffron, sugar, egg, salt, and flour. Save about 1 cup flour for rolling. Knead dough until it is smooth and does not stick to the sides of the bowl or board. Sprinkle dough with flour and let rise in the bowl for 45 minutes. Knead dough again on board until smooth. Divide into pieces and make desired shapes. Place on greased cookie sheets. Cover with a thin towel and let rise until almost double, at least 45 minutes. Brush with beaten egg and decorate with raisins. Bake 6-8 minutes at 350°. Cover and let cool on rack.

Mrs. William Taylor

LINDA'S SCANDINAVIAN RYE BREAD

Makes 2 loaves
3 cups rye flour
1/3 cup brown sugar
3 teaspoons salt
1 tablespoon grated orange peel
1 teaspoon anise seed
½ teaspoon soda
2 packages yeast
1 cup buttermilk
¼ cup molasses
¼ cup shortening
1 cup warm water
3-3½ cups flour, rye, white or
  whole wheat

Combine the first 7 ingredients in a large bowl. In a saucepan heat buttermilk, molasses and shortening until warm. Add warm water and buttermilk mixture to rye flour mixture. Stir and add the rest of the flour. Knead to form stiff dough that is smooth and elastic. Place in a greased bowl, turning to grease the top. Cover and let rise 1-1½ hours. Punch down and shape into 2 round loaves. Place on a cookie sheet and let rise for 1 hour. Bake at 350° for 45 to 50 minutes.

Mrs. Charles D. Hall

SALLY LUNN

Serves 10-12
1 package dry yeast
¼ cup warm water
2 tablespoons shortening
½ cup sugar
2 eggs
1 teaspoon salt
3½ cups flour, all-purpose
1 cup milk, warm

Soften yeast in warm water. Cream shortening and sugar. Beat in eggs and salt. Stir in 1½ cups of flour and beat vigorously. Stir in milk and yeast and mix well. Add remaining flour and beat again. Cover and let rise in a warm place for about 1 hour, until double in size. Stir down batter and spoon evenly into a greased bundt or tube pan. Cover, let rise again 30-45 minutes until double in size. Bake at 325° for 10 minutes and increase temperature to 375° for 20 minutes. Remove from pan while warm.

Mrs. Geoffrey Hill

VIRGINIA SPOON BREAD

6 servings
1 cup corn meal
2 cups water
1/2 teaspoon salt
2 tablespoons butter
4 eggs, beaten
1 cup milk, cold

Butter the sides and bottom of a 1 1/2 quart baking dish, at least 2 1/2 inches deep. Put the dish in the oven while spoon bread is being prepared. Stir meal into boiling water with salt. Stir for one minute, remove from heat, and add butter. Beat well. Add eggs and beat in cold milk. Pour into hot buttered baking dish. Bake at 375° for 25 minutes. This should be served from the baking dish *right* away.

Mrs. Hillard Willis

SWEET POTATO PONE

6 servings
2 large sweet potatoes, uncooked
   and grated
1/2 cup butter, melted
1 cup milk
1 egg, beaten
1 cup sugar
1 wine glass of sherry or whiskey
1 teaspoon each of allspice,
   clove, cinnamon, and nutmeg
1/2 teaspoon ginger
1/4 teaspoon salt
1 teaspoon vanilla

Grate raw potatoes. Add remaining ingredients. Put into a greased baking dish and bake, uncovered, in a 350° oven for 1 hour or longer. Suggestion: Cover if mixture seems to be drying too much on the top. Evaporated milk can be used, in which case less butter is necessary.

Mrs. Raymond Smith

WAFFLES CARDAMON

Serves 6
1 cup all purpose flour, sifted
2 tablepoons sugar
1 teaspoon baking soda
1/2 teaspoon salt
1 teaspoon cardamon
2 large eggs, separated
1/4 cup butter, melted
1 cup sour cream
1 cup buttermilk

Sift first 5 ingredients together. Beat egg yolks. Beat in butter. Add sour cream and buttermilk. Blend well. Mix with dry mixture. Beat egg whites until soft peaks form. Fold into cream mixture. Pour batter into waffle iron. Bake according to waffle iron directions. Serve with maple syrup or strawberries and sour cream.

Mrs. Tolson Meares

TARRAGON POTATO BREAD

Makes 2 loaves

6 to 6½ cups sifted all-purpose
   flour

2 packages active dry yeast

1½ cups milk

2 tablespoons sugar

2 teaspoons salt

2 tablespoons butter

1 can condensed cream of potato
   soup

½ cup sour cream

¼ cup snipped chives

1 teaspoon dried tarragon,
   crushed

In a large bowl combine 2½ cups of flour and all the yeast. In a pan heat milk, sugar, salt and butter, stirring until butter is melted. Add to dry ingredients in the bowl. Add soup, sour cream, chives, and tarragon. Beat at low speed for ½ minute and then at high speed for 3 minutes. By hand stir in enough of the remaining flour to make a moderately stiff dough. Turn out on a floured surface. Knead until smooth for 5 to 8 minutes. Place in a greased bowl, turning once to grease the dough. Cover and let rise until double, 50-60 minutes. Punch down. Cover and let rise for 10 minutes. Divide dough in half and shape into 2 loaves. Place in 2 greased 9" x 5" x 3" loaf pans. Let dough rise again until doubled in volume, about 30 minutes. Bake at 400° for 30 minutes, covering top loosely with foil if it seems to be browning too much the last 10 minutes. Remove from pans and cool on a rack.

Mrs. George Hero

ZUCCHINI BREAD

Makes 2 loaves

3 eggs

1 cup salad oil

2 cups sugar

3 cups flour, sifted

1 teaspoon salt

1 teaspoon baking soda

¼ teaspoon baking powder

3 teaspoons cinnamon

2 cups zucchini, grated

1 cup pecans, chopped

1 cup raisins

Blend eggs, salad oil and sugar. Combine dry ingredients. Alternately add dry ingredients and zucchini to egg mixture, blending until smooth. Add pecans and raisins. Bake in 2 greased loaf pans for 1 hour at 350°.

Mrs. Julian Arnold

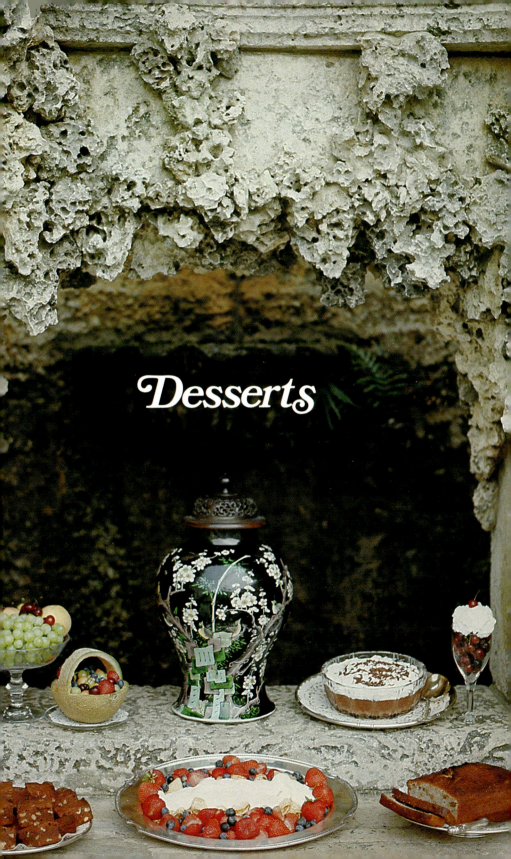

Desserts

DESSERTS

A priceless Chinese K'ang Hsi *famille noire* vase highlights an array of desserts. Part of an extensive collection of oriental works of art in the Lowe Art Museum, the vase has a black background with white flowers and was donated to the Museum by Mr. and Mrs. William Luban. It was photographed in the gardens of Vizcaya, the Italian Renaissance Palace built in 1912 by James Deering.

1-2-3-4 CAKE

1 cup butter
2 cups sugar
3 cups flour
4 eggs
1 cup milk
2 teaspoons vanilla
4 level teaspoons baking powder

With an electric mixer beat butter, sugar and flour thoroughly. Add eggs and beat 2 minutes. Add milk and beat 1 minute. Add flavoring and beat until mixed in. Lastly add baking powder and beat 1 minute. Bake in 2 greased and floured cake pans for 30 minutes at 325°.

Mrs. Peter Ray

APPLE DELIGHT CAKE

Serves 10
4 cups apples, diced and peeled
2 cups sugar
2 cups flour
1½ teaspoons soda
1 teaspoon salt
1 teaspoon cinnamon
2 teaspoons vanilla
2 eggs, beaten
2/3 cup oil
1 cup nuts, chopped
1 cup plumped raisins (optional)
6 tablespoons brandy (optional)

Mix apples and sugar and let sit until sugar is dissolved. Combine dry ingredients and mix with the apples and sugar. Add brandy and vanilla. Add eggs, oil and nuts. Pour into 9" x 13" baking pan and bake at 350° for 50 minutes. Cool and serve warm or frost. Can be frozen.

Variation:
Substitute 1 cup light brown sugar and 1 cup white sugar for 2 cups white sugar.

Mrs. Donald Clark
Mrs. Jack Pfleger, Jr.
Mrs. Peter Ray

MAC'S MOTHERS BUTTER CAKE

1 cup butter, at room temperature
1¾ cup sugar
5 eggs
2 cups cake flour
1 teaspoon vanilla
Pinch of salt
Pinch of cream of tartar

Cream the butter and add sugar gradually. Add the eggs *one* at a time beating 3 minutes on high speed after each egg. Add the flour and beat at low speed for 5 minutes. Add salt, cream of tartar and vanilla and mix. Pour into a greased bundt pan and cook for 1-1½ hours at 350°. This is good served with strawberries and whipped cream or vanilla ice cream.

Mrs. Hugh T. Whitehead

CHRISTMAS BOURBON CAKE

Serves 16
2 cups pecans, chopped
1 cup good bourbon
3½ cups sifted all-purpose flour
1½ teaspoons baking powder
Dash of salt
½ teaspoon nutmeg
½ teaspoon cinnamon
½ teaspoon cloves
2 cups butter
2½ cups sugar
8 eggs, beaten
1 teaspoon vanilla

Butter and flour 10" bundt pan. Combine nuts and ½ cup bourbon. Set aside. Sift next 6 ingredients together. Cream butter and sugar; add eggs to creamed mixture and beat well. Beat in vanilla. Stir flour mixture into creamed mixture. Stir in pecans which have been soaked in bourbon. Pour all into prepared pan. Bake at 350° for 60-70 minutes. Cool. Soak cloth in remaining ½ cup bourbon and wrap around outside of cake; then wrap over all with foil. Refrigerate for 2-3 days before serving. Always re-wrap after using with the bourbon soaked cloth and the foil. This keeps for weeks and a little bit goes a long way.

Mrs. Harry Taylor

CARROT CAKE

Serves 12
CAKE:
2 cups flour
2 cups sugar
2 teaspoons cinnamon
2 teaspoons baking soda
1 teaspoon salt
4 eggs
1 cup vegetable oil
3 cups carrots, grated
FROSTING:
8-ounce package cream cheese
1 box confectioners sugar
¼ cup butter
1 teaspoon vanilla
½ teapsoon maple extract
1 cup pecans, chopped
1-2 tablespoons milk

For the Cake:
Sift the dry ingredients together. Add eggs 1 at a time beating after each one. Beat in the oil. Mix in carrots. Bake in greased and floured cake pans for 30 minutes at 350°.

For the Frosting:
Cream the cheese and butter, and add sugar. Mix in vanilla, maple extract, and nuts. Add milk to obtain desired spreading consistency.

Mrs. Julian Arnold
Jack Pepper
Mrs. William H. Walker

BUCHE DE NOEL

Serves 10-12
THE CAKE:
4 egg yolks
1 cup sugar
½ teaspoon vanilla
4 egg whites
1 cup sifted cake flour
½ teaspoon baking powder
¼ teaspoon salt
4 tablespoons light rum
THE FILLING:
2/3 cup sugar
1/3 cup water
2 egg yolks
½ cup sweet butter, softened
1½ ounces unsweetened
    chocolate, melted
2 tablespoons rum
1 teaspoon instant coffee

To Prepare the Cake:
Beat 4 egg yolks until thick.
Gradually add ½ cup sugar. Stir
in vanilla. Beat in 4 egg whites
until soft peaks form. Gradually
add ½ cup sugar. Beat until stiff
peaks form. Fold in yolk mixture.
Sift together flour, baking
powder and salt; fold into egg
mixture. Spread evenly in
greased and floured jelly roll pan
(15½ by 10½ x 1 inch). Bake at
375° for 10-12 minutes. Loosen
edges and turn onto a dish towel
sprinkled with powdered sugar.
Sprinkle cake with rum. Roll up
cake in towel starting at large end
of cake. Cool.
To Prepare the Filling:
Heat sugar and water to boiling.
Cook to soft ball stage (240°). Beat
egg yolks until thick. Beat in hot
syrup gradually. Beat until cool.
Beat in softened butter, a
teaspoon at a time. Add melted
and cooled chocolate, rum and
coffee powder. Beat until thick.
Unroll cake. Spread the cake
with one-half of the filling. Roll
up the cake starting with the long
side. Diagonally, cut a piece from
one end and place it at the other
end of the log. Frost with
remaining filling and mark with
fork to resemble bark.
Mrs. Orin Ford Pearson

CHEESE CAKE

Serves 12
**1-1/3 cup finely crushed graham
cracker crumbs**
¾ cup walnuts, chopped
½ cup butter, melted
3 eggs, beaten
1 cup sugar
½ teaspoon salt
16 ounces cream cheese
1½ pints sour cream
2 teaspoons vanilla

Prepare crust by mixing the graham cracker crumbs, walnuts and butter thoroughly. Press onto bottom and up the sides of a lightly greased 10″ tube cake pan or springform cake pan. Prepare filling by beating eggs and then adding sugar and salt. Continue to beat and add softened cream cheese, beating until smooth. Fold in sour cream and vanilla. Pour into crust. Bake at 375° for 35 minutes. Cool for 3 hours. Refrigerate at least 5 hours.

Mrs. Frank C. Sargent, III

COOKIE'S CHEESE CAKE

Serves 12
3 tablespoons sugar
1-2/3 cup graham cracker crumbs
1 cup pecan pieces
1 cup butter, melted
3 large packages cream cheese
4 large eggs
¾ cup sugar
1 pint sour cream
¼ cup sugar

Grease a springform pan, and pack it with the combined 3 tablespoons sugar, crumbs, and pecan pieces. Place in 350° oven for 10 minutes. Cream the cheese and add the eggs one at a time. Add the sugar. Pour into the crust and bake at 350° for 30 minutes. Cool and top with the sour cream which has been beaten with ¼ cup of sugar.

Mrs. Kermyt W. Callahan, Jr.

CHOCOLATE ALMOND MOUSSE CAKE

Serves 10
**4 packages (4 ounce size) Baker's
German Sweet Chocolate**
½ cup water
**1-1/3 cups sweetened condensed
milk**
4 cups heavy cream
1 teaspoon vanilla
1 cup slivered toasted almonds
**2 packages lady fingers, cut in
half**

Combine chocolate and water in pan. Stir over very low heat until blended and smooth. Cool. Combine cooled chocolate, milk, cream, and vanilla in large mixing bowl and chill. Then whip until soft peaks form. Fold in almonds. Put lady fingers in the bottom and around the sides of a springform pan, cut side in. Pour in the mousse and freeze.

Mrs. Rodney G. Keep

MINIATURE LEMON CHEESE CAKES

Serves 24
2 large packages cream cheese
4 eggs, beaten
½ to ¾ cup sugar
1 tablespoon lemon juice
1 teaspoon vanilla
Vanilla wafers
1 pint sour cream
½ cup sugar

Mix cream cheese, beaten eggs and sugar. Add the lemon juice and vanilla. Mix well. Line cupcake pans with cupcake papers and put one vanilla wafer in the bottom of each paper. Pour mixture in to ½ full. Bake at 350° for 20 minutes or until golden on top. After cooled, top with the mixture of 1 pint sour cream and ½ cup sugar. You may also use whipped cream, cherry pie filling or fresh pineapple for a topping. Store in the refrigerator. This is a good dessert to serve for a buffet dinner. It is prettier if you remove the paper before serving.

Mrs. James A. Sawyer

CHOCOLATE MERINGUE LAYER CAKE

Serves 8
MERINGUE:
4 egg whites
¼ teaspoon cream of tartar
1 cup sugar
1/3 cup almonds, finely ground
FILLING:
2 egg whites
½ cup sugar
2 tablespoons sweet cocoa
1 cup butter, softened
¼ pound sweet chocolate, melted

For the Meringue:
Beat 4 egg whites with a pinch of salt and cream of tartar. Slowly add ¾ cup of sugar until the meringue is thick and smooth. Fold in the remaining ¼ cup of sugar and ground almonds. Spread 4 8-inch rounds of waxed paper with meringue and bake at 250° for about 15 minutes. Turn over and cook 5 minutes more.

For the Filling:
Beat egg whites over hot but not boiling water. Gradually beat in ½ cup sugar, sweet cocoa, softened butter, and sweet chocolate which has been melted. Beat well, and remove from heat to firm. Fill meringue layers with the filling and dust with confectioners sugar. Let ripen 24 hours.

Mrs. Tom Pennekamp

CHOCOLATE ICEBOX CAKE

Serves 10

2 or 3 packages lady fingers, cut in half

1 dozen eggs

2 small packages semi-sweet chocolate drops or 1 large package

1-2 teaspoons vanilla

2 cups whipped cream

Line springform pan with lady fingers, putting cut side in. Separate eggs and beat yolks until creamy and lemon yellow. Melt the chocolate drops over low heat and add vanilla. Add the hot chocolate to egg yolks and mix well. Beat egg whites until stiff and fold into chocolate mixture. Pour half into the pan and add a layer of lady fingers. Add the remaining chocolate; top with several lady fingers and chill overnight. Remove the sides of the pan and ice with whipped cream just before serving.

Mrs. David C. Schwartzburg

DEVILS FOOD CAKE

2 cups sugar

½ cup butter

2 eggs

2 teaspoons vanilla

½ cup cocoa, sifted

3 cups flour, sifted

2 teaspoons soda

½ teaspoon baking powder

2 cups cold water

Pinch of salt

CARAMEL FROSTING:

¼ cup milk

½ cup butter

1 cup brown sugar

1½ to 2 cups powdered sugar

½ teaspoon vanilla

Cream the butter and add the sugar. Mix and add eggs continuing to mix. Add vanilla. Add the dry ingredients alternately with the water. Beat well and bake for 35-40 minutes at 350° in 2 greased and floured cake pans or an 8" x 12" pan. Frost with caramel frosting.

Caramel Frosting:

Bring milk, butter, and brown sugar to a boil. Cook for 2 minutes after coming to a boil. Remove from heat and add the sugar and vanilla. Beat until smooth and spread on cake.

Mrs. Malcolm Weldon

FAVORITE DEVILS FOOD CAKE

2½ cups flour
1 teaspoon baking soda
1 rounded teaspoon baking powder
¼ teaspoon salt
½ cup butter
2 cups sugar
3 eggs, separated
1 teaspoon vanilla
1 cup buttermilk
2/3 cup cocoa dissolved in ½ cup boiling water

Sift flour, soda, baking powder and salt together. Cream the butter and slowly beat in the sugar and egg yolks. Add the flour mixture alternately with the milk. Then add the cocoa and vanilla. Fold in stiffly beaten egg whites and bake in 2 greased and floured cake pans for 25 minutes at 375°. Frost with favorite chocolate frosting.

Mrs. Jack Courtright
Mrs. Hagood Clarke
Mrs. F.E. Kitchens

FAVORITE CHOCOLATE CAKE FROSTING

½ cup butter
4 tablespoons cocoa
6 tablespoons sweet milk
1 box powdered sugar
1 teaspoon vanilla
1 cup pecans

Bring first three ingredients to a boil. Add sugar, vanilla, and pecans, pour over warm cake.

Mrs. Hagood Clarke

FUDGE CREAM CHEESE CAKE

Serves 12
½ cup plus 2 tablespoons butter, soft
8 ounce package cream cheese
2¼ cups sugar
1 tablespoon cornstarch
3 eggs
1½ cups plus 3 tablespoons milk
1½ teaspoons vanilla
2 cups self rising flour
¼ teaspoon baking soda
4 envelopes or 4 ounces unsweetened chocolate

Grease and flour a 13"x 9" pan. In a small mixing bowl add 2 tablespoons butter, cream cheese, ¼ cup sugar, cornstarch, 1 egg, 3 tablespoons milk and ½ teaspoon vanilla. Beat until smooth. Combine remaining ingredients in a large bowl and beat. Spread ½ of the chocolate batter into cake pan. Spoon the cheese mixture over the chocolate batter, spreading carefully to cover. Spoon the remaining chocolate batter over the cream cheese and spread to cover. Bake at 350° for 50 to 60 minutes.

Mrs. Dwight Plyler, Jr.

FUDGE CAKE

Serves 12
½ cup Hershey's cocoa
2/3 to 3/4 cup strong coffee
1 teaspoon vanilla
2 cups sugar
½ cup butter
½ cup sour cream
' ½ teaspoon baking soda
2 cups regular flour
⅛ teaspoon salt
3 egg whites, beaten stiff

Dissolve cocoa in hot coffee. Stir well and add vanilla. Cream butter and sugar. To this add cocoa mixture, sour cream mixed with baking soda, and flour which has been sifted with salt. Beat well. Fold in stiffly beaten egg whites. Bake in 3 greased and floured 9 inch layer pans at 350° for 15 to 20 minutes. Cool in pans. Before icing swab layers lightly with rum.

Mrs. Thomas J. Cogswell

COFFEE AND RUM ICING FOR FUDGE CAKE

6 tablespoons soft butter
4 cups powdered sugar
1 teaspoon vanilla
6 tablespoons strong coffee (if weather is humid you may want to reduce this by half)
1 tablespoon rum

Cream butter and add powdered sugar. Add vanilla and then coffee to thin. Add rum when icing is almost the right consistency.

Mrs. Thomas J. Cogswell

FUDGE CUPCAKES

Chocolate lovers, they are yummy!

Makes 16 Cupcakes
1¾ cup sugar
1 cup flour
4 eggs
4 squares semi-sweet or unsweetened chocolate
1 cup butter
1½ cups pecans, chopped or to taste
1 teaspoon vanilla

Combine sugar, flour, and eggs. Blend, do not beat. Melt chocolate and butter in a saucepan, add nuts and stir. Cool a little. Combine flour mixture, chocolate mixture and vanilla. Blend and pour into lined muffin tins about ¾ full. Bake at 325° for 30 to 40 minutes.

Mrs. James A. Sawyer

HERSHEY BAR CAKE

This is a very moist and smooth cake.

1 cup butter
2 cups sugar
4 eggs
1—10-ounce plain Hershey bar
15-ounce can Hershey syrup
2½ cups flour
1 teaspoon baking soda
1 cup buttermilk
1 teaspoon vanilla

Cream butter and sugar well. Add eggs one at a time mixing after each. Melt candy in a double boiler. Add syrup to melted candy. Add chocolate mixture to the butter, sugar, and egg mixture. Sift flour. Dissolve soda in the buttermilk. Add the flour and milk alternately. Add vanilla. Bake at 325° in a large 12 cup Bundt or tube pan which has been greased and floured, for 1½ to 2 hours.

Mrs. Phillip Newcomm

FANTASTIC HEALTH FOOD FRUITCAKE

10 pounds of fruitcake (100 servings)
1 cup butter
1 cup brown sugar
¾ cup dark honey
8 eggs
1 tablespoon mace
2 tablespoons cinnamon
2 tablespoons nutmeg
2 tablespoons cloves
2 tablespoons vanilla
2 tablespoons rum or rum flavoring
1 pound organic raisins
1 pound organic currants
1½ pounds unsulphured apricots
¾ pound whole wheat flour
2 tablespoons brewers' yeast
1 pound dates, pitted
1 pound pecans, chopped
1 pound walnuts, chopped
3 tablespoons grated fresh orange peel
3 tablespoons grated fresh lemon rind

Soak raisins, currants and apricots in warm water overnight. Cream together butter, sugar and honey in large 8 quart container. Add eggs, two at a time. Mix dry spices together and add to mixture, along with flavorings. Drain the soaked fruit and dust with a mixture of stoneground whole wheat and brewers' yeast (or a mixture of flour and wheat germ). Add to creamed butter and sugar mixture above. Dust nuts and dates with remainder of flour and add to above mixture. Add grated peels. Mix carefully so that no flour shows. Mixture will be thick and dark. Pour into oiled and papered pan about 2 by 8½ by 12 inches or several smaller pans. Gently drop pan a few times onto a hard surface to pack mixture. Bake at 300° for 3 hours, or until a test straw comes out clean. Let cool and cut into convenient sized cakes. Wrap in foil or transparent wrapping and keep in refrigerator or freezer.

Mrs. Donald Clark

THE PHILLIPS' DARK FRUITCAKE

Makes 10-12 cakes
2 pounds cherries
2 pounds pineapple
½ pound citron
½ pound orange
2 pounds currants
2 pounds white raisins
½ pound lemon
1 cup rum for soaking fruit
1 pound butter
1 pound dark brown sugar
1 cup boiling water
½ teaspoon salt
1 teaspoon soda
1½ teaspoons cinnamon
2 teaspoons cloves, powdered
3½ teaspoons allspice
1 cup molasses (dark black)
1½ cups flour
2 pounds pecans, chopped
1 dozen eggs, beaten
4½ cups flour
1 cup wine or rum

Soak fruit for 2 days in 1 cup rum (more if desired, keep adding). Stir occasionally and cover. Cream butter and sugar. Pour 1 cup boiling water over salt, soda, and spices. Add molasses and stir. Sift 1½ cups flour over fruit and nuts and toss lightly. This keeps fruit and nuts from sinking to bottom. Add beaten eggs to butter and sugar mixture. Add flour, wine, spices and fruit which has soaked for 2 days and then tossed with flour. Line greased pans with brown paper and grease again over the paper. Pour mixture in the pans. Bake at 250° for several hours until small crack forms in center and a toothpick inserted into crack comes out clean. Remove from pans immediately.

Mrs. George Baya

OATMEAL CAKE

1 cup quick oatmeal
1¼ cups boiling water
½ cup butter
1 cup white sugar
1 cup brown sugar
2 eggs
1 teaspoon vanilla
1 teaspoon soda
1½ cups self-rising flour
Pinch salt
1½ teaspoons cinnamon

Pour boiling water over oatmeal, and let stand until cool. Cream butter and the sugars and beat in the eggs. Then add oatmeal and vanilla. Sift dry ingredients together and add to creamed mixture. Beat well and bake in 2 9-inch greased and floured pans at 350° for 30-35 minutes. Good with a chocolate icing.

Mrs. John Brendle

MANGO CAKE WITH LEMON ICING

Serves 10
CAKE:
1½ cups raisins
½ cup shortening
1½ cups brown sugar (well
  packed)
2 eggs
1½ cups mango pureé
3 cups sifted cake flour
1½ teaspoons baking soda
¾ teaspoon salt
1½ teaspoons cinnamon,
  ground
¾ teaspoon cloves, ground
¾ teaspoon nutmeg, ground
ICING:
1/3 cup butter
3 cups sifted powdered sugar
1 tablespoon water
grated rind of 1 lemon

For the Cake:
Pour boiling water over raisins to soften. Let set aside a few minutes and then drain. Cream shortening. Add sugar and beat until fluffy. Add eggs one at a time and beat well after each addition. Add mango pureé and mix. Sift together flour, soda, salt and spices. Stir into creamed mixture. Mix well and then add raisins. Pour into oiled and floured 9″ x 13″ pan and bake at 325° for 50 minutes or until cake tests done. Cool before frosting.
For the Frosting:
Cream the butter and add sugar, water, and grated rind. Beat rapidly until creamy enough to spread.
Mrs. R. Lowell Goldman

ORANGE SLICE CAKE

Serves 20
1 teaspoon baking soda
½ cup buttermilk
1 cup butter
2 cups sugar
4 eggs
1 teaspoon salt
3½ cups flour
2 cups nuts, chopped
1 pound orange slice candy
1 pound sliced dates
1 can coconut (optional)

Dissolve soda in the buttermilk. Cream butter, add sugar, and then eggs. Alternately add ½ the flour, salt mixture with the buttermilk. Roll the nuts, candy and dates in the remaining flour. Add these to the batter with coconut. Bake in a greased tube pan for 2½ hours at 250°.
Mrs. Dwight Plyler, Jr.

ROARING GAP POUND CAKE

1 cup butter
½ cup Crisco
2½ to 3 cups sugar
6 eggs
½ teaspoon baking powder
3 cups flour
¼ teaspoon salt
1 cup milk
1 teaspoon vanilla extract
1 teaspoon lemon extract or
   1 teaspoon grated lemon rind

Cream butter and shortening. Gradually add sugar, creaming well. Add eggs one at a time beating well after each addition. Add sifted dry ingredients gradually with milk and continue beating. Add flavorings and turn into a greased and floured tube pan. Bake at 325° for approximately 1½ hours or until done.

Mrs. Arthur Spaugh

SEVEN-UP POUND CAKE

Serves 16-20
CAKE:
3 cups sugar
1½ cups butter
5 eggs
3 cups flour
2 teaspoons almond extract
1 7-Up (7 ounces)
ICING:
1½ cups sugar
1/3 cup cold water
1 tablespoon white Karo syrup
Pinch cream of tartar
2 egg whites

For the Cake:
Cream sugar and butter together. Beat until light and fluffy. Add eggs one at a time and beat well. Add flour. Beat in almond extract and 7-Up. Pour batter into well greased, floured jumbo fluted mold. Bake for 1 to 1¼ hours at 325°.

For the Icing:
In saucepan mix all ingredients together except egg whites. Bring to a soft boil. Remove from heat. Beat egg whites. Fold into cooked mixture. Beat together until thick enough to spread.

Mrs. John Patterson

CHRISTMAS SPICE CAKE

Delicious and simple.

1 cup vegetable oil
2 cups self-rising flour
2 cups sugar
3 whole eggs
1 heaping teaspoon cinnamon
1 heaping teaspoon nutmeg
1 heaping teaspoon ground
   cloves
1 junior size or 2 small jars Puree
   of Prune baby food

Put all ingredients into a bowl and mix well. Pour into a well-greased bundt pan or tube pan. Bake at 325° for 45 minutes or until done. Cool. Place on a cake plate and garnish with fresh holly.

Mrs. David C. Schwartzburg

SOUR CREAM POUND CAKE

1 cup butter
3 cups sugar, sifted
6 jumbo eggs
2½ cups flour, sifted
8-ounce carton sour cream
¼ teaspoon baking soda
1 tablespoon vanilla

Butter bundt pan generously. Sprinkle with flour. In mixing bowl, cream butter until fluffy. Add sugar and continue creaming. Add eggs, beating well after each egg. Add flour, alternating with sour cream (a bit at a time) beating well. Add baking soda and vanilla. Bake at 325° for 1 hour and 20 minutes. Remove immediately. Turn on cake platter while hot.

Mrs. D. Alan Nichols
Mrs. Jane Warren

SPICE CAKE

Serves 20
½ pound butter
½ cup vegetable oil
3 cups sugar
5 eggs
3 cups all-purpose flour
½ teaspoon mace
½ teaspoon allspice
¼ teaspoon nutmeg
½ teaspoon cloves
½ teaspoon salt
½ teaspoon baking powder
1 cup plus 2 tablespoons milk
½ teaspoon vanilla

Cream butter, oil, and sugar together until light and fluffy. Contine to cream, adding the eggs, one at a time. Sift flour, spices, salt and baking powder together. Repeat sifting. Add the dry mixture to the egg mixture alternating with the milk until all of the flour and milk are combined. Beat in the vanilla and pour the batter into a greased and floured tube pan. Bake at 325° for 1 hour and 15 minutes or until done.

Mrs. Arthur Spaugh

STRAWBERRY MERINGUE CAKE

Serves 15-17
2-layer size yellow cake mix
1 cup orange juice
1/3 cup water
4 egg yolks
1 teaspoon grated orange peel
4 egg whites
¼ teaspoon cream of tartar
1 cup sugar
1 quart fresh strawberries
2 cups whipping cream
¼ cup sugar

Combine cake mix, orange juice, water, egg yolks and orange peel. Beat 4 minutes on medium speed of electric mixer. Pour into 2 greased and waxed paper-lined 9" pans. Beat egg whites with cream of tartar to soft peaks; gradually add the 1 cup sugar, beating to stiff peaks. Gently spread meringue evenly over batter. Bake at 350° for 35-40 minutes. Cool. Carefully remove layers from pans, keeping meringue side on top. Set aside a few berries for garnish and slice remainder. Whip cream with the ¼ cup sugar. Spread 2/3 of the whipped cream over meringue on bottom cake layer. Arrange sliced berries on whipped cream. Add top layer, meringue side up. Garnish with remaining whipped cream and whole berries.

Mrs. Don Jefferson

WHISKEY CAKE

Serves 24
2 cups granulated sugar
2½ cups firmly packed light
    brown sugar
5½ cups flour, sifted
¼ teaspoon salt
1 teaspoon ground mace
1½ cups sweet butter
6 eggs
2 cups bourbon
3 cups pecans, chopped

Grease and flour 10" tube or bundt pan. Mix sugars. Sift flour, salt and mace together. Cream butter until fluffy. Add one half of the sugar mixture and beat until smooth. Beat eggs till fluffy. Gradually add sugars beating constantly until smooth. Blend in butter and egg mixture. Alternately, add flour and bourbon, beginning and ending with flour. Stir in pecans. Pour into prepared pan. Bake at 300° for 1½ to 1¾ hours or until cake shrinks from sides. Cool for 15 to 20 minutes, then turn cake onto cake rack and cool. This keeps well if well-sealed, but DO NOT FREEZE.

Mrs. Orin Ford Pearson

WINE OR WHISKEY CAKE

Serves 8
4 whole eggs
1 package yellow cake mix
3 ounce package instant vanilla
   pudding
¾ cup white Chablis or cream
   sherry or 2 ounces whiskey
½ cup salad oil
¼ teaspoon almond flavoring
1 teaspoon vanilla

Combine all ingredients. Beat for
4 to 5 minutes. Pour into greased
and floured 10″ bundt pan. Bake
at 350° for 45 to 50 minutes.
Remove from pan immediately.
Cool on wire rack.

Variation:
Add to batter 1 cup chopped nuts
and 1 cup chopped cherries.

Mrs. William Atwill
Mrs. Jack White
Mrs. Thomas Wood

MOIST BROWNIES

Makes 16 Squares
½ cup butter
2 ounces unsweetened chocolate
1 cup sugar
1 teaspoon vanilla
2 eggs
2/3 cup flour
½ cup nuts
¼ teaspoon salt
½ teaspoon baking powder

Melt butter and chocolate in pan.
Stir in sugar, vanilla, eggs, flour,
nuts, salt and baking powder.
Blend well. Pour into greased
8″ x 8″ pan. Bake at 350° for 30-35
minutes. Recipe can be doubled
and baked in a 9″x 13″ pan for
same length of time.

Mrs. Julian Arnold
Mrs. Richard O. Dowling
Mrs. F. E. Kitchens

ICING:
2 ounces bittersweet chocolate,
   melted
1/3 cup sour cream
1 teaspoon vanilla
⅛ teaspoon salt
2½ cups powdered sugar

Melt the chocolate in top of
double boiler and add the sour
cream, vanilla and salt. Remove
from heat and beat in powdered
sugar. Spread on cool brownies.

Mrs. Julian Arnold

QUICK CREAM CHEESE BROWNIES

Serves 40
1 family size package walnut
  brownie mix
1 teaspoon vanilla
¼ teaspoon almond extract
16 ounces cream cheese (room
  temperature)
¾ cup sugar
1 teaspoon vanilla
2 tablespoons flour

Prepare brownies as directed adding vanilla and almond. Spread in a greased 9 x 13 x 2 inch pan. Beat cream cheese with sugar until fluffy. Add vanilla, then flour and beat well. Spread cream cheese over brownies with a butter knife. Swirl cream cheese into chocolate for a marbeled effect. Bake at 350° for 35 minutes.

Mrs. Taffy Gould Beber

BUTTERSCOTCH BARS

Serves 12
½ cup butter
2 cups brown sugar
2 eggs
¾ cup nuts
1½ cup flour
¼ teaspoon salt
1 teaspoon vanilla
Powdered sugar

Melt butter and sugar, cool slightly. Add eggs and stir, add other ingredients. Pour into greased and floured 7" x 11" pan. Bake at 325° for 25-30 minutes. Cool slightly. Cut into strips and roll in powdered sugar.

Mrs. Thomas P. Wenzel, Jr.

BUTTERSCOTCH BROWNIES

½ cup butter
1 box brown sugar, light
2 eggs
2 cups flour
1 teaspoon baking powder
½ teaspoon salt
1 teaspoon vanilla
½ cup pecans, chopped

Melt butter in large pan, add sugar and then eggs. Sift dry ingredients together and add to sugar and butter. Mix well. Add vanilla and pecans. Mixture will be very stiff. Spread in buttered 9" x 13" pan and bake for 30 minutes at 325°. Do not overcook.

Mrs. R. Layton Mank

AUNT PAT'S BUTTERSCOTCH ICEBOX COOKIES

Makes 7 dozen
1 cup butter
1 box brown sugar, light
2 teaspoons vanilla
2 beaten eggs
3¾ cups flour
1 teaspoon soda
¼ teaspoon salt
2 cups pecans, whole or chopped

Cream butter and sugar well. Add vanilla, then the eggs. Sift dry ingredients and beat into sugar mixture. Add pecans and mix well. Form into rolls and chill thoroughly, several hours or overnight. Slice and bake at 350° for 8-10 minutes.

Mrs. Barbara Bachmann

CHRISTMAS COOKIES

Makes 40 cookies
1 cup butter (softened to room temperature)
2 cups flour
4 heaping tablespoons powdered sugar
1 teaspoon vanilla
½ cup pecans, coarsely chopped

Mix the first 4 ingredients thoroughly and then add pecans. Roll in balls, and then roll balls in the powdered sugar. Bake at 350° for 8-10 minutes or until they are brown on the bottom. Roll them in powdered sugar again before storing.

Mrs. Jack Courtright

CHRISTMAS KARO LACE COOKIES

Makes 4 dozen cookies
1 cup sifted flour
1 cup flaked coconut or nuts (almonds or pecans, chopped)
½ cup Karo crystal clear syrup, light
½ cup firmly packed brown sugar
½ cup butter
1 teaspoon vanilla

Mix the flour and coconut. Combine the syrup, brown sugar, and butter in a heavy saucepan. Bring to a boil over medium heat, stirring constantly. Remove from the heat, and gradually blend in the flour mixture and then the vanilla. Drop onto a foil covered cookie sheet by scant teaspoonfuls 3 inches apart. Bake in a 350° oven 8-10 minutes. Cool 3-4 minutes on wire racks until the foil peels off. Remove the foil and place the cookies on a rack covered with absorbent paper. Keep in an air tight container.

Mrs. Malcolm D. McNaughton

CHOCOLATE MERINGUE KISSES

Makes 3 dozen
2 egg whites
Dash of salt
⅛ teaspoon cream of tartar
1 teaspoon vanilla
¾ cup sugar
6-ounce package semi-sweet
　chocolate chips
½ cup pecans, chopped

Beat egg whites with salt, cream of tartar, and vanilla until soft peaks form. Slowly add sugar, beating until stiff peaks form. Carefully fold in chocolate chips and nuts. Drop by rounded teaspoonfuls onto a well greased cookie sheet. Bake in slow oven at 300° for about 25 minutes.

Mrs. Bishop Davidson
Mrs. James A. Sawyer

DATE BALLS

1 pound dates, cut up
1 cup butter
2 cups sugar
5 cups Rice Krispies
2 cups nuts, chopped
Powdered sugar

Cook the dates, butter, and sugar together until sticky. Then pour over the Rice Krispies and nuts and combine well. Let cool a bit and roll into balls. Then sprinkle with powdered sugar.

Mrs. John Brendle

JOHNNIE'S RICH DATE DROPS

Makes 6 dozen
1½ cups walnuts, chopped
2 teaspoons imitation maple
　flavoring
1 cup butter, softened
½ cup white sugar
1 cup brown sugar, packed
2 eggs
1 teaspoon vanilla
¼ teaspoon salt
2¼ cups flour
1 tablespoon baking soda
2 cups dates, chopped

Combine chopped nuts with maple flavoring and set aside. Cream butter and sugars until light and fluffy. Add eggs and vanilla and beat well. Add sifted dry ingredients and mix thoroughly. Stir in dates and nuts. Drop by teaspoonfuls onto ungreased cookie sheet. Bake at 350° for 10-12 minutes until lightly browned.

Mrs. Edward Weed

FORGOTTEN COOKIES

Makes 50 cookies
2 egg whites
2/3 cup sugar
1 teaspoon vanilla
Pinch of salt
6 ounces chocolate chips or 1 cup
    nuts

Beat egg whites until peaks begin to form. Add sugar gradually and continue beating until stiff peaks form. Add remaining ingredients and drop by spoon onto cookie sheet. Put into oven that has been preheated to 375°. Turn the oven off and leave overnight.

Mrs. Robert Bartelt

HAUREKAKOR

Makes 3 dozen
½ cup butter
¾ cup sugar
1 cup oatmeal
2 tablespoons sifted flour
1 teaspoon baking powder
1 egg

Melt butter and remove from heat. Stir in the rest of the ingredients. Drop by small spoonfuls on very well greased and floured cookie sheet, 3 inches apart. Bake at 375° for 6-8 minutes. Cool on the sheet for a few minutes until set. These are very thin and crunchy cookies, which will burn easily if not watched carefully.

Mrs. Orin Ford Pearson

ICE BOX COOKIES

Makes 12 dozen
3 cups flour
½ teaspoon double acting
    baking powder
½ teaspoon baking soda
1 teaspoon salt
1 cup butter
1 cup brown sugar, firmly
    packed
1 cup granulated sugar
2 eggs
1 teaspoon vanilla
1 cup nuts, finely chopped

Sift flour, measure, and resift 3 times with baking powder, soda and salt. Cream butter with sugars thoroughly. Add eggs, vanilla, and nuts. Mix well. Add flour mixture in 4 or 5 portions, mixing thoroughly after each addition. Divide dough into 4 portions. Shape each portion in a roll ¾ inch across. Wrap in wax paper. Chill several hours until dough is stiff enough to slice. Cut slices ¼ to ⅜ inch thick with a sharp knife. Bake on ungreased cookie sheet at 350° for about 10 minutes, or until lightly browned. Remove from pan to cake racks.

Mrs. Bishop Davidson

JILL'S COOKIES

¼ pound butter
Pinch salt
2/3 cup raw sugar
1/3 cup milk
½ teaspoon baking soda
1 cup rolled oats
1 cup flour

Cream butter, salt and sugar. Dissolve the soda in the milk. Add the flour and the oats alternately with the milk. Roll out on a greased cookie sheet. Score in squares with a knife. Bake at 350° until crisp.

Mrs. William Mooney

LEMON COCONUT SQUARES

Serves 24
1½ cups flour
½ cup brown sugar
½ cup butter (1 stick)
2 eggs
1 cup brown sugar
¼ teaspoon salt
1½ cups coconut, shredded
1 cup nuts, chopped
½ teaspoon vanilla
2 tablespoons flour
½ teaspoon baking powder
1 cup powdered sugar
1 tablespoon butter
Strained juice of 1 lemon

Mix the first 3 ingredients and press down in a buttered 9" x 13" pan. Bake at 275° for 10 minutes. Combine the next 8 ingredients and spread on the top of baked mixture. Bake 20 minutes at 350°. While warm spread with a frosting made of the powdered sugar, butter, and lemon juice.

Mrs. Frederick A. Alders

Variation:
Add 4 ounces of Chocolate chips to batter before second baking.

SUNSHINE SQUARES

½ cup butter
¼ cup powdered sugar
1 cup flour
2 eggs. beaten
1 cup sugar
½ teaspoon baking powder
¼ teaspoon salt
2 tablespoons flour
3 tablespoons lemon juice
Lemon rind

Cream first 3 ingredients and press in a 9 inch square pan. Bake 15 minutes at 350°. Add together the beaten eggs, the sugar, baking powder, salt and flour. Then add the lemon juice and lemon rind. Pour over a crust and return to a 350° oven for 25 minutes. When cool, dust with powdered sugar.

Mrs. Thomas J. Cogswell

PRALINE COOKIES

Makes 6 dozen
2/3 cup butter
1 cup sugar
½ cup dark syrup molasses
2 eggs
1 tablespoon vanilla
1¾ cup sifted flour
½ tablespoon baking soda
½ tablespoon cinnamon
¼ teaspoon salt
1 cup nuts

Slowly melt butter and cool. Add sugar and molasses and mix well. Add eggs and vanilla and beat well. Sift together the flour, soda, cinnamon and salt. Add to the mixture. Add nuts. Drop on greased and floured Teflon coated cookie sheet, leaving plenty of room between because they spread out. Bake at 375° for 5-8 minutes. Watch carefully because they burn easily. Remove from cookie sheet immediately and cool on wire racks. Store in air tight container as soon as cooled.
Mrs. James Billings

POTATO CHIP COOKIES

Makes 6 to 8 dozen
1 cup butter
1 cup margarine
1½ cups sugar
2 teaspoon vanilla
2 egg yolks
4 cups pre-sifted flour
1½ cups potato chip crumbs
    (crushed to about dime size)
1 cup pecans, chopped

Cream butter, margarine and sugar with an electric mixer. Add vanilla and egg yolks; beat until well blended. Gradually add flour, beating after each addition. Blend in potato chips and pecans. Drop by teaspoonfuls on a lightly greased cookie sheet. Bake in preheated oven at 350° to 375° for 12 to 15 minutes or until nicely brown.
Mrs. Frank Marston

RUM BALLS

1 pound dates, finely chopped
1 cup rum
1 cup nuts, chopped
coconut, shredded

Cover dates with rum and let sit overnight. Mix nuts with date mixture, then roll into balls. Roll in coconut. Can be kept for a long time in a covered container.
Mrs. Fred E. Luhm

SCOTCH COOKIES

1 cup sweet butter
1 cup sugar
1 egg
3 cups flour
½ teaspoon baking soda
1 teaspoon cream of tartar
¼ teaspoon salt (only if
   margarine is used)

Mix ingredients in order given.
Roll out (not too thin) and cut.
Bake at 350°. Decorate as desired.

June Coonse Hoagland

TOFFEE SQUARES

Makes 3½ to 4½ dozen
1 cup butter
1 cup brown sugar
1 egg yolk
1 teaspoon vanilla
¼ teaspoon salt
2 cups all-purpose flour
1 bar German sweet chocolate
1 cup nuts, chopped (optional)

Cream butter and sugar. Add egg
yolk and vanilla. Gradually add
sifted flour and salt. Spread thin
on a 13" x 10" pan leaving about
an inch border. Bake 20-25
minutes at 350°. Break up the
chocolate and as it softens on top
of cooked mixture spread evenly
over top. Cut while warm. It can
be refrigerated or frozen.

Variation:
Add chocolate chips and nuts to
batter before baking.

Mrs. John Aurell
Mrs. Conway Hamilton

BUTTER PIE CRUST

Enough for 2 pies
4½ cups all-purpose flour
1½ cups shortening (1 cup
   Crisco and ½ cup butter)
1½ teaspoons salt

Cut shortening into flour and salt
mixture till crumbly. Store in
refrigerator until needed. Add 2
to 3 tablespoons cold water to
about half of the mixture for one
2-crust pie. Bake for 10-15
minutes at 450°

Mrs. Richard O. Dowling

FLAKY PIE CRUST

Makes 2 pies, 9 inches
4 cups unsifted flour
½ teaspoon salt
1-1/3 cups vegetable oil
2/3 cup milk

Mix all of the ingredients with a fork. Roll dough between pieces of waxed paper. The dough will be moist and sticky. Arrange the dough in a pie pan by peeling one piece of wax paper off the dough and inverting the dough into the pie pan. Then carefully peel away the remaining wax paper and crimp the edges of the dough.

Mrs. Harper Davidson

HEAVENLY PIE CRUST

1½ cups shortening
3 cups sifted flour
1 egg
1 teaspoon salt
1 teaspoon vinegar
5 tablespoons ice water

Cut shortening into the flour and mix until crumbly. Beat the egg and add salt, vinegar, and water. Mix with the flour mixture, and make into 2 balls. Chill 15-20 minutes. Roll between 2 sheets of wax paper.

Mrs. Orin Ford Pearson

CHEESE PIE

Serves 8
1½ cups graham cracker crumbs
5 tablespoons butter, melted
11 ounces cream cheese
2 eggs
½ cup sugar
1 teaspoon vanilla
2 cups sour cream
¼ cup sugar

Line 9" pie plate with crumb and butter mixture. Beat cream cheese until smooth. Add eggs, one at a time, beating after each. Continue beating at a low speed and add sugar and vanilla. Pour into pie crust and bake 20 minutes at 350°. Blend sour cream with sugar and spread evenly over cheese mixture. Turn off heat and return the pie to the oven for 4 minutes. Cool and then chill. Before serving, garnish the pie with whole strawberries, or pass a bowl of strawberries and juice from a package of frozen strawberries.

Mrs. Tolson Meares

BRANDY ALEXANDER PIE

Serves 8
1½ cups fine graham cracker crumbs
1/3 cup butter, melted
1 envelope unflavored gelatin
1/3 cup sugar
⅛ teaspoon salt
½ cup cold water
3 egg yolks, beaten
¼ cup creme de cacao
¼ cup cognac
3 egg whites
1/3 cup sugar
1 cup heavy cream, whipped
4 ounce bar of sweet baking chocolate for curls

Prepare a 9" graham cracker crust by combining the graham cracker crumbs and melted butter; then press into 9" pie plate and bake at 350° for about 10 minutes. Cool completely. In a small saucepan, combine gelatin, sugar and salt. Stir in the water and egg yolks. Cook over low heat, stirring constantly until gelatin dissolves and mixture thickens slightly. Remove from heat; stir in creme de cacao and cognac. Chill until partially thickened. Beat egg whites to soft peaks. Gradually beat in 1/3 cup of sugar until stiff; fold in thickened gelatin mixture. Whip cream; fold into mixture and chill again until mixture mounds slightly. Pile mixture into pie crust and chill several hours or overnight. Top with chocolate curls. To make chocolate curls, have a bar of sweet baking chocolate at room temperature. Place the bar flat on firm surface. Hold bar firmly; press a floating blade potato peeler against chocolate and draw from one end of bar to the other.
Mrs. Orin Ford Pearson

CHESS PIE

1 cup dark brown sugar
½ cup granulated sugar
1 tablespoon flour
2 eggs
2 tablespoons sweet milk
1 teaspoon vanilla
½ cup butter, melted
Graham cracker crust or uncooked pie shell (see Index)

Mix the sugars and the flour. Beat in eggs, milk, and vanilla. Add melted butter, and beat until just blended. Pour into crust or pie shell and bake at 375° until set or for 45 minutes. Serve with whipped cream or pecans.
Mrs. Warren Samuel Tucker, Jr.

CHOCOLATE CHIFFON PIE

Serves 6-8
1 envelope unflavored gelatin
¾ cup water
2 squares of chocolate, unsweetened
1 cup sugar
4 eggs, separated
¼ teaspoon salt
1 teaspoon vanilla
1 pie crust, baked (see Index)

Soften gelatin in ¼ cup cold water. Put ½ cup water in top of double boiler, and add 2 squares of chocolate. When chocolate has melted add ½ cup sugar, the egg yolks slightly beaten and the salt. Cook until of custard consistency, stirring constantly. Add softened gelatin to the hot custard and stir until dissolved. Cool and add vanilla. When mixture begins to thicken, fold in stiffly beaten egg whites to which the other ½ cup of sugar has been added. Fill baked pie shell or graham cracker crust and chill. A thin layer of whipped cream may be added just before serving.

Mrs. Edward C. Vining

TOASTED COCONUT PIE

Serves 8
3 eggs beaten
1½ cups sugar
½ cup butter, melted
4 teaspoons lemon juice
1 teaspoon vanilla
1-1/3 cup flaked coconut (3½ ounce can)
9-inch unbaked pastry shell
Whipped cream for garnish
Toasted coconut for garnish

Thoroughly combine eggs, sugar, butter, lemon juice and vanilla. Stir in coconut. Pour into pie shell. Bake at 350° for 40-45 minutes or until knife inserted in middle comes out clean. Cool. Garnish with whipped cream and toasted coconut. To make scalloped edge on pie shell, mold pastry around a bowl, shape with tablespoon measuring spoon.

Mrs. G. William McMillan

FRENCH SILK PIE

1 scant cup sugar
½ cup butter
2 squares unsweetened
  chocolate, melted
1 teaspoon vanilla
2 eggs
Baked pie shell (see Index)
½ pint whipped cream to which
  4 tablespoons sugar has been
  added
Shaved chocolate

Cream sugar and butter. Add chocolate and vanilla. Add 1 egg at a time and beat 5 minutes after each egg at high speed. Pour into baked pie shell. Top with whipped cream and shaved chocolate. Refrigerate until served.

Mrs. W. Samuel Tucker, Jr.
Mrs. Hugh T. Whitehead

KEY LIME PIE I

2 baked pie crusts or graham
  cracker crust (see Index)
1 can sweetened condensed milk
6 egg yolks
½ cup key lime juice
6 egg whites
1 tablespoon cream of tartar
1 cup sugar

Whip milk and egg yolks together until light and creamy. Use a regular electric beater, medium high speed, about 8 minutes. Add the lime juice and let rotate low speed for 1 second. Fold a few times with a rubber spatula to be sure juice is thoroughly blended. Pour into baked pie shell and let stand. Beat the egg whites with the cream of tartar for 5 full minutes. Add one cup sugar and beat 5 full minutes again. Put on the pie and brown in the oven at 350°. This makes two 8-inch pies or one large 10-12 inch pie.

Fern Butters
Former owner of the Fern Inn
on Islamorada, Florida

KEY LIME PIE II

Serves 8
¼ teaspoon cream of tartar
4 egg whites
1 cup sugar
4 egg yolks
½ teaspoon salt
½ cup sugar
1/3 cup key lime juice
1 teaspoon lime rind, grated
2 cups whipped cream

Sprinkle cream of tartar on egg whites; beat until frothy. Very gradually add 1 cup sugar. Beat until very stiff and glossy. Lightly grease a 9″ pie pan and spread the mixture making a slight depression in the center. Bake 20 minutes at 275° and increase to 300° for 40 minutes. Turn oven off and open door so that the meringue will cool slowly. Beat egg yolks; add salt, ½ cup sugar and the lime juice. Cook in a double boiler for 10 minutes or until thick; cool. Fold in lime rind and 1 cup of whipping cream. Put in pie crust. Top with whipped cream to which a bit of sugar has been added and chill for at least 4 hours before serving.

Mrs. Dale Moseley

NO-BAKE LEMON CHIFFON PIE

Serves 8-10
3-ounce package lemon Jello
½ cup sugar
2/3 cup hot water
1/3 cup hot lemon juice
1 teaspoon lemon rind, grated
1 cup undiluted evaporated milk
2 tablespoons lemon juice
9-inch graham cracker crust

Dissolve the Jello and sugar in hot water and hot lemon juice. Chill to the consistency of unbeaten egg white. Add lemon rind. Chill evaporated milk in the freezer for 15-20 minutes or until ice crystals form. Whip until stiff. This takes about 1 minute. Add 2 tablespoons lemon juice and whip for 2 minutes longer or until very stiff. Fold into the Jello mixture and spoon into the pie shell. Chill until firm.

Mrs. Robert Hance

LEMON CREAM PIE

Serves 8
1 cup sugar
3 tablespoons cornstarch
¼ cup butter
1 tablespoon lemon peel or key lime peel, grated
¼ cup lemon juice or key lime juice
3 egg yolks
1 cup milk
1 cup dairy sour cream
9 inch baked pie shell (see Index)
½ cup heavy cream

Mix sugar and cornstarch in a sauce pan. Add butter, lemon peel, juice and egg yolks. Stir in milk and cook over medium heat, stirring until thickened. Cool. Fold in sour cream, and spoon mixture into pie shell. Chill 2 hours. Whip cream and spread over all before serving.

Mrs. R. James Kaylor

LEMON MERINGUE PIE

Serves 8-12
1½ cups sugar
¼ teaspoon salt
1/3 cup plus 1 teaspoon cornstarch
1½ cups water
4 egg yolks, slightly beaten
2 tablespoons lemon peel, grated
2 tablespoons butter
½ cup lemon juice
2/3 cup egg whites (takes about 4 large eggs)
¼ teaspoon salt
¼ teaspoon cream of tartar
2/3 cup sugar
10 inch baked pie shell, cooled (see Index)

In a heavy 2 quart saucepan, combine sugar, salt and cornstarch. Stir in 1½ cups water and bring to a boil stirring constantly. Boil 1 minute or until thick and translucent. Remove from heat and stir a bit of hot mixture into the egg yolks, stirring well. Then pour all back into the saucepan, add grated lemon peel and stir until mixture boils again. Boil 1 minute more. Remove from heat and add the butter, stirring until melted. Gradually stir in the lemon juice. Pour into the pie shell and let cool while making the meringue. Beat egg whites until foamy. Add salt, cream of tartar and the sugar, 1 tablespoon at a time, while beating at high speed until shiny and soft peaks form. Arrange on top of filling and bake 12-15 minutes at 375°. Pie must be completely cool before serving.

Mrs. Richard O. Dowling

CAKE TOP LEMON PIE

Serves 6-8
1 tablespoon butter, melted
1 cup sugar
2 tablespoons flour
⅛ teaspoon baking powder
1 lemon, grated (rind and juice)
2 eggs, separated
1 cup milk
9 inch pie crust (see Index)

Combine butter, sugar, flour, baking powder, lemon and beaten egg yolks. Stir in milk. Fold in stiffly beaten egg whites. Pour into unbaked pie shell. Bake at 425° for 15 minutes, reduce heat to 350° and finish baking until delicately browned.
Mrs. Robert White

JOYCE'S QUICK LIME PIE

1 can sweetened condensed milk
1 can limeade, 6 ounce size
4½-ounce Cool Whip
Lemon peel

Mix all ingredients. Grate lemon rind over the top and refrigerate
Mrs. Harper Davidson
Mrs. Richard Skrip

MY MOM'S PECAN PIE

Serves 8
1 cup light brown sugar
½ cup white sugar
½ cup butter
3 eggs
1 cup pecans
1 unbaked pie shell (see Index)

Boil sugar and butter until it just starts to bubble or makes a syrup. Beat eggs until light, and then add the syrup a little at a time. Continue to beat. Pour into the pie shell and sprinkle with pecans. Bake at 350° for 20 minutes and turn the oven to 400° and bake for 15 minute longer.
Mrs. Julian Arnold

REAL SOUTHERN PECAN PIE

Serves 6-8
2 eggs, beaten well
1 cup white sugar
1 cup white corn syrup
2 tablespoons butter, melted
¼ teaspoon salt
1 cup chopped pecan meats
A few whole pecans
9 inch unbaked pie shell (see Index)
Vanilla ice cream (optional)

Preheat oven to 400°. Mix eggs with sugar, syrup, butter, salt and chopped pecans. Pour into the pie shell and decorate with whole pecans. Bake at 400° for 15 minutes. Reduce heat to 350° and bake for 35 minutes more. Serve with vanilla ice cream after letting the pie stand at room temperature for a few hours.
Mrs. Jay Van Vechten

TINY PECAN TARTS

These make a nice party food as they may be eaten with the fingers.

Serves 20-22

CRUST:

3 ounce package cream cheese

½ cup butter

1 cup sifted all-purpose flour

FILLING:

1 egg

¾ cup dark brown sugar

1 tablespoon butter, melted

1 teaspoon vanilla extract

2/3 cup coarsely chopped pecans

For the shells combine cream cheese and butter; blend in flour. Refrigerate about 1½ hours. Shape into balls about 1" in diameter and press into tiny ungreased muffin tins. For the filling beat the egg with a hand mixer; add brown sugar, melted butter, and vanilla. Continue beating until well mixed. Stir in pecans. Pour into prepared shells and bake at 325° for about 25 minutes. Cool before removing from pans.

Mrs. J. Michael Garner

PUMPKIN CHIFFON PIE

Serves 8

1 envelope unflavored gelatin

¾ cup brown sugar (firmly packed)

½ teaspoon salt

1 teaspoon cinnamon

½ teaspoon nutmeg

½ cup milk

¼ cup water

3 eggs, separated

1½ cups pumpkin (canned)

¼ cup sugar

Whipped cream

9 inch baked pie shell (see Index)

Mix gelatin, brown sugar, salt and spices. Stir in milk, water, egg yolks and pumpkin. Mix and cook over medium heat stirring constantly until gelatin is dissolved and mixture is thoroughly heated. This should take about 10 minutes. Remove from heat, and chill in the refrigerator until mixture mounds slightly when dropped from a spoon. Beat egg whites until stiff. Beat in sugar. Fold gelatin mixture into egg whites. Turn into baked pie shell and chill until firm. Serve with whipped cream.

Mrs. Andrea Ferguson

SHERRY PIE

Serves 8
½ cup butter
1 cup flour
¼ cup light brown sugar
½ cup nuts, chopped
½ pound of marshmallows
½ cup sherry
½ pint whipped cream

Melt the butter in a 9″ pie pan in a 375° oven. Mix flour, brown sugar and nuts; add to melted butter and brown for 30 minutes, stirring occasionally. Reserve a bit to sprinkle on pie filling and pat down the rest to form a crust after it cools. Melt marshmallows with the sherry and cool. Fold the whipped cream into the marshmallow-sherry mixture until well blended. Pour into the pie shell and sprinkle the top with the reserved crust crumbles. Refrigerate until serving time. Serve cold.

Mrs. Robert Hays

STRAWBERRY WHIPPED CREAM PIE

Serves 8
CRUST:
23 Ritz crackers, broken into
   small pieces
1 cup pecans, coarsely chopped
3 egg whites
1 teaspoon vanilla
1 cup sugar
FILLING:
1 cup whipping cream
2 tablespoons sugar
1 large package frozen
   strawberries, sweetened to
   taste and well drained

Crust:
Beat egg whites until stiff. Add sugar, continue beating until well mixed. Fold in other ingredients. Spread in well greased pie plate. Bake 30 minutes at 350°. Let cool thoroughly.
Filling:
Whip cream until stiff. Add sugar and beat well. Fold in strawberries. Pour into cold pie crust. Refrigerate 2 hours before serving.

Mrs. Boyce Ezell, III

MOTHER'S APPLE CRISP

Serves 6
1 quart apples, peeled, cored and sliced (5 or 6 large apples)
½ cup water
Dash of salt
¾ cup flour
¾ cup plus 2 tablespoons sugar
6 tablespoons butter
1 teaspoon cinnamon

Place apples, water and salt in a buttered baking pan. Mix flour, sugar and butter together until crumbly. Sprinkle flour mixture on apples, then sprinkle cinnamon on top. Bake at 400° for 10 minutes or at 350° for 30 minutes. Serve warm with whipped cream, ice cream or cream.

Mrs. Barbara Bachmann

APPLE MACIE

Serves 6
¼ cup butter
2 cups milk
2½ cups white bread, crust removed and cut in cubes
1 cup sugar
2 eggs, slightly beaten
1 teaspoon vanilla
¼ teaspoon nutmeg
1 apple, peeled and diced
½ cup crushed pineapple, drained
½ cup raisins

Heat butter and milk together and pour over bread. Add sugar and eggs, beating well, then add remaining ingredients. When well blended, pour into buttered baking dish and cook for 45 minutes at 350°. Serve with hard sauce or whipped cream.

Mrs. J. Michael Garner

ORIGINAL BANANAS FOSTER

Serves 6
12 tablespoons butter
6 teaspoons brown sugar
6 ripe bananas (not overripe), slice lengthwise
Cinnamon
6 ounces white rum
6 teaspoons banana liqueur
Vanilla ice cream

Place butter and brown sugar in a chafing dish over medium heat. When butter starts to bubble add bananas. Sprinkle with cinnamon. Cook until tender, but not mushy. Pour in rum and liqueur. When warm ignite the mixture. When alcohol burns off serve over vanilla ice cream.

Harold Wirth

BRANDY ALEXANDER FRAPPÉS

Serves 6-7
1 quart vanilla ice cream
½ cup brandy
½ cup creme de cocoa
1 square chocolate to make curls

Remove ice cream to refrigerator ½ hour before serving. Combine ice cream, brandy, and creme de cacoa in blender. Blend at high speed until smooth. Turn into chilled sherbet glasses to serve. Let chocolate warm to room temperature. With a sharp paring knife cut into thin curls from back of chocolate square.

Mrs. George Hero

BOURBON MACAROON DESSERT

Serves 20-25
4 dozen macaroons
bourbon
½ gallon coffee ice cream
½ gallon almond butterscotch
  ice cream

Dip both sides of macaroon in bourbon, just moist, do not soak. Then press firmly on bottom of angel food cake pan or spring form pan, and pack firmly with the coffee ice cream. Then pack with the nut ice cream. Put into freezer immediately. Freeze at least 8 to 12 hours or longer. Unmold when ready to serve onto a chilled silver tray. Cut with a very sharp knife.

Mrs. T. Grady

CHERRIES IN THE SNOW

Serves 6
2 envelopes Dream Whip
1 cup cold milk
1 teaspoon vanilla
8-ounce package cream cheese
1 cup sifted confectioners sugar
1 angel food cake
1 can cherry pie filling

Mix Dream Whip, milk and vanilla, and beat until stiff. Then add softened cream cheese. Gradually add the sugar beating until smooth. Grease two 9" pans or one 9" x 13" pan and spread a thin layer of cream cheese mixture on pan bottom. Cut angel food cake in slices and place over cheese. Spoon remaining cream cheese mixture over the cake. Spoon pie filling over everything. Chill in the refrigerator at least 8 hours before serving.

Mrs. Robert Bartelt

BUTTERSCOTCH BREAD PUDDING

Serves 4
3 slices raisin bread
3 teaspoons butter, softened
¾ cup light brown sugar, firmly packed
3 eggs
1 cup evaporated milk
Dash of salt
½ teaspoon vanilla

Trim crusts from bread, spread with butter and cut into ½ inch squares. Butter inside of upper part of 1 quart double boiler and spread with brown sugar. Place bread cubes on top of sugar. In bowl beat eggs, evaporated milk, salt and vanilla with wire whisk. Pour over bread cubes; do not stir. Place over boiling water and cook, covered, for 1 hour or until knife inserted comes out clean. Watch water in bottom of double boiler during cooking, and add more if necessary. Serve in small bowls, spooning sauce over custard portion.

Mrs. Tolson Meares

CHOCOLATE MARSHMALLOW DESSERT

Serves 8
1 pound marshmallows
1 cup hot coffee
1 pint whipping cream
1½ squares bitter chocolate, shaved
1 cup pecans, chopped

Dissolve the marshmallows in the coffee or combine the two in a double boiler. When dissolved, cool and add whipped cream, shaved chocolate, and chopped nuts. Put the mixture in the refrigerator for several hours and then spoon into sherbet dishes.

Mrs. William H. Walker

CHOCOLATE MOUSSE I

Serves 6
1 cup chocolate chips
5 tablespoons boiling water or coffee
4 eggs, separated
2 tablespoons liqueur (rum or orange)
1 cup heavy cream, whipped

Use a blender to break up the chocolate chips. Add water or coffee and continue to blend. Add egg yolks and liqueur. Turn into a bowl and fold in the whipped cream. Fold in beaten egg whites and chill.

Mrs. Karl Noonan

CHOCOLATE MOUSSE II

Serves 8
3½ ounces of dark sweet
   chocolate
2 tablespoons water
¾ cup sugar
3 tablespoons water
2 cups heavy cream, whipped
3 tablespoons sugar
1 teaspoon vanilla
4 egg whites, stiffly beaten
2 packages lady fingers
Rum or white port

Melt over low heat the chocolate and 2 tablespoons of water. The mixture should form a smooth paste. Add ¾ cup sugar, 3 tablespoons water and bring to a boil. Remove from heat, cool, and chill. Beat 1½ cups whipping cream until stiff. Fold in 3 tablespoons sugar and the vanilla. Fold into the chilled chocolate mixture. Fold in the stiffly beaten egg whites. Line a Charlotte mold with lady fingers that have been dipped in rum or white port. Pour in the chocolate mixture. Place another layer of dipped lady fingers over the top. Chill. Best to make a day ahead, if possible. Unmold and frost with remaining ½ cup of cream, whipped. Garnish with shaved chocolate if desired.

Mrs. Steve Pease

COCONUT TORTE

Serves 8
1 cup Graham cracker crumbs
½ cup grated coconut
½ cup walnuts, chopped
4 egg whites
¼ teaspoon salt
1 teaspoon vanilla
1 cup sugar
Butter crunch, butter brickel, or
   vanilla ice cream

Combine crumbs, coconut and nuts. In another bowl beat the egg whites, salt and vanilla until peaks form. Gradually add the sugar and beat until very stiff. Fold graham cracker mix into egg white mix, and spread in a well greased 9" pie plate. Bake at 350° for 30 minutes or until an inserted toothpick comes out clean. Cool, cut into wedges, and top with ice cream.

Mrs. R. Layton Mank

CHOCOLATE OMELET

Serves 6

4 egg whites

2 tablespoons water

4 egg yolks

¾ cup semi-sweet chocolate bits melted and cooled

½ cup sour cream

¼ cup sifted powdered sugar

1 tablespoon butter

½ cup whipping cream

2 tablespoons creme de cacao, optional

Chocolate curls

Beat egg whites until frothy, add water and beat to stiff peaks. Beat egg yolks until thick and lemon colored and then beat in the chocolate, sour cream, and sugar. Fold egg yolk mixture into egg whites. Melt butter in a 10″ oven proof skillet and heat until a drop of water sizzles in the pan. Pour in the egg mixture spreading to the edges. Reduce heat to low and cook 6 minutes. Finish cooking in a 325° oven for 10 minutes or until a knife inserted off center comes out clean. Loosen omelet around the edges and invert to a warm platter. If desired, sprinkle with additional sifted powdered sugar. Whip cream to soft peaks and stir in creme de cacao. Garnish the creme with chocolate curls and serve with the omelet.

Mrs. William Atwill

BOBBIE AND CAROL'S CREPES SUZETTE

Serves 10

CREPE BATTER:
3 eggs
¼ cup sugar
1½ cups milk
1 cup flour
2 tablespoons butter
½ teaspoon vanilla
2 tablespoons brandy or orange
  liqueur
ORANGE BUTTER:
6 tablespoons sweet butter
3 tablespoons sugar
Grated rind of 1 orange
2 tablespoons orange liqueur
SAUCE:
1 cup granulated sugar
6 tablespoons sweet butter
½ cup strained orange juice
1/3 cup orange liqueur
¼ teaspoon orange extract
Skinned sections of 2 oranges
Slivered rind of 1 orange
1/3 cup orange liqueur

Crepes:
Place ingredients in the blender and blend for 1 minute at top speed. Dislodge any unblended bits of flour with a scraper and blend 3 seconds more. Cover and refrigerate 2 hours or overnight. Preheat lightly greased skillet to a medium temperature. (If skillet is too hot crepes will not spread, if too cool, they will run.) Pour 1 tablespoon batter from tip of spoon for each crepe, spread to 3 inches in diameter by tipping pan. Brown lightly on both sides. They freeze beautifully if placed on wax paper with wax paper inserted between each crepe.

Orange Butter:
Spread crepe with orange butter made by beating butter until light and fluffy and slowly adding rest of the ingredients. Spread a little orange butter on each crepe. Fold crepes into triangles.

Sauce:
In serving pan have slivered rind of 1 orange, granulated sugar, butter, orange juice, and orange liqueur and ¼ teaspoon orange extract. Cook until syrupy. Add skinned orange sections. Put crepes in sauce. Pour warm ignited liqueur over crepes.

Mrs. Jack Courtright

FLAN

Serves 6
1-2 teaspoons sugar
5 eggs
1½ cups sugar
Pinch of salt
2 cups boiling milk
2 teaspoons vanilla

You need a 1 quart heavy flan mold. Sprinkle 1-2 teaspoons of sugar evenly around the bottom of the flan mold and carmelize. To carmelize, set electric range burner fitting the size of the mold to "medium." Place mold on burner and watch closely, turning as sugar turns gold and them medium brown. Be careful not to let it get dark brown or burned. Set aside. Beat eggs; add 1½ cups sugar, salt and beat again. Add boiling milk slowly. Add vanilla. Strain entire mixture through a strainer, into the flan mold. Put mold into a pan filled with water. Water should be almost to top of custard level for proper baking. Bake at 350° for about 50 minutes. Test with silver knife inserted in center coming out clean. Cool in refrigerator. To invert, first run a wet knife around edges to separate from mold. Place custard plate on top and then invert. The caramel will be on top.

Mrs. Alan Greer

CARAMEL CUSTARD

Serves 6
CUSTARD:
½ cup granulated sugar
5 eggs
½ cup granulated sugar
Pinch of salt
¼ teaspoon vanilla
3½ cups milk
FRUIT FOR CENTER
   GARNISH:
½ pint fresh strawberries
1 cup pineapple, cubed
½ pound green grapes

Have on hand one 5-cup mold or flan pan which looks like a ring mold. Sprinkle ½ cup sugar in small heavy skillet. Cook slowly over low heat, stirring with wooden spoon, until melted to a golden syrup. Be careful not to burn. Pour immediately into 5-cup mold, tilting to coat the sides. Let cool. In large bowl, beat with wire whisk the eggs, sugar, salt and vanilla. Mix well. Gradually add milk, until smooth. Place ring mold into shallow baking pan. Remove about 1 cup of the mixture and pour the rest into the mold. Place the pan on the middle rack of preheated oven and pour remaining 1 cup of mixture into mold. Pour hot water 1″ deep around the outside of the mold so that the water will surround the mold. Bake at 325° for 55 to 60 minutes or until knife comes out clean when inserted in center. Remove mold from the pan of hot water and let cool completely. Refrigerate to chill at least one hour. (Can be made a day ahead.) To serve, loosen edge of custard by going around edges with sharp knife. Cover with wet serving plate and quickly invert and shake gently to loosen. Fill center with fruits.

Mrs. Robert White

GOODIE'S DANISH RUM PUDDING

Serves 8
1 tablespoon gelatin
¾ cup water
3 egg yolks
6 tablespoons sugar
¼ cup light rum
1 cup whipping cream
1 pint raspberries

Soften gelatin in cold water in a heavy sauce pan. Beat egg yolks and sugar until lemon colored. Add rum. Dissolve gelatin over low heat, stirring constantly. Gradually add dissolved gelatin into egg and rum mixture. Refrigerate, and when mixture thickens to a beaten egg white consistency, fold in the whipped cream. Refrigerate until firm. Serve with raspberries; use 1 package of frozen berries, and thicken juice with corn starch if desired.

Mrs. Lindsey D. Pankey Jr.

ELEGANT DESSERT

Serves 8-10
12 macaroons (almond or coconut)
½ cup Grand Marnier or any good brandy
20-24 ounce jar bing cherries, drained
1 quart vanilla ice cream.

Soak the macaroons in the brandy for about 20 minutes. Crumble together and add the cherries and the ice cream. Place in your loveliest silver shell and put in the freezer until serving time. It does not freeze hard.

Mrs. Emil Gould

FRESH FRUIT, GLAZED

Serves 8
1 cup Burgundy
¼ cup sugar
⅛ teaspoon ground cloves
¼ teaspoon cinnamon
Dash ground cardamon
1½ teaspoons grated orange peel
8 medium size fresh pears, peeled, pitted, and halved
Vanilla ice cream

Make a syrup of the Burgundy, sugar, cloves, cinnamon, cardamon, and orange peel. Poach the pears in the syrup until just tender. Drain and reserve the liquid. Chill the fruit, and store the liquid at room temperature. Serve the fruit with vanilla ice cream topped with the liquid.

Mrs. George L. Irvin, III

BRIDGE CLUB'S FAVORITE ICE CREAM PIE

Serves 6-8

1 graham cracker pie crust, baked

Vanilla ice cream, softened

2 egg whites

¼ cup sugar

¼ teaspoon salt

20 large marshmallows

1½ tablespoons water

Hot fudge sauce or syrup

Make graham cracker pie crust and bake as directed. Cool completely. Fill with soft vanilla ice cream. Freeze. Prepare a meringue by beating egg whites till foamy. Add ¼ cup sugar and salt and beat until stiff. Melt 20 large marshmallows with 1½ tablespoons of water and then fold into the egg whites. Spread the meringue over the top of the frozen pie being sure to spread entirely up to the edge of the crust. Brown under a broiler a few seconds. Freeze again. To serve, cut into wedges and pour hot fudge sauce or syrup over each slice.

Mrs. Bruce Reinertson

KOLACKY-SLOVAK NUT ROLL

Makes 40 slices

½ cup lukewarm water

2 envelopes yeast

2 tablespoons sugar

½ cup butter

4 cups flour

1 cup warm milk

3 egg yolks

1 teaspoon salt

2 tablespoons sugar

4½ cups English walnuts, packed in cup

2 cups sugar

2 teaspoons cinnamon

½ cup butter, melted

1 tablespoon canned milk

3 tablespoons honey

Combine water, yeast and sugar and let stand. Blend butter and flour as for pie dough. Combine warm milk, egg yolks, salt and sugar. Add yeast mixture to this and combine with flour mixture. Dough should be consistency of pie dough. (Add more flour if needed.) Cover and let rise until double. Punch down and divide into 4 pieces. Roll each one out into a 6" x 12" sheet of dough. Make the filling by mixing the walnuts, sugar, and cinnamon. Add butter, milk and honey and mix thoroughly. Spread filling evenly on sheets of dough and roll up like a jelly roll. Place all 4 on a greased cookie sheet and grease tops of rolls. Cover and let rise until double. Bake for 30 minutes at 350°. Especially good for Christmas.

Mrs. Julian Arnold

CHAMPAGNE MANGOES

Serves 6
2 ripe mangoes
10½ ounce package frozen
   raspberries
1 bottle ice cold champagne

Chill champagne glasses. Peel
and slice mangoes. Chill.
Partially thaw raspberries. Before
serving, place slices of mango in
champagne glass and top with
1 tablespoon of whole raspberries.
Fill glasses with champagne and
serve at once.

Mrs. Karl Noonan

MANGO MOUSSE

Serves 4
5 ripe mangoes
1/3 cup key lime juice
2 egg whites
1/3 cup sugar
Pinch of salt
½ cup heavy cream

Peel and dice mangoes. Purée
pulp of 3 of the mangoes in a
blender. Add key lime juice. Beat
egg whites until frothy. Add
sugar and continue beating until
egg whites are stiff. In a separate
bowl whip cream until stiff. Fold
egg and cream mixture together
gently. Add 1 cup of the mango
purée and fold. Add the
remaining purée and fold again.
Gently fold in the diced mango
and spoon into individual dishes
or 1 large dish and refrigerate at
least 3 to 4 hours before serving.

Mrs. Art Roberts

PEACH COBBLER

Serves 8
1½ pounds fresh peaches, sliced
   and peeled
Juice of 1 lemon
½ cup butter
2/3 cup sugar
1 tablespoon flour
Nutmeg
1 cup sugar
1 cup flour
2 teaspoons baking powder
2/3 cup milk
Brown sugar, light

Mix the first 6 ingredients. Heat
to a boil. Pour in a deep baking
dish. Mix next 4 ingredients and
pour over the peach mixture. Do
not stir. Bake at 350° for 40
minutes. After 15 minutes
sprinkle a bit of brown sugar over
the top.

Mrs. Dale Moseley

PEACHES AND CREAM DESSERT SOUP

Serves 4
1½ pounds freestone peaches or nectarines, peeled and cut into quarters
Water
½ cup sugar
Juice of ½ lemon
3 or 4 gratings of whole nutmeg or ¼ teaspoon powdered nutmeg
Pitcher of heavy cream

In a saucepan, cover the peaches with water and bring them to a boil, with the sugar, lemon juice, and nutmeg added. Simmer until the peaches are tender, (about 15 minutes). Cool and purée. Chill and serve as a dessert with a pitcher of cream and crisp thin cookies.

Mrs. Murray McClain

PEARS IN RED WINE

Serves 6
6 fresh pears (firm)
Juice of ½ lemon
6 whole cloves
¾ cup sugar
¾ cup water
1 cup dry red wine
1 stick cinnamon
½ lemon, thinly sliced

Peel pears, brush with lemon juice and place a clove in the blossom end of each pear. Combine sugar, water, wine, cinnamon stick and lemon slices. Place pears standing up in a deep casserole. Pour wine mixture over the pears. Cover and bake in a hot oven at 400° for 30 minutes, basting occasionally. Uncover and bake 15 minutes longer. Chill and serve with remaining sauce.

Mrs. William Mooney

PRUNE WHIP

Serves 4
4 teaspoons cold water
½ teaspoon vanilla
4 egg whites
1 cup sugar
½ cup cooked prunes, chopped
¼ cup pecans, chopped

Add water and vanilla to egg whites and beat very stiff. Add sugar gradually and continue beating. Add prunes and pecans. Put in ungreased pan, and cook in slow oven for 1 hour at 250°.

Mrs. Lester R. Johnson, Jr.

POACHED PEARS WITH VANILLA SAUCE

Serves 8
8 whole ripe pears
8 cups water
3 cups sugar
Peel from 2 lemons
10 cloves
A piece of vanilla bean
SAUCE:
1½ cups heavy cream or half
   and half
1 vanilla bean
3 egg yolks
¼ cup sugar
Pinch of salt
1/3 cup heavy cream, whipped

Peel pears with a vegetable peeler, leave whole. Simmer 2 quarts of water and sugar with lemon peel, cloves and piece of vanilla bean for 10 minutes. Add the pears and simmer until tender. Let the pears cool in syrup and refrigerate. Remove them to a pretty bowl with a slotted spoon at serving time. To make the vanilla cream sauce, scald the cream or half and half with split vanilla bean. In the top of a double boiler beat egg yolks, sugar and salt. Gradually pour in the hot milk, beating constantly. Cook mixture over simmering water stirring briskly until it is thickened and coats a spoon. Cool sauce and fold in heavy whipped cream. Spoon some sauce over the pears and pass the rest separately.

Mrs. John Renuart

STRAWBERRY CREAM

Serves 8
1 quart strawberries
Superfine granulated sugar, to
   taste
Brandy, to taste
1 pint heavy cream
2 tablespoons Kirsch
Toasted almonds, for garnish

Wash and hull strawberries. Dust with sugar until sweet. Sprinkle lightly with brandy. Whip cream stiff, flavoring with Kirsch. Fold strawberries carefully into cream. Place in crystal bowl. Refrigerate for at least 2 hours before serving. Garnish with strawberries and toasted almonds.

Mrs. George L. Irvin, III

STRAWBERRY DELIGHT

Serves 6-8
1 package strawberry Jello
½ pint heavy cream, whipped
4 cups angel food cake
Fresh strawberries in season, for garnish

Make Jello the speedy way with ice cubes. Put in freezer 15 to 20 minutes (to shaky consistency). Whip with Beater. While Jello is setting, whip cream. Add angel food cake to the Jello. Fold in the whipped cream and pour into a 9″ x 9″ glass dish. Chill and serve when firm. Garnish with fresh strawberries.

Mrs. Andrea Ferguson

STRAWBERRY MOLD

The coloring in this mold is beautiful.

Serves 6
20 ounces frozen sliced strawberries, thawed
1 cup syrup from berries
3-ounce package lemon Jello
1 cup hot water
1 tablespoon lemon juice
8-ounce package cream cheese, softened

Drain the defrosted strawberries and reserve 1 cup of the syrup. Dissolve the package of lemon Jello in 1 cup hot water. Add the cup of syrup, lemon juice and mix well. To the softened cream cheese, add half of the Jello mixture gradually, stirring well to blend. Pour into 1 quart mold. Chill until firm. Add strawberries to remaining gelatin mixture and stir gently. Pour into mold over the firm cheese mixture. Chill until firm.

Milly Wasman

MANGO ICE MARCELLA

Serves 8
1 quart water
1½ cups sugar
1½ cups puréed mango
3 egg whites

Mix all ingredients and place in an ice cream machine, and you have got instant Italian ice. You may substitute the puréed mango with any fresh puréed fruit except lemon, lime, or orange. Use more sugar if you intend to store for more than 4 days. Serve as a dessert or between courses.

John Baratte

LEMON ICE CREAM

This is a very rich ice cream and it stores well.

4 eggs separated
1 cup sugar
4 tablespoons cold water
2 lemons
Grated rind of one lemon
1 pint heavy cream

Mix yolks, ½ cup sugar, water, lemon juice and grated lemon rind. Cook in top of double boiler until thick. Cool. Beat egg whites, gradually adding rest of sugar (½ cup) and continue beating until stiff.

Pour *cooled* custard over stiff egg whites, folding thoroughly. Whip cream and fold into above mixture. Freeze. To serve: Line glass dessert saucers with paper thin slices of lemon. Place mound of ice cream in center. Or: Cut stem-end off of lemon and hollow out the pulp. Place ice cream in the lemon and freeze until serving time.

Mrs. Tom Huston

KEY LIME SHERBET

Serves 10-12
1 envelope unflavored gelatin
2 cups milk
1½ cups sugar
½ teaspoon salt
2½ pints light cream
2/3 cup key lime juice
3 drops of yellow food coloring
   (optional)

Sprinkle the gelatin over ½ cup of milk in a heavy saucepan to soften. Combine sugar, salt, 1½ cups milk and cream in mixing bowl, and whisk until the sugar is dissolved. Add the key lime juice and whisk until well mixed. Heat gelatin over very low heat until dissolved, stirring constantly. Slowly stir gelatin mixture into lime mixture. Put into 2 glass dishes and freeze until the edges are solid and the middle part is firm but not frozen. Remove the semi-frozen mixture from one glass dish into a chilled mixing bowl. Beat at high speed until the mixture is smooth but not melted. Work quickly! Return to dish and refreeze. Do the same for the second glass dish. Serve with a simple sugar cookie.

Mrs. Lindsey D. Pankey, Jr.

Restaurants

RESTAURANTS

Beautiful Biscayne Bay reflects the lights of downtown Miami at night.

MOUSSE DE POMPANO ROYALE— SAUCE FLEURETTE

The Bath Club—Miami Beach

Serves 16

5 pounds fresh fillet of pompano
Salt and fresh ground white pepper to taste
1½ quarts fresh light cream
½ quart cognac
3 to 4 whites of eggs
2 quarts fish stock
SAUCE FLEURETTE
1 pint Hollandaise sauce (see Index)
2 tablespoons shallots, chopped
2 tablespoons tarragon, chopped
2 white of leeks

1 carrot
2 onions studded with cloves
2 tablespoons crushed peppercorns
½ quart dry white wine
½ quart water
4 stalks of celery
Pinch of saffron
Heads and skin from pompano
1 red snapper head, quartered
1 pound butter
4 or 5 laurel leaves
Pinch of thyme

Method:

Clean pompano of heads, skin and bones. Take fillet and pass through finest blade of meat grinder. Put in freezer until ice cold, but not frozen. Put in food chopper, add 3-4 egg whites, salt and pepper. Mix well, but do not overwork. (Should be of rubber consistency.) Start to add light cream a little at a time. Make sure cream mixes well. After 1 quart cream is mixed, add cognac. (Attention: You do not want the mousse to be like cottage cheese). Add ½ quart of cream. Should have a nice white gloss and stand in peaks like meringue. Mold in spoon-like quenelles and place in 4" deep buttered pan. Add fish stock. Poach approximately 10 minutes.

Sauce Fleurette:

Cut vegetables into ½ inch pieces. Put in heavy duty sauce pot with 1 pound of butter. Braise vegetables for 10-15 minutes. Add fish bones, heads, etc., with bay leaves, peppercorns and thyme. Braise 10-14 minutes (covered). Add white wine and cold water. Cook for 30-45 minutes. At the last minute add saffron and cook 2-3 minutes more. (Note: do not let stock boil, but simmer.) Strain through cheesecloth. Put on the stove and bring to a boil. Add white roux until consistency of heavy cream. Strain through French China cap. Cook shallots until transparent. Add chopped tarragon. Add to sauce. Simmer 4-5 minutes at slow boil. Put aside when it cools down and add Hollandaise. Coat mousse with sauce on silver oval dish. Garnish with fleurons, lemon slices and truffle slices.

CONCH FRITTERS
Burdines—Miami

Serves 6
1½ pounds fresh conch, minced
1½ pounds onion, minced
1 large green pepper, minced
6 eggs, slightly beaten
1 cup flour
1 cup milk
1 ounce lime juice
1 teaspoon Tabasco
**1 tablespoon Worcestershire
    sauce**
½ teaspoon dry mustard
1 ounce dry white wine
1 teaspoon white pepper
1 teaspoon salt
¼ cup bacon fat, for frying

After mincing the first three ingredients, add the other ingredients and mix thoroughly. Drop silver dollar sized rounds of dough into a well greased, with bacon fat, frying pan. Cook over high heat until browned on both sides.

CHICKEN IN CHAMPAGNE SAUCE
Cafe Chauveron—Bal Harbour

Serves 4
2-3 pound chicken, cut up
4 shallots, finely chopped
Salt and pepper to taste
1/3 cup white port wine
**4 ounces dry champagne or dry
    white wine**
½ pound butter
2 ounces brandy
3 cups light cream
**1 cup thick white sauce (see
    Index)**

Sauté chicken and shallots in butter. When lightly browned, season with salt and pepper, and cover. Cook slowly for 25 minutes. Remove the chicken and pour off the cooked butter. Bring the brandy, port and champagne to a boil; simmer for 5 minutes, stirring up the pan drippings. Add the thick white cream sauce and the fresh light cream. Continue cooking over a hot fire for 6 minutes, stirring constantly. Do not boil. Place the chicken back in the sauce and simmer for 5 minutes. Serve at once.

LOBSTER SANTINO
Casa Santino–Miami

Servs 8
4 — ¼ pound Maine lobsters
2 tablespoons olive oil
2 cloves garlic, chopped
2 shallots, chopped
18 fresh clams
½ cup dry white wine
8 large shrimp
12 fresh mussels
¼ teaspoon salt
8 red pepper seeds (optional)
¼ teaspoon pepper
2 bay leaves
16-ounce can of tomato with purée, crushed
1 pound linguine

Split lobster in half lengthwise and discard intestinal tract and sac. Gently sauté garlic and shallots in olive oil in a large pan. Place lobster cut side down in a pan and sauté until it starts to turn red. Turn lobster over and add the clams and wine. Cover and cook for 5 minutes. Add the shrimp, mussels, crushed tomatoes and seasoning. Bring to a boil, reduce heat, and simmer for 20 minutes. Meanwhile, heat a large pot of boiling water. Add 1 tablespoon of salt. Cook linguine until tender but still firm (according to directions on package). Strain. Place pasta on large platter. Place lobster and fish around pasta and pour sauce over dish. Sprinkle with parsley.(Casa Santino suggests Frascati or Soave wine.)

COTELETTE DE VEAU A LA BEAUX ARTS
The Coral Gables Country Club–Coral Gables

Serves 4-6
4-6 lean veal cutlets
1 cup flour, sifted
4 ounces butter, melted
2 ounces white wine
Juice of 1 lemon
1 pound lump crabmeat
2 cups Hollandaise sauce (see Index)
12-18 green asparagus spears, cooked

Dust the veal cutlets with flour and sauté slowly on both sides in clarified butter until golden brown. Add lemon juice and white wine to the pan. Let the cutlets simmer for a few minutes to keep warm. Heat the crabmeat in a separate pan. Fold in half of the Hollandaise sauce. Place equal parts of crabmeat on each cutlet. Place 3 warm asparagus spears on each cutlet and crabmeat. Cover with the remainder of the Hollandaise and heat under the broiler. Serve immediately.
Leonardo Trompetto

PAELLA
Centro Vasco—Miami

Serves 6-8

1/3 cup olive oil

3-pound fryer chicken, cut in 12 pieces

½ cup ham, diced

½ pound garlic-flavored sausage, sliced

1 large onion, chopped

1 clove garlic, minced

3½ cups whole tomatoes

3½ teaspoons salt

⅛ teaspoon powdered saffron

¼ cup boiling water

1 cup regular raw rice

¼ teaspoon black pepper

1 pound raw shrimp

1 pound raw scallops

1 dozen scrubbed little neck clams in the shell

1 package (10 ounces) frozen green peas

1 can pimientos (4 ounces) cut in strips

Heat olive oil in a 15" pan. Add chicken and brown lightly over medium heat. Add ham, sausage, onion and garlic. Saute over low heat for 10 minutes. Add tomatoes and 1 teaspoon of the salt. Cover and simmer for 30 minutes. Combine saffron in boiling water and stir into the chicken along with the rice, remaining 2½ teaspoons of salt and ¼ teaspoon of pepper. Simmer another 25 minutes, stirring occasionally. Add scallops, clams and shrimp. Cook 10 minutes longer or until shrimp are done and clams have opened, stirring once. Precook frozen peas in 1½ quart sauce pan as directed on the package. Drain. Toss with pimientos. Stir into chicken and seafood mixture.

RIVERGATE SNAPPER
Cye's Rivergate—Miami

Serves 2

¼ pound of butter

2 — 12-ounce fillets of snapper

Salt and pepper to taste

2 tablespoons cream

2 teaspoons lemon juice

Paprika

Melt the butter in a small saucepan. Brush a baking pan with melted butter and place fillets on it. Sprinkle fillets lightly with salt and pepper. Add 1 tablespoon of cream to each fillet. Add 1 teaspoon of lemon juice to each fillet and 1 tablespoon of melted butter to each fillet. Sprinkle fish lightly with paprika. Bake at 450° for 20 minutes.

COTE DE VEAU A LA CREME
Chez Vendome – Coral Gables

Serves 2
2 veal chops (10 ounces)
10 medium mushrooms,
   quartered
2 ounces Apple Jack Brandy
6 ounces whipping cream
1½ teaspoon butter
Salt and pepper
Cooking oil
Parsley

Season both sides of the chops with salt and pepper and dredge in flour. Heat butter and a dash of cooking oil in a saucepan. When butter is melted, place veal chops in the pan and cover. Cook 5 minutes on each side, covered, on medium heat as chops should not be too browned. Remove chops from the pan. Sauté in the pan for 4 minutes. Replace chops in the pan to heat. Pour in 2 ounces of Apple Jack Brandy and flambé. When the flame extinguishes, add the whipping cream and cook 2-3 minutes without the lid until sauce thickens. Place chops in a serving dish. Salt and pepper to taste. Pour sauce with mushrooms over the veal and sprinkle with parsley.

Guy Toussaint
Chef des Cuisines

ROAST DUCK
Famous Restaurant – Miami Beach

Serves 4
6-8 pound duck
3 garlic cloves
½ teaspoon salt
Dash pepper
¼ cup onion, finely chopped
¼ cup celery, chopped
¼ cup chicken fat
½ pound stale bread
Dash of thyme
¼ teaspoon poultry seasoning
1 egg

Wash duck carefully inside and out, removing all innards. Finely chop 3 garlic cloves. Salt and pepper the outside of the duck and also the cavity. Rub bird with garlic inside and out. Allow to stand overnight in the refrigerator. Remove from the refrigerator 1 hour before roasting. Stuff and place duck on a rack in a roasting pan. Roast uncovered, basting occasionally with pan drippings. Roast 12 to 15 minutes per pound at 425°.

Stuffing:
Sauté onion and celery in chicken fat. Soak bread in water and squeeze dry. Combine the remaining ingredients and loosely stuff the duck.

COQUILLES SAINT JACQUES
The Fisherman—Ft. Lauderdale

Serves 2
1 quart water
5 ounces bay scallops
5 ounces shrimp, uncooked,
  cleaned and peeled
3 tablespoons butter
5 ounces shallots
2 large mushroom caps, sliced
3 ounces crab meat
3 ounces lobster meat
chopped parsley
1 recipe medium white sauce
  (see Index) Worcestershire
  sauce, salt, pepper, lemon
  juice and Accent to taste
GARNISHES:
2 lemon wedges, 2 sprigs parsley

Bring water to a boil. Add scallops and shrimp; bring to a boil and cook until just tender, 5-7 minutes. Remove shrimp and scallops to a platter and strain the liquid, reserving 1½ cups. Melt butter in a saucepan. Add the shallots and sliced mushrooms and sauté for a few minutes. Next, add the shrimp, scallops, crab, lobster and parsley, and a dash of sauterne. Make white sauce using 1½ cups of the seafood cooking liquid. Add to the seafood. Bring to a boil. Add a dash of lemon juice, salt, pepper, Worcestershire sauce and Accent. Boil 5 minutes. Serve in au gratin dishes or shells with a lemon wedge and a sprig of parsley. Delicious as an appetizer or a main course at lunch.

CREAMED SPINACH
The Forge—Miami Beach

Serves 8-10
3 pounds fresh spinach
1½ cups thick white bechamel
  sauce (see Index)
¾ cup mayonnaise (see Index)
½ cup heavy cream
1 clove garlic, finely chopped
Grated nutmeg
Salt and pepper to taste

Boil and strain spinach in a large pot of water. Drain it carefully and chop it finely. Add white sauce (bechamel), mayonnaise, heavy cream, garlic, nutmeg, salt and pepper to taste, and mix all together. Heat before serving.

CAESAR'S SALAD
Grentner's International – South Miami

Serves 4-6
1 clove garlic
½ cup salad oil
2 cups day old French bread, cubed
1 egg
1 lemon
½ teaspoon salt
¼ teaspoon pepper
Worcestershire sauce to taste
4-8 anchovy fillets (according to taste)
2 heads Romaine lettuce
½ cup Parmesan cheese, grated
3 tablespoons wine vinegar
Additional grated cheese

Crush garlic in a small bowl and cover with oil. Refrigerate covered, 30 minutes or more. Put ¼ cup of the garlic oil in a medium skillet and fry bread cubes until brown on all sides. Set aside. Cook egg 1 minute in boiling water. Remove and cool. In a small bowl combine the lemon juice, Worcestershire, salt, pepper and mix well. Mash anchovies with a fork around the inside of large wooden salad bowl. Into the same bowl place lettuce which has been torn into bite-sized pieces. Lettuce should be well drained and cold. Drain remaining oil from garlic. Pour over the lettuce. Toss to coat evenly. Pour on lemon mixture. Toss well. Add cheese and vinegar and toss. Add bread cubes next and toss again. Sprinkle teaspoon of Parmesan cheese over each serving.

MUSTARD SAUCE
Joe's Stone Crab – Miami Beach

Makes 6 cups sauce
4 ounces English mustard
1 quart mayonnaise (see Index)
½ cup A-1 Sauce
½ cup Lea and Perrins Worchestershire sauce
1 pint light cream

Beat above ingredients until mixture reaches a creamy consistency. Serve with cold stone crabs and other seafoods.

ROAST PORK CHUNKS CUBAN STYLE
La Tasca—Miami

Serves 8-10
3 pounds pork, cut into chunks
Oil
2 bay leaves
6 cloves garlic, minced
½ lemon, squeezed
1 teaspoon oregano
1 teaspoon paprika
Salt and pepper to taste
2 large onions, thinly sliced
4 tablespoons butter
2 garlic cloves, minced
1 lemon, squeezed

Remove excess fat from the pork. Saute pork in a small amount of oil in an ovenproof casserole with bay leaves, garlic, juice of ½ lemon, oregano, paprika and salt and pepper to taste. When pork is lightly browned, cook in the oven for 1 hour at 350°. Sauté onion in a little butter, garlic, and remaining lemon juice and pour over the pork at serving time.
Claudio Martinez

PEA POD PORK
Mai Kai—Ft. Lauderdale

Serves 1 generously
¼ pound pork tenderloin, sliced
4 tablespoons peanut oil
1 teaspoon salt
1 tablespoon cooking sherry
½ cup chicken stock
¼ cup celery, sliced
¼ cup Bermuda onion, sliced
3 drops sesame oil
½ teaspoon msg
1 teaspoon potato starch
½ pound fresh Chinese pea pods

Slice pork thinly; heat peanut oil over high heat. Add salt and pork and stir-fry for 2 minutes. Add sherry and stir-fry for 1 minute. Add chicken stock, celery, onions, sesame oil and msg and stir for ½ minutes. Add 1 teaspoon starch or enough to slightly thicken the mixture. Add the peapods and stir for 15 to 20 seconds. Remove and serve.

SNAPPER FILLET
Marcella's—North Miami

Serves 6
1 red snapper, filleted
Milk to cover
⅛ teaspoon each of mint,
  rosemary, sage, salt, pepper
1 clove garlic, smashed
12 large mushrooms, sliced
6 ounces prosciutto (6 servings)
Handful sliced almonds
6 tablespoons butter
2 tablespoons olive oil
Flour
Juice of 1 lemon
¼ cup dry white wine
½ package bread sticks, crushed
Butter
Baking paper

Have the snapper boned and the skin removed so that the flavor will be more delicate. Cut fillets in 3 pieces each, on a diagonal. Pound them between a cloth. Put fish in a bowl with milk to cover. Add mint, rosemary, sage, salt, pepper and garlic. The fish should be left in the bowl for 3 to 4 hours. Slice the fresh mushrooms and reserve them. Cut the prosciutto in slices and reserve them. Sauté a large handful of sliced almonds in 2 tablespoons of butter. Reserve them. Sauté the mushroom slices and prosciutto slivers in 2 tablespoons of butter and reserve it. Remove fillets from milk and flour lightly. Add 2 tablespoons of olive oil to the skillet. Heat and add floured fish fillets and then the butter. Turn when golden brown. Drain oil from the skillet and add lemon juice, white wine and herbs. Cool about 10 minutes, covered. Cut baking paper into large heart pieces. Put some of the buttered almonds in one half of paper hearts, reserving half of them. Place fish fillets on the almonds. Cover with prosciutto and mushroom mixture. Sauté half a package of breadsticks, crushed in a few tablespoons of butter and put this mixture on top of mushroom-prosciutto mixture. Put reserved almonds on top. Beat the egg and baste edge of paper hearts with it. Roll the edges carefully. Pierce the paper and blow with air to inflate. Bake at 400° for 15 minutes.

Chef Walter

(This recipe was demonstrated at a Beaux Arts meeting by Walter, Marcella's chef)

CORNED BEEF MAJOR
Marshall Major's—South Miami

Serves 4
1 pound of second cut corned beef
½ pound imported swiss cheese
1 can sauerkraut
Hot dinner rolls or toasted rye bread
Dijon mustard
4 kosher pickles
4 parsley sprigs

In a casserole place corned beef and cover with thinly sliced cheese. Place sauerkraut around the edge of the casserole. Put in the oven at 325° for 7-10 minutes (or until the cheese has melted). Serve immediately with hot bread after draining the juice from the sauerkraut. Accompany with a good mustard and garnish with pickles and sprigs of parsley. I prefer the second cut corned beef since it is a little fatter and does not dry out when baking.

MULLIGATAWNY SOUP
Miami Lakes Country Club—Miami Lakes

Serves 4
1 large frying chicken
2 celery stalks, cut
2 carrots, cut
2 onions, chopped
3-4 quarts water
1 onion, finely minced
2-3 tablespoons butter
2-3 tablespoons flour
1 tablespoon curry powder
1 tart apple, grated
Rind of 1 lemon, grated
Juice of 1 lemon
Salt and pepper to taste
Cooked white rice

Cook a large frying chicken and celery, carrots and onions in 3 or 4 quarts water. Remove the chicken when done and cool, then dice. Continue to simmer the stock. In another kettle, sauté a minced onion in butter until it begins to brown. Add enough flour to make a roux. Cook. Add curry powder, apple and a little grated lemon rind. Add enough strained chicken stock to make a creamy soup. Simmer 10-15 minutes and correct the seasonings. Add the lemon juice and the chicken. Serve with boiled rice.

VEAL OSCAR
The Miami Marriott—Miami

Serves 8
2 pounds veal cutlets
1 cup flour
Salt and pepper to taste
1 cup clarified butter
½ pound crabmeat, picked over
¼ cup clarified butter
2 pounds asparagus spears, cooked
Hollandaise sauce, (see Index)
2 tablespoons horseradish, drained

Flatten cutlets with flat side of cleaver until cutlets are very thin, but not torn. Dredge cutlets in flour which has been well seasoned with salt and pepper. Sauté cutlets in clarified butter to golden brown. In a separate pan, sauté crabmeat in butter just to heat. Place 4 cooked, drained asparagus spears on top of veal cutlet. Place 1½ ounces of sautéed crabmeat on top of asparagus. Prepare Hollandaise sauce adding horseradish. Cover crabmeat with 2 ounces horseradish Hollandaise sauce, leaving tips of asparagus exposed. Place under broiler for a few seconds until golden brown. Serve hot.

VEAL CHOP PIEDMONTESE
Raimondo's—Miami

Serves 6
6 loin chops of veal (1 inch thick)
Olive oil
Salt and pepper, to taste
Sage, to taste
3 sweetbreads, poached, cleaned and pressed under a weight for one hour
1 cup milk
½ cup flour
¼ cup drawn butter
2 shallots, chopped
12 large mushroom caps
1 cup Madeira wine
1 cup heavy cream
1 lump sweet butter

Sauté veal chops in enough olive oil to cover the bottom of a frying pan, until golden, but do not overcook (they should be juicy). Season with salt, pepper, and sage and place on a serving platter. Cut the sweetbreads in half, dip in milk, and coat with flour. Sauté in the drawn butter until done. Place one on each chop. Sauté shallots and mushroom caps in the remaining butter. Add Madeira and reduce until wine is ¼ its original volume. Blend in heavy cream. Remove all excess fat and bind sauce by mixing in the lump of sweet butter. Pour over hot chops and sweetbreads.
Raimondo Laudisio

VEAL PAPRIKASH
Piccadilly Hearth —Miami

Serves 25
10 pounds veal, cubed
20 medium onions, finely chopped
4 large green peppers, diced medium
4 tablespoons butter
1 cup paprika, or to taste
1 quart sherry
6 large fresh tomatoes, peeled and chopped
Water if necessary
2 pints sour cream
Roux (butter melted, add flour, stir till brown)
¼ cup ground cardamon
2 tablespoons nutmeg
Salt and pepper to taste
1 cup cognac

Sauté onions and peppers in butter until golden. Mix veal with paprika, add to onions and sauté until brown. Add sherry and tomatoes. Simmer approximately 20 minutes, or until veal is tender, depending upon size of pot. Add a little water if necessary to keep meat from sticking. Put small amount of sauce from pot in another pan. Add sour cream slowly and mix. Now add to the main ingredients. Thicken with roux. Add cardamon, nutmeg, salt and pepper. Cook until blended. Just prior to serving, add cognac, and simmer only until heated through. Serve with noodles or spaetzle.

BAKED CLAMS
The Quintessence—South Miami

Serves 6
1 ounce butter
1 ounce flour
1 pint whipping cream
2 tablespoons Parmesan cheese, grated
¼ teaspoon white pepper
⅛ teaspoon salt
6 ounces crabmeat
36 large fresh clams in the shell
Bread crumbs
Paprika

Melt butter in a saucepan. Add flour and cook over low heat, stirring for 5 minutes to remove floury taste. Add whipping cream and blend to make a smooth cream sauce. Add cheese, white pepper and salt. Chop crab and add to the sauce. (Open clams by heating them in a 450° oven for 3 minutes.) Place clams on a flat tray and bake in a 400° oven for 2-3 minutes until the edges begin to curl. Remove from the oven and add 1 heaping teaspoon of sauce to each. Sprinkle with bread crumbs and paprika. Bake at 400° until bubbly and golden brown.
Elmer J. Deihl

SALAD DRESSING
The Mutiny at Sailboat Bay – Coconut Grove

Makes 2 cups
1 cup mixed olive oil and
cooking oil
1/3 cup vinegar
2 tablespoons soy sauce
3 scallions, chopped finely
Msg to taste
1 tablespoon garlic salt
1 tablespoon sugar
Dash Tabasco
Capers, optional

Mix all ingredients together and chill.

CAPON-ROCHAMBEAU
The Riviera Country Club –Coral Gables

Serves 6
DUXELLES:
¼ cup butter, melted
½ pound mushrooms, chopped
3 tablespoons onions, minced
⅛ teaspoon thyme
2 bay leaves, chopped
Salt and pepper to taste

6 — 6-ounce chicken breasts,
boneless
Salt and pepper to taste
1 cup butter, melted
1 quart Burgundy
3 shallots, minced
12 mushrooms, sliced
1½ cups basic brown sauce (see
Index)
6 large mushroom cups, lightly
sautéed
6 tablespoons Bearnaise sauce
Capers
Watercress

To prepare the duxelles: Sauté onions and mushrooms in butter with thyme, bay leaves, salt and pepper for 5 minutes. Set aside and drain off excess juice. Keep cool. Stuff the breasts, which have been spread wide open and seasoned with salt and pepper, with the cold duxelle and secure them tightly. Sauté chicken in ½ cup melted butter until golden brown. Add the Burgundy and let it reduce to 1/3 the original amount of liquid. Reserve the liquid. In another pan sauté the shallots and mushrooms. Set aside. Add brown sauce to the reduced pan liquids and heat them together. Sauté the mushroom caps and reserve them. Arrange the chicken on a platter with the shallots and sliced mushrooms around them. Cover with the wine sauce. Put a sautéed whole mushroom on top of each piece and fill it with Bearnaise sauce to which a few small capers have been added. Garnish with watercress.
Chef Gerard Ondaro

MUSHU PORK
The Tiger Tiger Teahouse—Miami

Serves 4
PANCAKES:
2 cups unsifted all-purpose flour
¾ cup cold water
Lard
FILLING:
1 cup fungus (dried Chinese wood ears)
Water
1 cup dried lily flowers (golden needles)
1 pint vegetable oil
½ pound pork, shredded
4 eggs, lightly beaten
½ teaspoon garlic, minced
4 cups American cabbage, thinly shredded

½ cup mushrooms, sliced
½ cup fresh snow peas
½ cup carrots
½ cup canned bamboo shoots
½ cup scallions, green and white parts
1 teaspoon msg
2 teaspoons sugar
½ teaspoon salt
2 tablespoons cooking sherry
4 tablespoons dark soy sauce
2 tablespoons sesame oil
2 tablespoons oyster sauce
¼ teaspoon white pepper, ground

Pancakes:
Place 2 cups unsifted all-purpose flour in a mixing bowl. Stir in approximately ¾ cup cold water. Adjust the amounts of water and flour as necessary to make a dough that is not too sticky. Turn out on a lightly floured surface and knead until smooth. Place in a bowl, cover with a damp cloth, and let stand at room temperature for ½ hour. On a floured surface, with floured fingers, roll the dough into a long roll 1½ inches in diameter. Cut into ½ inch slices, making 16 pieces. Roll each piece between your hands to make a smooth ball. In the palm of your hand flatten one ball slightly. Spread one side of it with a teaspoon of lard. Flatten another ball and place it over the lard. Press to flatten slightly. On a floured surface, with a floured rolling pin, roll the double pancakes into a paper-thin circle about 6 to 7 inches in diameter. In a hot, dry skillet, over low heat, fry one double pancake at a time for about ½ minute on each side (do not overcook) do not fry until pancake colors. While still hot, use your fingers to pull the pancakes apart into 2 pancakes. If they are to be served soon, place them on a towel and cover them with another towel. If they are to wait a long time they must be wrapped airtight. (They may be stacked on top of each other, wrapped airtight, and frozen.) The pancakes must be steamed before serving. (If they have been frozen they must be thawed first, unwrapped.) To steam: place a large strainer or colander over a large saucepan of shallow boiling water. Place a damp towel in the strainer. Cover them with a dry towel and then cover the saucepan with a pot cover. Steam over moderate heat for about 10 minutes.
Continued

Filling:
The ingredients for the filling may be prepared for cooking even a day ahead, or shortly before serving. Soak fungus (dried Chinese wood ears) in boiling water to cover. Let stand for 15 minutes. Change the water twice. Rinse well, drain and dry. Prepare dried lilly flowers (golden needles) in the same manner as the fungus. Cut off and discard any hard parts. Chop the remainder coarsely. Immediately before serving heat vegetable oil in a wok over high heat. Add shredded pork and cook, stirring, for ½ minute. Add eggs, lightly beaten, and stir until scrambled. Pour into a strainer or colander and set aside. In the hot wok, heat 2 tablespoons vegetable oil. Add garlic, then add American cabbage, mushrooms, snow peas which

have been cut the long way into matchstick-thin slices, carrots cut into matchstick thin slivers about 2 inches long, finely shredded canned bamboo shoots, fungus, dried lilly flowers, and scallions cut into 2-inch lengths. Stir briefly for a few seconds. Stir in the cooked and drained pork and scrambled eggs. Add msg, sugar, salt, sesame oil, oyster sauce, and ground white pepper. Stir well. Cook for only a few seconds. Do not overcook.

To Serve:
Fold the pancakes in quarters, serve 4 to a portion. Place the filling in one large serving dish or in four individual dishes. Put a generous amount of filling in the center of pancake, then fold up one end, and roll from opposite sides to enclose the filling. Hold it in your hands and eat from the open end.

PAPALINA
Vintino's Piccolo Mondo—Miami Beach

Serves 8-10
1 pound fettucini or thin egg
   noodles
7 tablespoons butter
2 tablespoons olive oil
½ pound mushrooms, sliced
5 zucchini, thinly sliced
Salt and pepper to taste
½ cup dry white wine
1½ cups heavy cream
4 tablespoons butter
¼ teaspoon nutmeg
White pepper
5 egg yolks
1½ cups Parmesan cheese,
   grated

Cook fettucine or noodles as directed on the package. Drain and add 4 tablespoons butter. Sauté mushrooms and zucchini in 3 tablespoons butter and the olive oil. Add salt and pepper to taste. Drain juices off and return to the skillet. Add wine and simmer for 5 minutes. Add vegetable mixture to noodles and toss lightly. In the top of a double boiler, mix together the heavy cream, 4 tablespoons butter, nutmeg, white pepper and salt to taste. When butter is melted, add 5 egg yolks, beating continuously until slightly thickened (custard-like). Add 1½ cups cheese and stir until melted. Pour sauce over fettucini and mix. Place in a buttered baking dish. Sprinkle with cheese and bake for 10 minutes at 350°.

COSTOLETTE ALLA VALDOSTANO
Sorrento Restaurant—Miami

Serves 3
3 veal chops
3 pieces Fontina cheese, thinly sliced
1 cup flour
2 eggs, well beaten
1 cup bread crumbs
¼ pound butter
Salt and pepper to taste

Slice each chop horizontally to the bone. Insert a slice of cheese into pocket. Dip chops in flour, in egg, and finally in bread crumbs. Sauté in hot butter on both sides until golden brown. This should take 10 to 15 minutes. This dish has been derived from Piedmont, Italy and should be served with artichokes au gratin.
Vincent Amanzio

LOBSTER OR SHRIMP A LA CHEF JAMES
Vinton's Townhouse Restaurant—Coral Gables

Serves 4
½ pound scallions
¼ pound butter
4 cloves garlic, chopped finely
4 lobsters, 1 pound each (or 2 pounds of shrimp, cleaned and shelled but raw)
1 #2 can of whole peeled tomatoes
1 cup chablis
1 tablespoon oregano
Salt and pepper to taste
Parsley, chopped (garnish)

Cut root end off scallions. Wash and slice down to the green part. Sauté in butter with garlic. Split the lobster in half lengthwise and pull meat out of tail. Pull the claws off the body and crack each one. When the onions and garlic are golden, add the lobster meat and claws and the rest of the ingredients. Simmer until the lobster is cooked. Garnish with chopped parsley.
James Bernhardt

SEAFOOD BAKE
The Yellow Rolls Royce—Fort Lauderdale

Serves 4-6
1 green pepper, diced
1 cup celery, diced
8 ounces crab meat
1 cup shrimp
½ cup scallops, slightly cooked
1 cup mayonnaise (see Index)
Salt and pepper to taste
1 cup buttered bread crumbos

Mix all together. Add salt and pepper to taste. Pour into individual serving dishes, cover with the bread crumbs and bake for 30 minutes at 350°

SEA TROUT RUDI
MÉNAGE – COCONUT GROVE

Serves 4

1 medium onion, sliced and salted

Pinch of ground black pepper and salt

1 dressed sea trout, 3-4 pounds

2 cups dry red wine

2 tablespoons flour

2 tablespoons melted butter

Heart shaped fried white bread croutons

Scatter the onion slices over the bottom of a large baking dish. Sprinkle the salt and pepper lightly over the trout, and place the trout over the onions. Pour the wine over the fish, bring it to a boil and reduce the heat. Cook until the fish flakes with a fork. Drain the wine into a small sauce pan. Blend the flour and butter, add to the wine, then mix well and cook for 30 seconds. Pour mixture over the trout. Quickly glaze under the broiler. Serve on a platter, garnish with the croutons.

Variation:

Grouper or snapper may also be used.

Chef Rudi Berggold

COUNTRY CAPTAIN CHICKEN
ZODIAC RESTAURANT— NEIMAN MARCUS
BAL HARBOUR

Serves 4

3½ to 4 pound young, tender fryer, cut up

Flour, salt and pepper

Lard

2 onions, finely chopped

2 green peppers, chopped

1 small garlic bean, minced

1½ teaspoons salt

½ teaspoon white pepper

3 teaspoons curry powder

2— 20-ounce cans tomatoes

½ teaspoon chopped parsley

½ teaspoon powdered thyme

¼ pound almonds, scalded, skinned and roasted to golden brown

3 heaping tablespoons dried currants

2 cups cooked rice

Parsley for garnish

Remove the chicken skins and roll pieces in flour, salt and pepper. Brown in the lard. Remove the chicken from the pan, but keep it hot. (This is a secret of the dish's success.) Into the lard in which the chicken has been browned put the onions, peppers, and garlic. Cook very slowly, stirring constantly. Season the mixture with salt, pepper and curry powder, to taste. Add the tomatoes, parsley and thyme. Put chicken in roaster pan and pour mixture over it. If it does not cover the chicken, rinse out the skillet in which mixture has been cooked and pour over the chicken also. Cover the roaster tightly. Bake in moderate oven about 45 minutes, or until chicken is tender. Place the chicken in the center of a large platter, pile the rice, cooked very dry, around the chicken. Now drop the currants into the sauce mixture and pour over the rice. Scatter the almonds over the top. Garnish with parsley.

INDEX

A

Ambrosia, Heavenly Florida, 170
Anchovy sauce, 196

Appetizers
Angels on horseback, 7
Anne's artichokes, 7
Asparagus roll-ups, 7
Avocado shrimp paste, 8
Biscuit sausage, 8
Bollos, 8
Broccoli dip,9
Caviar mousse, 9
Cheese ball, 10
Cheese bureks, 11
Cheese canapes, 11
Cheese crunches, 12
Cheese paté, 12
Icebox cheese wafers, 12
Clam canapes, 9
Clams casino, 10
Hot clam dip, 10
Crab cocktail, 13
Crab and cheese dip, 13
Emilio's conchitas, 13
Greek crabmeat pastries, 14
Hot crabmeat dip, 14
Coconut chips, 15
Curry dip, 15
Mrs. Smith's egg ring, 15
Egg salad spread, 16
Eggplant caviar, 16
Deep fried Indian eggplant, 16
Smoked fish, 17
Green chilies and cheese dip, 17
Liptauer with accompaniments, 18
Liptauer cheese, 18
Mango delight, 18
Barbecued meatballs, 19
Mushrooms Gruyere, 19
Marinated mushrooms, 20
Mushroom roll, 20
Chicken liver paté, 21
Country paté, 21
Paté in jelly, 23
Paté Esso, 22
Fried plantain chips, 23
Salmon mousse, 24
Smoked salmon, 24
Salsa fria, 24

Guacamole, 24
Apricot sausage balls, 25
Scallops and mushrooms, 25
South Florida scallops, 26
Seafood in dill pesto, 27
Seviche Domning, 26
Shrimp dip, 27
Marinated shrimp, 28
Pickled shrimp, 28
Spicy shrimp cocktail, 28
Delicious spinach, 29
Original spinach, 29
Spanokopita, 30
Steak tartare Baratte, 31
Steak tartare Shepherd, 31
Party tomatoes, 32
Ann's raw vegetable dip, 32
Apple crisp, Mother's, 248
Apple delight cake, 217
Apples flambe, 162
Apple Macie, 248
Apricot chicken, 135
Apricot sausage balls, 25
Arroz con pollo, 128
Artichokes
Ann's artichokes, 7
with chicken, 133
Green bean salad, 166
hearts in Parmesan custard, 145
Italian, 145
salad, marinated, 163
and rice salad, 163
stuffed with shrimp, 88
Asparagus
Chicken with, 129
Ginny's, 145
roll-ups, 7
salad, 164
and shrimp au gratin, 89
Aspic, Snappy Tom, 172
Avocado
dressing, 183
mousse, 164
Roquefort, 164
salad, Naples, 165
shrimp salad mold, 165
shrimp paste, 8
soup, 37

B

Seasons in the Sun
Beaux Arts, Inc.
The Lowe Art Museum
1301 Stanford Drive
Coral Gables, Florida 33146

Please send me _____ copies of your book at $9.95 per copy plus $1.50 postage.

Florida residents please add 4% sales tax for each book. Enclosed is my check for $ _____
(Make checks payable to Beaux Arts, Inc.)

Name _____

Address _____

City/State/Zip _____

Seasons in the Sun
Beaux Arts, Inc.
The Lowe Art Museum
1301 Stanford Drive
Coral Gables, Florida 33146

Please send me _____ copies of your book at $9.95 per copy plus $1.50 postage.

Florida residents please add 4% sales tax for each book. Enclosed is my check for $ _____
(Make checks payable to Beaux Arts, Inc.)

Name _____

Address _____

City/State/Zip _____

Seasons in the Sun
Beaux Arts, Inc.
The Lowe Art Museum
1301 Stanford Drive
Coral Gables, Florida 33146

Please send me _____ copies of your book at $9.95 per copy plus $1.50 postage.

Florida residents please add 4% sales tax for each book. Enclosed is my check for $ _____
(Make checks payable to Beaux Arts, Inc.)

Name _____

Address _____

City/State/Zip _____